Population and Food

Population
and
Food

Edited by

Robert S. Leisner

and

Edward J. Kormondy

American Institute of Biological Sciences

WM. C. BROWN COMPANY PUBLISHERS
Dubuque, Iowa

BIOLOGY SERIES
Consulting Editor
E. Peter Volpe

Foundations for Today
A joint publishing venture between
Wm. C. Brown Company Publishers/BioScience

Printed in the United States of America

Contents

Introduction

"Ecology," "Population and Food," "Pollution" are timely topics because of their significance in man's quest for survival. Little wonder then that these titles were selected for the first three collections of articles which have appeared in *BioScience* since January 1968. In responding to the critical issues of our times, *BioScience,* the official publication of the American Institute of Biological Sciences, has consistently devoted a considerable portion of its pages to environmental matters. Of the many articles of high quality bearing a significant environmental message which have been published in the last three years, eight have been selected for these first three anthologies.

Why an anthology when *BioScience* is already available in most college and university libraries, as well as in many high schools? A collection of readings provides a focus for a reader on a single topic, isolating that topic from other articles that appear in a given journal and providing thereby a more comprehensive feel for the particular issue in its various dimensions. More importantly, it provides an inexpensive sourcebook for the many courses, seminars and study groups which are currently dealing with the topic: to attempt to have fifty, or even ten people trying to read a given article from one library copy is certainly foolhardy; to reproduce copyrighted articles with the convenience of xerography borders on illegality. Many of us have been gravely concerned that scientists speak too much and too often to their own kind on critical contemporary problems: an anthology at least allows the potential for reaching that other audience, the lay public.

Doubtless as concern continues in the matters of population and the environment, there will be more articles of value for yet further anthologies. As anxiety mounts over such other issues as control of human evolution, biological effects of chemotherapy as well as of "drugs," surgical engineering by organ transplant or the use of prosthetics, the pages of *BioScience* will certainly reflect these problems and thus suggest the compilation of articles into other anthologies at given intervals. Time will tell.

Population Resources
and Technology

Harrison S. Brown

In large regions of the world today gains in food production are being more than eaten up by increased population. Birth control can help, but only if coupled with a much greater rate of economic development, which can only be made possible with generous help from the industrial countries. (BioScience *18*, no. 1, p. 31-33)

In 1954 the United Nations estimated that by 1980 the population of the world would lie between 3.3 and 4.0 billion persons, and it gave 3.6 billion as the most likely figure. By 1965 the population had already reached 3.3 billion and the United Nations demographers were estimating that the 1980 world population would lie between 4.1 and 4.5 billion, with a medium of 4.3 billion. Thus, in the span of but a decade the estimate for the most likely population in 1980 was moved upward by about 20%.

This substantial change in estimate resulted directly from the fact that the world rate of population increase has itself increased to levels considerably higher than were deemed plausible in the early 1950's. During the last half-century the rate of population increase has more than doubled, moving from somewhat less than 1% per year to 2.1% per year today. It is quite conceivable that the rate of increase might grow eventually to about 3% per year, corresponding to a doubling of world population every 23 years.

Today, the population of human beings is somewhat over 3.3 billion persons. Projections made on the basis

The author is a professor of geochemistry in the Division of Geological Sciences, California Institute of Technology, Pasadena. This paper is reprinted with permission from Volume II, *Proceedings of the XVII International Horticultural Congress,* p. 19-24.

of plausible extrapolations of the rate of population increase indicate that world population might well grow to about 7.5 billion by the turn of the next century, only 34 years from now.

Approaching Catastrophe

In 1950 many students of the population-resource situation concluded that a major world catastrophe was in the making. Today, when we view the

WORLD POPULATION SOARS

2000 SIX BILLION

1960 THREE BILLION

1930 TWO BILLION

1830 ONE BILLION

AD   500   1000   1500   2000

(Courtesy of the American Society of Agronomy, from "Careers in Agronomy," 1966.)

1

growth of world population in relation to what mankind is doing about the situation, that catastrophe appears a near-certainty. We are faced by the fact that in large regions of the world gains in food production are being more than eaten up by increased population, with the result that we are now experiencing actual reductions in *per capita* food production in many nations in which most people are already hungry. Further, with respect to other aspects of economic development, increased rates of economic growth are being in substantial part wiped out by increased rates of population growth.

Time does not permit our going into the reasons for these ominous changes in any detail today. Instead, I would like to confine my remarks to a brief statement concerning steps the more economically well-off nations might take in the all-too-short time that is still available. I feel justified in doing so, for what we do or don't do in this regard is certainly bound to have profound effect upon the quality of human life.

Clearly, an improvement in the situation would result were we to decrease the rate of population growth. Equally clearly, an improved situation would result were we to increase the rate of economic development, including food production. What many of us have failed to appreciate fully, however, is that these two factors are strongly coupled. We have thought so much in terms of the potential magic that could be wrought by the "perfect contraceptive" that we have failed to appreciate that, in the absence of a greatly improved economic situation in the poorer regions of the world, it is doubtful that even the most perfect contraceptive imaginable would have a truly major effect. Oversimplified, Indian families must have some reasonable assurance of security in old age before they are likely to use a contraceptive, no matter how perfect it might be from the point of view of cost and convenience.

Not Contraception Alone

I hope that I am not misunderstood concerning this point. I believe that accelerated research on human fertility is essential. We need better contraceptive techniques and we need to understand far better than we do now the cultural problems involved in the individual decisions to limit family size. Almost all of us applaud the recent relaxation within our own government and others which permits greater freedom in discussing contraceptive techniques, in carrying out educational programs concerning birth control, and in helping with the establishment of population policies. This change of attitude has been terribly important. I simply wish to underscore the fact that while all of this is necessary it is by no means sufficient. We cannot look upon contraception as a panacea which, if only the churches and the politicians approve, will enable us quickly and inexpensively to improve the world's lot. To repeat, techniques of birth control can help enormously, but only if coupled with sustained economic development at a rate which is considerably greater than that which the poorer nations of the world are experiencing today.

Economic development can be likened to a vast fabric of interwoven threads of different kinds, all of which are necessary yet none of which by itself is sufficient. To mention but a few of the more obvious components, economic development involves the evaluation and development of land and mineral resources, the construction and operation of power plants and factories, the improvement and expansion of farming, the development of transportation and communications systems, the construction of housing, the development of systems of education, as well as the elimination of certain political, social, and cultural institutions, the modification of others and the introduction of still others.

Here, as in the case of birth control, we must beware of the "quick fix," the gimmick, the magic solution. Too often we have looked to land reform or to increased fertilizer production or to the desalting of water as being "cure-alls" for agricultural illnesses. Similarly, it does little good to educate people unless their talents can be put to use; nor is it useful to build complex factories unless there are adequately trained persons available to operate ment of the poorer nations requires massive, sustained, and balanced efforts over a broad front. Unfortunately, the efforts thus far have not been massive enough, nor have they been sustained, them. Briefly, the economic development of the poorer nations requires massive, sustained, and balanced efforts over a broad front. Unfortunately, the efforts thus far have not been massive enough, nor have they been sustained, nor have they been adequately balanced.

More Aid Mandatory

It is absolutely clear that the poorer nations cannot, without help, extricate themselves from the vicious circle in which they now find themselves. That help must come predominantly from the industrial countries of Western Europe, North America, and the western Pacific which, with less than one-fifth of the world's population, produce and consume more than one-half the world's product. At present, aid from these nations remains at about $6 billion a year.

George D. Woods, President of the World Bank, estimates that about $3 to $4 billion more of development finance could be effectively used by the developing countries at the present time. As time goes by, considerably more even than this could be absorbed. He stresses that the capacity of the industrial nations to provide aid also is rising and points out that the national income in these areas is increasing at the rate of $40 to $50 billion a year.

We are faced, however, by the sad fact that for the past 5 years aid contributions from these countries have remained static. Indeed, as a proportion of their incomes, aid contributions have decreased from 0.8% to 0.6%.

The amount of assistance the industrial countries are providing for the developing countries is far indeed from being commensurate with the magnitude of the crisis which confronts us. In the case of the United States, a part of the inadequacy of our own contribution stems from a failure on the part of our Congress to fully recognize the seriousness of the situation and take appropriate action to place the tactics and strategy of aid on as sound and continuing a basis as our defense organization. Most of us would agree that it would be far easier to use economic and technical aid to prevent new crises than to wait until crises appear and then resort to military force.

Certainly a nation which can afford to spend $50 billion annually for defense and $5 billion annually for space and which has a rapidly rising per capita income ought not shrink from thinking in terms of U.S. aid expenditures which are two, three, five, or even ten times greater than our present expenditure of about $3 billion annually. Nor should we look upon such massive injections of aid overseas as gifts. Quite apart from the effects of such investments on economic growth overseas, were they properly handled they could also have an accelerating effect upon our economy. The production of electrical generators, steel plants, and farm machinery for shipment overseas could keep our own people employed much as the production of military equipment does at the present time.

If aid programs are to be successful, we must appreciate the need for continuity and we must appreciate the timescale involved. The economies of the poorer countries cannot be brought up to reasonable levels overnight. The changing of cultural and political patterns requires a great deal of time. Indeed, in our planning it is essential that we think in terms of 10, 25, and even 50 years.

The Short-Term Fallacy

Today, in the face of Congressional attitudes, programs are started, then often stopped without being given a reasonable chance. Personnel turnover is rapid. It is extremely difficult to maintain any real continuity either of programs or people. More than in any area of government activity with which I am familiar, the attitudes of Congress inhibit the initiation of imaginative and creative programs. Equally important, it is difficult to plan ahead on a time-scale appreciably longer than the magical 2-year Congressional cycle. There are so many pressures in the direction of making a good showing within a short time, our aid efforts have tended to emphasize short-term proj-

ects at the expense of long-term efforts. As a result, our overall showing during the last two decades has been remarkably poor, particularly when compared with the need. I often feel that if we had taken at least a 20-year view of the problem when we first started our assistance efforts abroad, they would now be much further ahead than they actually are.

The problem of adequate balance in our aid efforts is equally critical. A banker tends to think in banker's terms; an agriculturalist tends to think in terms of agriculture; an educator tends to think in terms of education. As a result of the tugging and hauling, our aid programs in some countries are often analogous to the proverbial house which was designed by a committee and which turned out to be a giraffe.

Here I would like to stress that our Agency for International Development is itself far less to blame for these troubles than is our Congress. I know many dedicated, selfless men in the organization who work day and night trying to keep essential programs going and to make sense of a situation the magnitude of which dulls the senses. But the organization and its predecessors have been beaten, trampled upon, and derided to such an extent over the years, I sometimes wonder that it is able to function at all. Indeed, I find it little short of amazing that it is still able to carry out meaningful programs.

Economic development can be effectively blocked at any one of numerous points by failure to fully anticipate needs. The economy of a given nation might improve with breathtaking speed, only to be halted by a lack of trained manpower able to assume supervisory positions. Agricultural production might increase at a satisfactory rate, only to be halted by lack of adequate agricultural research. We must always be on the lookout for the missing nail which might lead to our losing the shoe, the horse, the king, and eventually the war.

The Missing Nail

I would now like to take advantage

of being with a group of fellow-scientists to draw attention to one of the "nails" which has been almost completely absent from most country-development programs. The missing nail is the development of adequate indigenous scientific-technological competence.

As a nation develops economically, it is certain to be faced by a multiplicity of problems of a technical nature which are peculiar to that country. If those problems are to be solved, the nation must have available its own group of applied scientists, its own facilities for research and development, and administrative organizations which will enable industry and government to mobilize research efforts effectively. This "problem-solving competence" must be backed by competent scientific and engineering staffs in the universities and by a research tradition and a scientific attitude. It must also be backed by an appreciation within the government itself of the need to support and nurture scientific activity.

Unfortunately, the need for this "problem-solving competence" is often completely ignored — it being more or less tacitly assumed that technology can be transferred intact and that should problems arise they can be solved in Europe or in the United States. Yet it would appear obvious that the technical problems of developing the Amazon basin must of necessity be solved in Brazil; they certainly can't be solved in Iowa.

Resource Drain

Finally, I would like to stress that the economic development of the poorer nations will place a tremendous drain upon the earth's available resources. We have seen that by the year 2000 the population of the world might well grow to 7½ billion persons, about 6 billion of whom will be living in the presently underdeveloped nations of the world. If by some miracle all these persons were to be brought up to the level of living now enjoyed by the people of the United States, we would need to extract from the earth over 50 billion tons of iron, one billion tons of copper, an equal amount of lead, over 600 million tons of zinc, and nearly 100 million tons of tin in addition to huge quantities of other substances. These quantities are several hundred times the present world annual rates of production. Their extraction would virtually deplete the earth of all high-grade mineral resources and would necessitate our living off the leanest of earth substances: the waters of the sea and ordinary rock.

Although depletion of the earth's buried high-grade resources should be a matter of serious concern to us all, it is by no means an immediate threat nor is it an insurmountable problem. Given the necessary technology, which I am convinced can be developed, the earth has ample resources to enable persons the world over to lead abundant lives, even were the population to grow eventually to a considerably higher level than that now anticipated in the year 2000. In principle we can feed, clothe, and support a population of, say, 10 billion persons, at a reasonably high level of consumption for an indefinitely long period of time.

The Basic Problem

Our basic problem, really, is not that of supporting comfortably the distressingly large numbers of people who we now know will inevitably inhabit the earth in the decades ahead. I am convinced that technically this can be done. Our basic problem is that of getting from here to there successfully with a minimum of chaos and human suffering. We are called upon to make the most difficult transition the community of man has yet been called upon to make — that of bringing birth rates in balance with rapidly lowering death rates on a world-wide scale. At the same time we are called upon to rapidly improve the economic well-being of the world's people. Although this transition is feasible from a technological point of view, it might well turn out to be impossible politically.

Here indeed is the great potential tragedy of our age! Our science and our technology have given us the power to create a world in which virtually all people can lead free and abundant lives. We have the power to create a civilization as yet undreamed of in its beauty and its accomplishments. Yet somehow we can't seem to organize ourselves to use that power effectively to solve mankind's basic problems.

Will future generations point to ours as that which made possible the realization of this higher level of human culture? Or will they point to ours as the generation which failed humanity at the most critical period of its history?

I fear that there is no middle ground.

Can We Prepare for Famine?

A Social Scientist's View

E. James Archer

The crises resulting from overpopulation are described and a program for responsible action is proposed. The concept of family planning is questioned; the need for population management is urged. The establishment of a university-consortium to operate a National Center for Population Studies is urged. Informing the public is essential. (BioScience 18, no. 7, p. 685-690)

Since the writings of Malthus, we have heard that the growth of the world's population will outstrip our ability to feed that population. Almost as frequently we have heard from the optimists that in view of our great technological advances "something will turn up" to prove Malthus wrong. Perhaps the optimists will be correct, but on the chance that they will be wrong, it might be prudent to consider some alternatives.

With increasing frequency we are reminded of our exploding population and our much slower progress in increasing our food production. If one were an optimist, he would dismiss the prediction of widespread famine, but if one were more cautious, he would look at the evidence which has prompted Paddock and Paddock to write the book, *Famine 1975! America's Decision: Who Will Survive* and the President's Science Advisory Committee (PSAC) to issue a three-volume report entitled, "The World Food Problem."

The Paddock and Paddock book concentrates on the exploding population. It points out four principal population dynamics and several false hopes for controlling the population growth. I would like to identify these four population dynamics and some of the false hopes:[1]

1. The Death Rate

Most people think that the population explosion is due to an *increased* birth rate, i.e., number of births per 1000 people. This is a gross oversimplification. As Robert Cook, the president of the Population Reference Bureau said, "We've been trying for years to get people interested in death rates, to get people to understand that the 'explosion' is due primarily to falling death rates and not to changing birth rates."

The relationship is quite simple: *Only* live people have babies and live people *do* have babies. The more people you save from death due to typhoid, cholera, diphtheria, smallpox, malaria, and bubonic plague, the more people will be around to have babies.

In many underdeveloped countries the death rate has been cut in half since World War II. The relationship between death rate and population explosion is nicely illustrated by the following observation, "If by 1975 the death rate in Guatemala fell somewhere near the 1950 United States level (9.6) — a not unlikely development — this alone would increase the number of women reaching the beginning of the child-bearing period by 36 percent and the number at the end of the child-bearing period by 85 percent."

[1] Except where noted all quotes are from Paddock and Paddock.

2. The Younger Generation

Nearly one-half of all the people in the underdeveloped countries are under the age of 15. Young people marry and married people have babies. One statistical prediction presents the case: by 1975 there will be 60% more marriages formed in Latin America than in 1960. Sixty per cent more marriages formed in 1975 will mean 60% more babies in 1976. Again, it is not the birth rate, i.e., births per 1000 population, which accounts for the explosion, rather there are just more people in the child-bearing ages.

3. The Birth Rate

For many years it was thought that a birth rate of 45 per thousand was the physiological maximum. This figure was based on the observation that of 1000 people 500 will be women. Of that number, 410 were either too old or too young or sterile. Of the remaining 90, we could find another 45 who were pregnant or who just had a child and had not had time to conceive and deliver another child. However, with a shift to a lower average age (Population Dynamic Number Two) we find a few instances of birth rates exceeding the "classical limit" of 45/1000. For example, in 1963, Costa Rica had a birth rate of 50.2/1000.

We also see an interaction of some of these Population Dynamics in that those techniques which lower the death

A paper presented at the Midwest Conference on Graduate Study and Research, March 26, 1968, Chicago, Ill. The author is a Professor of Psychology at the University of Colorado, Boulder.

rate generally also improve the health of the individual and people who are both young *and* healthy, are more fertile, have more frequent intercourse, and if a child is conceived, it is more likely to come to full term, i.e., there will be fewer miscarriages and still births.

4. Man's Reproductive System

"Man has been evolving and reproducing for a million years. Those who expect science to be able to find quickly a birth control method which can successfully circumvent this million years of such single-mindedness both overestimate modern science and underestimate the efficiency of the reproductive system which evolution has provided man."

Now the optimists will react with a list of things that will assure themselves that all is well. For example, they might cite the control of population in Japan, but that is a very special case and not applicable to other areas. Specifically, Japan has a literacy rate which is so high that they don't even bother with this measure in their census taking today. In 1948 Japan showed an illiteracy level of 1.1%. In contrast, Africa's is 84% and Latin America's is about 40%. Japan also had legalized abortions in 1948. The impact of this decision is best seen in the following statistics: In 1955 there were 1.2 million abortions performed. Even assuming the higher proportion of males at birth, because these 1.2 million conceptions did not come to full term, Japan will have approximately 0.5 million *fewer* women entering the child-bearing age next year than would have occurred in the absence of the abortions which took place in 1955.

Japan has a large medical profession as compared to the underdeveloped nations. If we look at the number of inhabitants per physician ratio, we see Japan's is 900:1, but Mexico's is twice that ratio. Pakistan has a ratio of 11,000:1 and Ethiopia has 96,000:1. If you think the intrauterine device (the IUD) is the answer, you have another problem. Who will insert it?

The IUD is another false hope of avoiding widespread famine due to the exploding population. Consider these data. The designer of the most widely used IUD claims it can be inserted in 6 minutes. One well trained team even managed to insert 75 IUD's in a 3-hour session — that is one IUD insertion every 2 minutes and 24 seconds. While this sounds good, it must be recognized that 850,000 women entered the child-bearing age in India alone last year and the number will increase in succeeding years. You cannot insert IUD's fast enough.

The hope of the Pill is equally discouraging. Its use requires daily attention plus motivation. Remember also when a woman goes off the Pill, or forgets to take it regularly, her fertility is actually increased. Furthermore, because of the undesirable side-effects, the Pill is not recommended for all women. Until a "morning after" or monthly pill is developed, the Pill as it is now known is only promising and not an answer.

Let me mention a few other hopes which the optimists cite but which also appear to be *false* hopes. We have frequently heard, and the PSAC report emphasizes this point, that what we need to do is to improve the agricultural production of the developing countries. One way to do this is to send them seeds, stock, and fertilizers; then they can raise more food to feed their exploding population and all will be well.

First, many strains of wheat and corn which do very well in the United States either perform poorly or even fail to come to seed in other climates and on other soils. You cannot export seed; you have to develop the appropriate strains and agricultural technology in the field where the grain is to grow. For example, it is estimated that corn production in Mexico has been increased about 200% by the work of the Rockefeller Foundation program. This sounds great and may seem to be the obvious solution, i.e., we export the know-how and all will be saved. There are a few hitches, however. First, half of the increased yield was due to double cropping (but getting in two growing seasons is not always possible). Second, the research program did *not* find just *the* right strain of corn to grow in Mexico. The soils, micro-climates, macro-climates, and irrigation conditions are so different in different areas that about a dozen different strains are needed — each appropriate to its growing conditions. Third, the program took 25 years. We just do not have 25 years.

Look at it this way — in the best of our agricultural research and training institutions, how long does it take you to train one plant pathologist? One geneticist? And remember, he comes from and lives in an environment that financially supports him, offers rewards for successful work, and has a supporting intellectual climate of chemists, biochemists, cell biologists, plant physiologists, biophysicists, and agricultural engineers. Finally, he has the elaborate infra-structure of an agricultural extension system to communicate his work to the point of meaningful effect — the farmer. Even if we had all of the personnel, equipment, and financial resources available, we do not have the time — no matter how many chickens sit on an egg, it still takes 21 days to hatch it. The same principle applies to successive plant breeding tests.

Some of the optimists will feel safe because man will solve his food problems by "harvesting" the sea. Paddock and Paddock point out the special relish with which the word "harvest" is used. Hoping to harvest the sea in time to avoid major famines is truly a false hope. How little we know of the sea is shown in another PSAC publication entitled "The Effective Use of the Sea," which appeared in 1966. We are a long way from ever understanding the processes of turbulence which contribute to the essential stirring of the sea. The sometimes cyclic churning action brings necessary organic material to intermediate depths to provide food for plankton, which becomes food for shrimp, which become food for larger fish, which become food for man. We do not even have a satisfactory buoy network technology to enable us to study the microclimate of the seas. If you do not understand the climate on land, you will be a poor farmer and if you don't understand the "climate" in the ocean, you will be at least as poor a harvester of the sea. How long will it take to train an oceanographer? The climate for such personnel development is nowhere comparable to that which exists for training a plant pathologist.

Even if I have not persuaded the optimists that there is cause for concern about the population explosion, I hope I have brought the matter to their attention.

Let us now look at another aspect — the world's food supply. A few years ago this country was troubled with crop surpluses. You do not hear of these anymore because they no longer exist. Whereas we used to be concerned with the cost of storing our surplus crops, we now find that we could ship one-fourth of each year's production to India alone — and that would not be enough.

The PSAC report focuses its attention on the need to improve the economic development of the developing countries so as to produce the capital to invest in improving agricultural development. The PSAC report offers 46 recommendations. It is significant, disturbingly significant, that of the 46 recommendations, only one refers specifically to the population problem.

Here is a quotation and comment on this particular recommendation: *Population and Family Planning.*

"This policy has been stated forcefully and adequately in recent messages by the President and the Panel strongly endorses these statements. Family planning should be encouraged because of the long-range needs to decrease the rate of population growth and because of its value in improving economic benefits per capita. The Panel *cautions, however, that family planning will not in itself be a solution to the world food problem,* and that family planning alone will probably not significantly reduce the problem of the food needs within the next 20 years in the developing countries. Population numbers in the developing countries will continue to increase rapidly during the next 20 years because nearly half of the present population is less than 15 years old. In spite of the fact that population control is one of the

greatest problems facing mankind, there is an immediate need for increased supplies of food and better nutrition."

I disagree! First, the recommendation directs its attention at the effect rather than the cause. Developing countries need more food *because* of their exploding population — they would need less food if there were fewer people. Second, what is family planning? It is a decision made by a man and a woman about the size of their family. It is a decision based upon their personal wishes independent of their food supply. It is a decision based upon cultural norms as perceived by the procreating couple. For example, if Chilean couples are asked what they consider an ideal family size, they reply four children. They have no need for "planning" until they have had their fourth child. It takes very little arithmetic to see what this means in terms of population growth. *We do not need "family planning"; we need population management.* India has come to realize this problem too late and unless it adopts a proposal of compulsory sterilization of every man who has fathered two children, it will not manage its already excessive population.

Third, the PSAC report states, "In spite of the fact that population control is one of the greatest problems facing mankind, there is an immediate need for increased supplies of food and better nutrition." This, I believe, is remarkably short sighted. If we were to supply more food and improve nutrition, we would improve the health and fertility of an already mismanaged population. We would only exacerbate an already critical problem. How critical the problem is can be seen from a close-up view of Calcutta. It is so overpopulated now that 600,000 of its people sleep on the sidewalks. It is estimated that two-thirds of Calcutta goes to sleep hungry. Calcutta has a birth rate of 41 per 1000 now. Imagine the birth rate if the nutrition were improved.

The general tone of the PSAC report is best described by quoting two sections: One is just inside the cover and reads, ". . . Feed Them Also and Lift

Them Up . . ." — Psalms 28:9, the other is Section 3.10.1 entitled "Why?"

In the Panel's view, the concern of this country for the hungry nations is threefold:

"1. *Humanitarian.* We should help the less fortunate simply because they need help and we are able to help them. The benefits of altruism are by no means unilateral. The challenge of a difficult task and the moral uplift that comes only from doing for others are needed to temper and balance the leisure and affluence of American life. The real successes of the Peace Corps center in the fundamentally inspired, collective aim that is exemplified in the late Albert Schweitzer's dictum, 'It is only giving that stimulates.'

"2. *Security.* Populations in the developing countries double in 18 to 27 years; 55 to 88 years are required for populations to double in developed countries. By the year 2000, if present rates of growth continue, there will be more than four times as many people in the developing countries as are in the developed nations. To avoid a threat to the peace of the world as well as to our own national security, we cannot afford to be too little and too late with our development assistance. The expectations of the poor are demanding fulfillment. It is to be hoped that some measure of their ambitions can be realized by peaceful means."

(I must interrupt here and challenge the logic of this statement. It assumes that the population increase *will* take place and we should prepare to feed that increased population. It even seems to imply that an ever-increasing population for us in the United States is both inevitable and may be even desirable. It implies that our security is tied to the *number* of people we have rather than the quality of the life future generations live. It is remarkably condescending since it implies that those countries which are now "developing" will still be only developing in the year 2000, they will still be poor and we hope "some measure of their ambition can be realized.")

Continuing with the Panel's reasons for our improving the world's food supply, we have the third and most disturbing reason.

"3. *A Better Tomorrow for Us, Too.* This is a long-range goal, an economic reason for investment. An important way to expand our own economy in the future will be through further specialization and trade. As nations develop, they become trading nations and through trade, both parties to a transaction benefit. Trading partners are likely to be peaceful protagonists."

This *reason* sounds disturbingly like economic exploitation or it can easily be so interpreted by others. I suggest that we are less in need of a study of "The World Food Problem" with the PSAC orientation than we are in need of a study of "The World Population Problem" with an orientation which recognizes that this world has a finite size. We must recognize that the world's population may have already exceeded the allowable limits and, finally, that if man is going to live in an environment of high quality, he must learn to be a part of his environment — interacting with it and not just consuming and in some cases destroying it.

When we speak of the population explosion, we usually imply some other nation's explosion, but we had better start looking at our own population. Unless we can demonstrate that we can manage our own population, we can hardly hope to have others manage theirs. Why should they? The population of the United States has increased from 130 million in 1930 to over 200 million in 1967. The day the census clock ticked off the 200 millionth U.S. citizen, the President celebrated the event with a speech. He might well have used the occasion to ask, "Where are we going?" This is an increase of over 70 million in less than 37 years. With this enormous growth we have polluted our air, streams, lakes, and sea shores to a degree that in some cases they have been irreparably spoiled. We are consuming natural resources faster than they can be replaced and we are putting impossible pressures on our recreational and cultural facilities. Ecologically, we seem hell-bent on creating as degraded an environment as pos-

sible for those future generations who might survive us and we seem equally motivated to make sure that that future population is enormous.

What can we do about this problem? First, we need to decide if we want to do something about the problem. If you are a confirmed optimist then there is no problem. If, however, you have been persuaded that we have a problem, I suggest we decide to do something about it. *That* is the first step.

Secondly, I suggest that the universities are in the best position to deal with the problem. Just as some universities in the United States formed the University Corporation for Atmospheric Research (UCAR) to operate the National Center for Atmospheric Research (NCAR), so also could we establish a National Center for Population Studies. Such a Center could develop at least three major programs. One of these programs would be in the field of public information; the second would be in research on the biological, social, and humanistic problems; the third would serve as a legislative reference service.

The first would deal with public information. Here I see a very critical problem. The solution to the long-range problem of population management will depend on an informed and concerned public. Unless the majority of people in this country are convinced that there is a problem and that we can and should do something about it, there will be little hope of success. I would suggest that the Public Information Program of the Center could produce a series of television documentaries which would present the scope of the problem as it now exists and what would seem to be realistic predictions. As a starter, the producer of the documentaries could even consider televising the Paddock and Paddock book. I suggest television as the medium of communication to the public since this is the medium which will bring the information to the public. Few of my colleagues even know of Paddock and Paddock and, I suspect, fewer still have read the exchanges of letters on this general problem which recently have appeared in

Science. Unfortunately, the average citizen is even less likely to be aware of the problem and the prediction of the future. I believe a series of televised documentaries could correct this lack of information and understandable lack of public concern.

Unfortunately, the task of educating the public will be difficult and the difficulties are compounded by such TV programs as the recent NBC television special entitled "Feeding the Billions" (Frank McGee, Friday, February 23, 1968). This hour-long program spent the first 53 minutes on the many pilot programs underway for developing synthetic foods, improving marine aquaculture, and fresh-water fish farming. Only in the last 7 minutes did we get to hear from Drs. James Bonner and Harrison Brown of Cal Tech that we faced unavoidable famines and that our synthetic food production technology, our fertilizer plant projects in underdeveloped countries, and our "harvesting" from the sea would take more time than we had available.

Curiously, many people who were interviewed on that NBC Special freely admitted that we were coming up with too little and it would be too late, but the commentator smoothed over these rough spots with heavy doses of optimism.

The research programs of the Center would need to be quite diversified. In the *biological* research programs some effort might be directed to the general problems of contraception, but since other agencies are already providing considerable support in this area, it might be better to look at population genetic problems, especially behavioral genetics. As you know, whenever you impose any bias or limitation on procreation of a population, you will produce a pattern of changes as that population reproduces. Some of these changes in blood chemistry are reasonably easy to recognize. Some of the behavioral changes are less easily identified, however. For example, how a man or woman reacts to stress will be determined by many variables and one of these is genetic makeup. Unfortunately, the nature of the inheritance is not as simple as brown eyes are dominant over blue eyes. The genetic characteristic which is transmitted provides a disposition of the individual to react in a particular way *if* the social situation is appropriate and if the individual has not already learned some counter-reaction to stress. In short, the variables in behavioral genetics are at once more complex, show a greater degree of interaction, and are more important for the high quality survival of future generations than brown eyes are dominant over blue eyes.

For the social research programs, we have many problems to consider. Many of them deal with attitude assessment and attitude change. The following questions indicate the scope of appropriate research programs that need to be considered by social scientists. What are the factors which account for family size preference? How do these factors operate to determine family size? What can be done to modify the effect of these factors? What will be the secondary repercussions of modifying family size? For example, if the size of the school age population would become much more predictable, providing for educational facilities could be done with greater reliability. If the school boards and state legislators knew the size of the school age population in 1980, 1990, and 2000, they could better plan expenditures for education and would have less reluctance in doing so.

There are very serious problems to consider in the field of race relations. A population management program could easily be misinterpreted as a poorly disguised program of race extermination. In fact, if population management controls were applied differentially to the races, it *would* be a form of prenatal genocide. There would be many problems in "selling" a population management program, but if the people were informed, I am hopeful that they would demand such a program.

It is unfortunate that my discipline of psychology has not made greater efforts to study the factors which make for a human environment of high quality. Some of our research is far removed from this very critical problem. The factors which promote or inhibit the acquisition of a conditioned eyeblink are interesting, but knowledge of factors which will better enable man to resolve conflicts is more important. Discovering the factors which interfere with the learning of a list of nonsense syllables can be challenging, but determining the changes in human relations which result from commuting to work in a dirty, smelly, crowded, and noisy subway will be more important for both our survival as a species and our development as humane human beings.

Psychology, sociology, and anthropology should rise to the occasion and study human development under different environments. It is interesting to know of the warlike ways of the Mayutecs in Amazon country, but what are the factors in ghettos in our big cities which make for warlike subcultures?

The field of urban planning has assumed new prominence in the past few years because of our growing concern with the city and its core which is frequently found to be deteriorating. There is little evidence of an interest in building cities which strive to attain environments of high quality. While it is true that expediting the flow of traffic through or around a city adds a measure of pleasure, consider the ugliness that surrounds you as you come down the Kennedy Expressway from O'Hare Airport. It is an ugliness which overwhelms the visitor; but worst of all, the citizen of Chicago adapts to it (he has to), and he becomes insensitive to it. That insensitivity enables him to tolerate the ugliness of visual and auditory and olfactory noise which he finds in the Loop and many, many other parts of this and other cities. (I feel I can criticize Chicago's ugliness since I was born and raised here.)

Humanists frequently refer to the sanctity and dignity of each human individual — but what are they doing about it? What efforts are they making to assure that dignity? What efforts are they making to prevent man from sinking to a caged animal existence in the cities where the effects of our ever increasing population are so sharply seen? Could not the humanists and the behavioral scientists study the problem of determining maximum population density? Or more precisely, do we not need to formulate the relationship between population density and availability of recreational and cultural facilities which will contribute to a human environment of high quality?

My point is that the humanists have limited themselves to academia or to showplace cultural centers; the humanities have had pitifully little impact on man and his development of his environment. As we start to consider the kind of environment we want to live in, the humanities must play a more significant role than they have in the past. The humanities need to become a force in shaping our future, making the most of what has been and can be man's best efforts.

A National Center for Population Studies would employ the best available biological and social scientists and humanists. The latter two fields would be especially critical because the problems is *not* just a biological problem but rather one of social and cultural change.

We urgently need our most able humanists to turn their attention to the questions of the human environment. The humanists need to consider how and to what degree we can change our morality, as change we must, and still remain humane; they need to consider how we can make each man and woman aware of his role in a society without also destroying the qualities of individuality we hold so dear (and which in fact are essential to the continued development and improvement of our human environment); they need to participate in the planning of a human environment of the highest quality. Traditionally, humanists have been concerned with evaluating man's past and their occasional anticipations of the future have been deemed utopian. We live in a time when their function has become essential and utterly practical — man will not adjust biologically until his spirit demands it. We are in a time when the wisdom of the past should be used to divine man's future.

The third very important functional program of my proposed National Center for Population Studies would be a legislative reference program. There is going to be a need for appropriate state and federal legislation in many areas of population management. For example, last year the Legislature of the State of Colorado passed a "liberalized" abortion law. The law was not meant to manage our population, but it is a start in changing attitudes toward an even greater acceptance of abortion as a form of population control. It is only relatively liberal but is far ahead of anything like it in other states. If and when other states want to consider such legislation, they need not only a copy of the Colorado bill but they will need to know of its successes and its failures. In addition, they will want to know what has been tried or is being considered in other states and countries.

Your first reaction may be that *we* could never legislate how many children someone has, but this is not true. We actually pay a bonus to people for having children. Every April 15th you may discount $600 from your taxable income for each child you have. While the concept of a bonus may not have been intended, this is the effect.

Finally, I have deliberately chosen to restrict my proposal to a *National* Center rather than try for an *International* one. I am not being a provincial or an isolationist. I think our best contribution is not exporting foodstuffs to underdeveloped countries or even fighting wars in which they themselves do not believe. Rather, I think we should take a page from the Department of Housing and Urban Development approach which is trying to develop "model cities." We should try to develop

a "model country" where overcrowding, pollution of all sorts, and inhumanity toward one another is eliminated. The forced regulation of the lives of other people is imperialism. We will best serve a better world by showing leadership in developing a society worthy of emulation. We certainly cannot lead in any effective way if our own strength is sapped away while we "help" others.

I think that Paddock and Paddock are right when they conclude that there are some underdeveloped countries which are making so little progress in population control and so little progress in increased agricultural production that we cannot help them to avoid widespread famine without destroying our own society. Paddock and Paddock go so far as to suggest that the underdeveloped countries need to be divided into three groups: They draw the analogy of triage.

" 'Triage' is a term used in military medicine. It is defined as the assigning of priority of treatment to the wounded brought to a battlefield hospital in a time of mass casualties and limited medical facilities. The wounded are divided on the basis of three classifications:

(1) Those so seriously wounded they cannot survive regardless of the treatment given them; call these the 'can't-be-saved.'

(2) Those who can survive without treatment regardless of the pain they may be suffering; call these the 'walking wounded.'

(3) Those who can be saved by immediate medical care."

This concept can and must be applied to nations when the time of famines comes. Paddock and Paddock see the analogy as follows:

"(1) Nations in which the population growth trend has already passed the

agricultural potential. This combined with inadequate leadership and other divisive factors makes catastrophic disasters inevitable. These nations form the 'can't-be-saved' group. To send food to them is to throw sand into the ocean. . . . Nor can the national interests of the United States be excluded, whether political, military, or economic. American officials when applying triage decisions and shipping out *American* food are surely justified in thinking beyond only the food requirements of the individual hungry nations. They are justified, . . . , to consider whether the survival of a specific nation will:

(a) help maintain the economic viability and relative prosperity of the United States during the time of famines.

(b) help maintain the economic stability of the world as a whole.

(c) help create a 'better world' after the troubles of the time of famines have ended."

Let me put the problem another way. At the present time we have many people demonstrating and engaging in civil disobedience because of a war they feel is immoral. It is immoral, they say, to kill one or two thousand people on both sides a week. How will they react to triage? How will they react when it has become a national policy to let a particular group of nations suffer widespread famine while we withhold food from them? Panics? Riots? What unfriendly nations will fish in troubled waters and offer military weapons including ICBMs to large starving nations to blackmail us into sharing? How will the "moralists" react then?

The question is not *"Can* we prepare for famine?" The real question is "Are we *willing* to prepare for famine?"

Mariculture

Harold H. Webber

A review of the state of the art of mariculture is presented with reference to the current and potential yields of food from the sea as it is now garnered. The practices in use around the world in farming the edge of the sea are considered and specific techniques employed with molluscs, crustaceans, and finfish are described. (BioScience 18, no. 10, p. 940-945)

The potential, practicable production of human food and animal feed from the living resources of the world ocean, by current fishing techniques, has been variously estimated at 4 or even 10 times the current annual yield of about 53 x 10⁶ metric tons of fish and shellfish.

Since the basic source of all organic food materials originating in the sea is from the sun's energy, we can estimate production of organic material by the green plants of the sea. It is about 20 x 10⁹ metric tons per year. On a wet weight basis, this yields 200 x 10⁹ metric tons of living plant material per year. This is equal to (or greater than) the production of all plant life on land — including the forests and the uncultivated savannas from which man realizes little food.

Although we do not know the conversion efficiency of the several steps in food chains in the sea, or even the actual number of trophic increments from photosynthetic algae to marketable food fish, it seems reasonable to assume that herbivores are 20% efficient and that the carnivore links in the food chain are 10% efficient. Based on this assumption, and further assuming that harvestable marine fish are secondary carnivores, Graham and Edwards calculated that "considerably less than 60 x 10⁶ metric tons of marine fish are at present available for harvest on

The author is President, Groton Associates, Inc., Groton, Mass.

an annual basis." This amount would represent only 0.03% of the organic material estimated to be produced annually in the sea.

With a more optimistic judgment, and if man is to limit his marine food procurement to the exploitation of wild fish and shellfish populations as they occur in their natural habitats, *and* given the best international fisheries management, *and* advanced detection and catching methods, M. B. Schaeffer calculates that the earth's oceans may be capable of providing us with not much more than 200 x 10⁶ metric tons per year *on a sustained yield basis.*

In contrast to the 1500 x 10⁶ metric tons of human food being produced on the land, the current ocean yield is only about 3% of the total food now being generated. The marine resource will certainly be further exploited with the advancement of improved hunting-gathering techniques. It may even exceed the productivity of the most optimistic estimate as technologies devise more effective detection and the use of more efficient biological processing methods allow the extraction and use of more efficient biological forms closer to the primary productivity of the seas.

The frequent references to the disproportion of land and water surfaces of the earth ("70% of the earth is covered by water") has often promised an opportunity for greatly increased marine food production, on the tacit assumption that the productivity of the

water covered surfaces will approximate that of the land. But the vast pelagic expanses of the ocean which cover one-half of the surface of the earth are for the most part deserted by food animals. With few exceptions, it is only in the waters over the continental shelves (20% of the area of the earth), and within the 200 m depth range where nutrient concentrations are high, that the fisheries of the world are sufficiently productive to warrant the great expectations and justify the financial investment and the human effort.

It is particularly at the margin of the seas (probably not more than 3% of the ocean surface) that the profusion of marine life exists which, since prehistory, has been garnered by man as a food resource. It is here that there is sufficient nutrient concentration washed off the land and dispersed by turbulence and convection, and here where abundant solar radiation reaches deep into this rich nutrient solution.

It is in this narrow ribbon of shoreline, in the estuaries, the coastal lagoons, the marshlands and wetlands that rim the continents and islands that the marifarms will be located.

Some of the major fisheries of the world have come from this highly eutrophic boundary region. Here we gather the numerous molluscan delicacies: oysters, clams, mussels, abalone. Here we catch the shrimp, lobsters, and crabs which are dependent during their early stages of life on the waters at the land's edge for shelter and nursery grounds. And many valuable finfish are caught close inshore, where the waters are rich in the planktonic forms that start and support the food chain that ends in the marketable fish.

If man is to enhance the yield of these desirable foods, then he must begin to exercise control over their environment. He must protect them against the influences of pollution. He must limit predation and competition of the preferred species, control disease, and guard against the extremes of weather influences. In addition to such preventive measures, programs of improvement such as genetically increased growth rates, food conversion rates, resistance to disease, and adaptation to confined culture conditions must also be undertaken. It will be necessary to provide appropriate kinds and quantities of supplemental feeds and growth-promoting substances, and to devise the bioengineering systems for culturing dense populations.

When we exercise this much control and positive improvement over the environment, then we are beginning to practice mariculture, rather than the traditional hunting and gathering practices upon which we rely today.

Man is a terrestrial, air breathing animal who finds the more familiar land environment and its inhabitants more amenable to manipulation and control. It is therefore obvious that the innovation of agriculture, which probably occurred in the Neolithic age some 10,000 to 15,000 years ago, should precede the invention of mariculture. On the other hand, the sea and its creatures have been in a world apart, alien and enigmatic. The aquatic environment and the strange biotic interactions occurring in it become less hostile and intractable as we venture further into an understanding of the ocean's uncertainties. Land animal husbandry practices grew out of a familiarity with creatures like ourselves that are air breathing, warm blooded vertebrates, with familiar mechanisms for reproduction and nutrition, irritability to the environment, and behavior both within and among communities. These have not been appropriate guides to lead us into the hus-

banding of animals of the sea. The marine biologist and the fisheries scientist have a great deal more basic research to perform in these matters to support the developing technology that will bring aquaculture abreast of agriculture.

It is propitious now, under the pressure of the massive food demands of our rapidly growing populations and our increasing capability to cope with the more alien marine environment, to attack the problems of mariculture in a systematic way. However, it is urgent to say at this point that the immediate return from mariculture will probably contribute very little to relief from hunger of the undernourished peoples of the world. It is unlikely that the *caloric* requirements of the hungry peoples can ever be met from the sea. The contribution to the *immediate* alleviation of protein hunger will at best be small, relative to the need that we are confronting in the next two decades.

On the other hand, mariculture holds great promise as a business opportunity for the advanced nations of the world, where investment can be made in research, development, and engineering applications studies that will result in economic production of high value seafood products. A mari-farming venture can only be designed to market products in the developed countries where purchasing power is sufficient to support the current high prices, and where the more catholic tastes of affluent peoples promise high consumer acceptance.

We may expect, and plan for, a cost and commensurate selling price reduction to result from advancement of maricultural technologies, and as more extensive investment and research and development generate greater efficiencies. It is not presumptuous to assume an analogy with poultry and other advanced animal husbandry industries. In recent years these have realized high conversion rates of feed to marketable food, increased growth and survival rates, and generally very high levels of productivity in terms of capital and labor inputs. Advances have been achieved through the wise application of fundamental biological science in

genetics, nutrition, disease and pest control, behavior, and general physiology. Only when marine biology and physical oceanology provide the basis for similar applications of these fundamental sciences can mariculture make a significant contribution to programs that are required to alleviate the protein famine that confronts the developing nations. This achievement may well take the next two decades.

The inference that one might draw from the above is that mariculture is a brand new concept. But, in fact, this is far from the truth. There is abundant evidence for the existence of maricultural practices among the ancient cultures, recorded in the histories of the Mediterranean peoples and of the peoples of the Far East. Molluscs, such as oysters, were grown in Roman waters in suspended culture by techniques not unlike those used today in the Mediterranean and in Japan. In the Far East, juvenile shrimp, captured as a natural recruitment on tidal exchange in coastal waters and confined in lagoons, were cultured in a pastoral sense 2000 years ago. Here they grew to maturity on naturally available feeds, which flourished in the nutrient rich warm waters and in the bottom muds and sediments.

Since World War II, however, there has been a growing body of knowledge in the fields of marine biology and estuarine ecology which has reached a promising state of advancement. This knowledge should encourage the more venturesome entrepreneurs in our business community and governments to invest in the additional research and development required to establish a system of production from sunlight to market.

Molluscs

I should like to illustrate the concept with an existing maricultural enterprise which is emerging from an advanced developmental stage into what appears to be a very attractive business venture in marine animal husbandry.

By eclectically drawing on research results and culture techniques devised over the last half century by marine biologists around the world, and testing and validating these concepts against a long experience with molluscan forms in the Long Island waters, a commercial enterprise has assembled a complete system of oyster and clam production. Much of this technology was developed in the 1920's by Wells and Glancy of the New York State Fish and Game Commission and in the postwar years at the Bureau of Commercial Fisheries Biological Laboratory at Milford, Connecticut.

The American oyster *(Crassostrea virginica)* and the northern hard shell clam *(Mercenaria)* are the primary forms that are being reared for market. With small adaptations of the techniques briefly described below other pelecypods and such univalves as abalone can be cultured in essentially the same facility and by the same system. The European oyster *(Ostrea edulis),* the Japanese oyster *(Crassostrea edulis),* the Olympic oyster of our Pacific Coast *(Ostrea lurida),* the bay scallop *(Pecten irradians),* and our West Coast abalone *(Haliotis)* have all been raised from egg to market by the hatchery and nursery methods which shall be described here for oysters.

The production system starts with the maintenance of selected parents which are cultured in the laboratory as a source of egg and sperm. A breeding program has been undertaken with these parents, and selection for growth rate, size, meat quality, and certain shell characteristics is being made. Due to the very high fecundity of the oyster and the clam, very few breeding parents are required to support a very large business. Breeding stocks are kept in shallow plastic trays through which low temperature-controlled, natural sea water is kept constantly flowing. By keeping the temperature at essentially winter water levels, the parents are kept from spawning, but in a healthy state. No additional feed algae are required to supplement those that naturally occur in the excellent natural waters available in Long Island Sound. This water, as well as all the water used in the hatchery and nursery operation, is pumped from a selected point out in the phytoplankton-rich bay which has been proven

to be regularly free of toxic agents and pollution.

When spawning is desired, selected parent oysters are transferred to trays through which water that is precisely controlled for temperature is flowing. The parent oysters are subjected to a temperature regimen with a controlled rate of change which will induce gonadal development and result in spawning. This management of the reproductive system frees the marifarmer from the vicissitudes of the complex interactions of nature. Since spawning is now a totally predictable phenomenon, and can be achieved on command, he can be regularly assured of having a set of oysters.

In Long Island Sound there has not been a significant natural set of oysters in 8 years! Since industrial pollution, marina developments, channel dredging resulting in silting, and other human intrusions on the environment are likely to continue *and even increase,* dependence on a natural spatfall is too risky to justify an investment.

Male and female individuals are selected from the parent stock after they have been appropriately temperture conditioned and are placed in spawning trays where both eggs and sperm are ejected into the water where fertilization occurs. For the first 24-36 hr after fertilization no feeding of the zygote or the first larval stage is required. The larvae are then transferred to large tanks and fed known quantities of known species of algae from large pure-culture chambers.

Pure cultures of specific algal organisms, and mixed cultures of natural phytoplankton are used.

Seawater for this purpose is centrifuged and large detritus and suspended plants and animals are removed. Nannoplankton (2-10 μ cells) are retained in the water. Most of this water is piped to large tanks where it may be enriched with mineral nutrients if necessary These tanks are located under a translucent polyester/glass fiber roof where adequate light is provided to sustain photosynthetic activity. Due to the greenhouse effect, adequate heat, even in the wintertime, is available to support rich cultures of these desirable, nat-

urally occurring, small cell phytoplankton.

Other bay water which has been centrifuged passes through filters and high intensity ultraviolet light fields. Here any remaining bacteria and viruses are removed or killed. This sterile water is used for the pure algal cultures required for larval feeding. Several naked flagellates and diatoms are cultured for oyster larval forage. *Monochrysis lutheri, Isochrysis galbani, Dicrateria inornata, Cyclotella nana,* and *Chaetocerus calcitrans* are some of the most effective algal forms for feeding oyster larvae.

The larval growing tanks are monitored regularly. The tanks are emptied daily through fine mesh screens and the individuals sorted through meshes increasing in size with each day. The largest sizes are returned to freshly prepared rearing tanks. The use of fresh tanks daily eliminates the accumulation of staling products, and allows the maintenance of population density at an optimum. Those individuals which for one reason or another have slow growing rates, and are therefore small for their age-class, pass through the screens and are discarded. Thus there is a built-in mechanism for selecting the more vigorous individuals and for achieving a more uniform final product.

After 10 days the veliger larvae reach the umbo stage and are retained on a 325 μ mesh screen and are ready to set.

These larvae are then transferred to setting tanks which have had cultch distributed over the bottoms. These tanks are maintained at the appropriate temperature of 28 C (82.4 F) and setting occurs soon after the larvae are introduced.

After the set has been achieved, the cultch bearing the attached larvae, called spat, is placed into black polyethylene net bags, and the bags are suspended in large concrete nursery tanks. The water supply to these tanks is piped directly from the bay, but is supplemented with the rich culture of small phytoplankton that has been allowed to bloom in the enriched centrifuged water referred to earlier. Since the nursery tanks are housed in a building whose walls and roof are translucent corrugated polyester/glass fiber panels, a considerable amount of light and heat energy is provided. Water temperature is controlled in the nursery tanks, and gradually reduced to that of the natural waters of the bay in order to condition the larvae to be introduced ultimately into the "real world" of the open bay.

After a 3 or 4 week retention period, the spat, which grows very rapidly under these almost ideal conditions, reach about ½ inch in diameter. They are then ready to be moved out into natural waters, but they are still fragile enough to require protection from predators and silting. This frequently occurs in Long Island Sound and imposes enormous attrition on natural populations.

Still in the plastic bags, they are brought out onto rafts, floating in the bay alongside a pier. This makes them readily accessible to be monitored and tended. The rafts are designed to use the same bag supports which are used in the nursery tanks.

The young oysters are retained in suspended bag culture in the bay for a month, in which time, during the warm months of the year, they have grown to 1¼ inches, and are judged to be hardy enough to be out on oyster beds in the bay where they will be reared to market size.

These selected bottoms, which were hard to begin with, are specially prepared as any farmer would prepare his field to receive an agricultural crop. The bottoms are dragged or harrowed and vacuumed to clear them of debris and silt. They are also treated to kill predators: with CaO to kill the starfish, and with a chlorinated benzene to kill the oyster drill.

The oyster beds are regularly monitored by SCUBA divers who inspect the beds approximately twice a week during the warm weather months to check on growth condition. They inspect for disease, predators, and silting particularly. When any of these undesirable conditions is detected, prompt and effective remedial action can be taken.

Although the bottom on which the young oysters are placed is selected to enhance early growth of juveniles, for instance, because of higher temperature waters, it may not be appropriate for the final growth period. The oysters may therefore be lifted off the bottom and transplanted to other beds before they are finally harvested for sale.

A recent development in this oyster mariculture operation is the use of a heated sea water lagoon as a substitute for the indoor and outdoor nurseries. The heated effluent waters from a steam-electric power plant condenser cooling system is directed to a specially designed lagoon on which oyster rafts are floated, and in which a good growth of phytoplankton can be maintained. The heated water allows for an increased growth rate of the young oysters and a year round growing season, as opposed to the 5 or 6 month natural season in Long Island Sound. For this reason, and others noted above, the 5 year natural growth cycle can be cut to 2 to 2½ years. This system produces a high quality oyster which is exclusively sold as a half-shell table oyster, and commands a premium price in the marketplace.

The success of this economically sound venture in mariculture is based on a considerable resource in fundamental biological research and empirical evidence. It may be viewed as encouragement to induce us to undertake similar efforts with the other molluscan forms mentioned above.

TABLE 1. Yields of oyster meat (pounds per acre per year)

United States		
Public (average)		6
Private (average)		170
(maximum)		5000
France		
Flat (average)		320
Portuguese (average)		740
Australia		
(average)		120
(maximum)		4400
Philippines		
(maximum)		10,000
Japan		
(maximum)		50,000
Spain (mussels)		
(maximum)		500,000

Oyster production in other parts of the world in phytoplankton-rich waters in many instances may be higher in pounds per acre, but not necessarily on a dollar per acre basis.

Table 1 (Ryther 1968) assembles yields by countries and reflects the wide range of productivity in the various waters of the world. The Spanish mussel production is included because in the Bay of Vigo a happy set of circumstances allows for prodigious production on the ropes that are suspended from rafts to collect the mussels.

Crustaceans

Among the crustaceans, shrimp culture has been studied in Japan and the United States in sufficient depth now to justify a major effort. Shrimp mariculture is now being undertaken in Florida, and in other states with a coastline on the Gulf of Mexico.

Additional possibilities of achieving success among crustaceans such as the spiny lobster *(Panulirus)*, the American Maine lobster *(Homarus)*, the Dungeness crab of the Pacific Coast *(Cancer)*, the stone crab of Florida *(Menippe)*, or the common blue crab of the Atlantic coast *(Callinectes)* may have to be deferred until we learn more about their complex development stages. Furthermore we must recognize that with crustacean forms, which are in part dependent on other marine animals as feed to satisfy their high protein nutritional requirements, the feeding efficiency will be lower than in the filter feeding herbivorous molluscs.

Various shrimp of the Far Eastern coastal waters have been "cultured" for centuries by a rather unsophisticated pastoral art. In the tidewater ponds of Singapore, the Philippines, Taiwan and in the tambaks of Indonesia, and along the coconut-shaded Malabar coast of India, young shrimp are captured from the wild, or allowed to stock the shallow, brackish water ponds by a natural recruitment carried in on the tides. By a system of earthen dikes the juveniles are confined and provided with some protection and sometimes served some supplemental feeds, until they have grown to market size. Predator, disease, and competitor control and management of the physical environment in the ponds is primitive, even compared with the agricultural practices in these countries. However, the pasturing of shrimp has persisted as a practical means of providing this high value seafood to the peoples of Asia for many hundreds of years.

The most developed of this form of shrimp farming occurs in the Philippines, where the large Pacific shrimp (*Penaeus monodon*) called "hipon-sugpo" is a highly preferred food, and therefore commands a high market price. The shrimp are reared in a series of ponds formed by bunding the tidal marshlands. Primitive but effective sluice gates allow for tidal interchange of waters which bring in fresh nutrients, provide for some gas exchange, carry out staling products, etc., but unfortunately also stock the ponds with predators and competitors. The ponds are stocked by a rather elaborate system for capturing juvenile and post-larval forms in the shallow seas. Specialists in the art use bundles of twigs or reeds which are suspended in the coastal waters. These serve as lures to attract the young shrimp who feed on the epiphyton and small animals that aggregate on the reed surface. These "traps" are visited regularly, and the young shrimp are shaken off into earthen jars in which they are carried to the culture ponds. A quarter of a million young are stocked per acre of nursery pond, and are held for about 6 weeks. By this time they are nearly 2½ inches long. They are then moved to the rearing ponds where the stocking rate is about 5000 per acre. Some supplemental feeding is provided with clam and mussel meats and some low value trash fish meat. The primary feed for the shrimp is that wonderfully complex nutritious community of small plant and animal forms which the Filipinos call "lab-lab." Green *Chlorophyceae* and bluegreen *Cynophyceae* algae, copepods, rotifers, and a host of other forms growing in sheets covering the underwater surfaces provide a rich pasturage for the shrimp to forage, and growth is so rapid that in 6 to 8 months they may be harvested. They reach a size of 6 to 10 inches in this period, and weigh from 1 to 3 oz each. They are

captured by netting or sometimes the ponds are allowed to drain on a low tide and the shrimp are concentrated into a sump at the sluice gate and merely gathered.

What we have been discussing above can be called shrimp "ranching" based on stocks that are captured from the wild. True shrimp mariculture in which shrimp are grown under control from the egg to market is practiced now in Japan. This culture system, which is being conducted on a commercial basis by the Kuruma Shrimp Company, Ltd., was started and developed by Dr. Motosaku Fujinaga, who is a past director of the Research Bureau of the Japanese Government Fisheries Agency.

The Kuruma Shrimp Company, Ltd., located at Takamatsu on Shikoko Island, is culturing the Japanese wheel shrimp *Penaeus japonicus*, which is one of the primary shrimp of commerce in Japan. This is a large shrimp, 9 to 10 inches long, with brown and white vertical striping. Most of the brood females are supplied by commercial fishermen who bring them up in their trawl nets.

Gravid females are kept in carefully controlled tanks of sea water, and as soon as the eggs are released the mothers are removed to prevent them from eating the eggs. The eggs, which would ordinarily sink, are kept floating by compressed air agitation of the water, which is kept between 25.0 and 31.1 C (77 and 88 F). This hatchery period lasts between 13 and 14 hr before the naupilus larvae hatch from the egg.

A larval population density of about 10,000 per gal is maintained. After 36 hr and several molts, the naupilus changes to the protozoeal stage, at which time the larvae are provided with feed, for which a diatom (*Skeletonema costatum*) is cultured. The diatom is kept suspended by air agitation in order to make it readily available to the shrimp. During the next larval stages, the mysis, the diatom is supplemented with "meat" in the form of oyster larvae, brine-shrimp (*Artemia salina*), copepods, or mollusc meats. Each of the mysis stages lasts one day following

which the shrimp enters a post-larval period. At this stage it is important to keep an abundant supply of food available at all times to reduce cannibalism. After about 10 days of post-larval life in these conditions shrimp are moved to concrete outdoor rearing ponds about 2 ft deep. These ponds have a double bottom providing a means of aerating the sand at the bottom in which they burrow during the daylight hours; the shrimp are thus kept feeding and their bottom environment is well oxygenated. This mechanism results in high yields at the rate of 9000 lb. of shrimp per acre in 10 months, on an experimental basis.

After 10 to 20 days during which they are fed the meats of the short neck clam (*Tapes japonica*), the shrimp have attained a length of ¾ inch, and are moved to finishing ponds which are about 10 acres in area. Some are sold for stocking neighboring shrimp "farms" which do not operate hatcheries. The shrimp are harvested by dragging a special net. Shrimp are dislodged from the bottom sand, in which they prefer to remain, by jets of water just in front of the nets.

Mature shrimp are conditioned for shipment by being chilled to reduce metabolic activity, and thus increase survival during shipment.

Live shrimp are shipped in cardboard cartons in dry sawdust, which insulates them from rapid temperature change. In the winter months they can survive 4 days in shipment, and about 2 days in the summer.

Justification for this rather expensive shrimp farming lies in the high selling price for live shrimp used for tempura in Japan. The Japanese demand *live* shrimp for tempura, and are willing to pay as much as $3.50 per pound. Shrimp being one of their preferred foods it is in constant short supply, even with their extensive shrimp fisheries in native waters and around the world.

A shrimp farming operation such as described above may not yet be economical in the United States, but with the yields reported by Fujinaga, only relatively small advances in technology leading to cost reductions in feeding and handling may be required to make U.S. shrimp culture competitive with trawling.

As fishing costs continue to mount, the natural populations of shrimp are further exploited, and as production rates and maricultural developments improve, the value of this new technology will be increasingly significant.

Finfish

Finfish have been farmed and cultured in marine and brackish waters of the world dating back to ancient times. In some parts of the world finfish are reared by methods generally similar to those described for shrimp farming or "ranching" in the Philippines. Fry are caught on the tidal exchanges, and confined in coastal lagoons and ponds where they grow on natural foods.

In Japan an eel (Anguilla japonica) has been caught at entrances to rivers, and raised to market size in ponds in one year on a diet of low value fish and chrysalids of silkworms. The yellowtail (Seriola quinqueriadiata) is cultivated in the Inland Sea of Japan. This desirable fish is confined in tidal exchange ponds and fed on crushed mussels and cheap forage fish. It grows to marketable size in about 8 to 9 months.

On the Adriatic coast of northern Italy, in the estuaries where fresh and saline waters mix, fish of several species are reared in lagoons called "valli da pesca." Mullet (Mugil), seabass (Morone labrax), eels and others are captured on the tides, or sometimes caught in the sea and transferred to the ponds, to be nurtured by control of salinity, oxygen tension, and sometimes by artificial feeding. Production is sometimes very high, but devastating floods, winter temperatures, and other uncontrolled variables can destroy the fish crops. At last report there were about 50,000 acres in "valli" production, yielding about 130 lb. per acre.

In Far Eastern waters Chanos chanos, the milkfish or bango, is one of the most successfully cultured fish. It is a particularly favored food, and has assumed importance in certain traditional festive rituals. It is grown most successfully in the Philippines where about 200,000 acres of ponds are maintained,

and in Indonesia in about 300,000 acres. Chanos fry are captured close inshore and transferred to ponds prepared by diking the low coastal flats. Critical control of salinity in the "tambaks" or nursery ponds is required, and the muddy river waters mixed in the tidal exchange provides an opportunity to maintain optimum conditions.

Since the fry feed on that curious mixture of microscopic plants and animals called lab-lab, the soils in which the tambaks are constructed are selected for their high fertility to ensure luxurious lab-lab growth. Water depths are maintained from 1 to 4 ft as a function of the growth stage of the fish, and since the fish tend to concentrate in deep holes and thus exhaust their oxygen supply, it is critical to maintain uniform depths by grading level the pond bottoms.

Stocking density in these ponds ranges from 150,000 to 250,000 fry per acre. After about 6 weeks, the fry grow to a size of about 2 inches. These fingerlings can then be transferred to larger ponds to a density of about 200 to 600 per acre. Here they grow to market size. In Taiwan where milkfish ponds are heavily fertilized, they are stocked with 1200 fingerlings to the acre.

Production in the Philippines has been variously reported, with an average of about 500 lb. per acre, to a maximum of about 2000 lb. per acre.

In the fertilized ponds of Taiwan, production of milkfish has been estimated to be about 1000 lb. per acre.

A similar type of fish culture is in its beginning stages in the United States. The pompano of Florida (Trachinotus carolinus), which is one of the highest market value fish in our cuisine, can be managed similarly to the milkfish of the Far East. The young fry appear in the surf in Florida's Atlantic beaches in particularly dense populations north of Cape Kennedy. They can be readily netted and transported to ponds designed to shelter them until they reach market size. Supplemental feeding with trash fish and/or pellet rations promises to be an efficient and economic means of

producing a high value crop competitive with fishing the wild stocks.

As the biological and environmental parameters for optimum pond growth are established, we can expect to achieve higher efficiencies and economies, so as to make this highly valued fish more widely available in the U.S. market.

Laws and ordinances define the sea as in the public domain, and thus restrict private investment. Alleviation of restraints on the uses of the sea will be required before large scale mariculture can be practiced in the U.S. coastal waters.

Another prerequisite to encourage the further development of mariculture is the wise management of estuaries and coastal ecosystems by abatement of toxic pollution from industrial wastes and agricultural pesticides. Domestic waste disposal into our coastal and estuarine waters must also be managed so as to avoid over-enrichment, and the growth of useless microorganisms with the attendant oxygen depletion. Dredging, marina development, wetlands drainage, filling, and other deleterious influences on the environment must also be controlled so as to provide manageable sites, water quality, water flow patterns, etc., for mariculture systems.

Considerable additional investment in education, research, and engineering in the fields of marine biology and fishery science must be made in order to provide the basic resource — the knowledge and the trained personnel — to meet the needs of a new technology with which to achieve practical cultural control over the marine organisms for which a market demand exists, or can be encouraged.

For additional information, read:

Ansell, A. D. 1962. An approach to Sea Farming, New Scientist, 14: 408-409.
Bardach, J. 1968. Harvest of the Sea, Harper and Row, New York.
Chapman, W. M. 1965. Food from the Sea, Address before Agriculture Research Institute, Nat. Acad. Sci.
Emery, K. O., and Iselin, C. O'D. 1967. Human Food from Ocean and Land, Science, 157: 1279-1281.
Graham, H. W., and Edwards, R. L. 1962. The World Biomass Marine Fishes, Fish

in Nutrition, Fishing News (Books) Ltd., London, pp. 3-8.

Hickling, C. F. 1962. *Fish Culture,* Faber and Faber, London.

Isaacs, J. D., and Schmitt, W. R. 1963. Resources from the Sea, *International Sci. and Tech.,* pp. 39-45.

PSAC. 1966. Effective use of the Sea, *Report of Panel on Oceanography of the President's Science Advisory Committee.* xv + 144 pp. U.S. Government Printing Office, Washington, D.C.

Schaeffer, M. B. 1965. The Potential Har-

vest of the Sea, *Trans. Amer. Fish. Soc.,* **94:** 123-128.

Tham, Ah Kow. 1967. Prawn Culture in Singapore. FAO World Scientific Conf. on the Biology and Culture of Shrimps and Prawns, Mexico.

Biomedical Aspects of Population Control

William D. McElroy

The current rate of growth of the world population cannot be allowed to continue. The United States and other developed countries must take the leadership in setting up world-wide institutions in which maternal and child health care is intimately coupled with family planning and population control advice. (BioScience 19, no. 1, p. 19-23)

The population of the world is now growing at an unparalleled rate of 2% per annum. Translated into a head count, this means that 132 persons are added per minute to the present population; as time passes this figure will increase in magnitude. It took us over one million years — from the emergence of man from a primate stock to 1830 — to reach one billion individuals.

In 1930, 100 years later, we had increased to 2×10^9 and only 30 years later, 1960, we added a third billion. The Population Reference Bureau sets the world population as of January 1, 1968 at 3.44 billion individuals. The 4.5 billion mark is expected to be reached by about 1976.

The current 2% per year may not sound like an unusual rate of growth. However, a few calculations can demonstrate what exponentials really mean. Markert (1966) has shown that if this rate had existed from the time of Christ until the present time, the increase would be about 7×10^{16}. There would be over 20 million individuals in place of each person now alive or 100 persons for each square foot. At our present rate of 2% per year there would be over 150 billion people within two centuries.

The author is former head of the Biology Department, Johns Hopkins University, Baltimore, Maryland and currently Director, National Science Foundation.

This paper and the two following by Drs. Robinson and Thurston were presented at the Plenary Session, 19th Annual AIBS Meeting, Ohio State University, Columbus, on September 1968.

We are on the logarithmic phase of a typical growth curve after a long lag period. In nature no animal, plant, or bacterial population has ever maintained a logarithmic phase of growth for very long. The major factors that slow this rate of growth are exhaustion of food supply, accumulation of toxic products, decimation through disease, or the effects of some outside lethal agent which kills a high proportion of the population. Any one or all of these factors will force the population back into a lag phase. I leave it to your imagination which of these factors might apply to the human population. Of course, you will say that humans have intelligence and can intentionally modify some of these factors whereas a bacterial population cannot. I wonder if the present evidence does not support arguments to the contrary.

Some feel that the battle to feed the world population is now lost, and that it is a foregone conclusion that by 1985 we will have world-wide famines in which hundreds of millions of people will starve to death. I must admit that at this time I see no major crash program which would lead me to disagree with this conclusion.

If the world were divided into two groups, the so-called "have" and the "have not" countries, only about one-third of the total population would be found to live in the "have" nations where per capita income is high, food supplies ample, and literacy nearly universal. How to feed, educate, house, and find meaningful employment for the remaining two-thirds of the world population is the number two problem of the world. It might even replace the search for peace as the number one problem if we do not act soon.

We can no longer wait to deal with this set of problems even though the population growth may presently seem unimportant to some here in the United States. We must depress and actually reverse this logarithmic phase of growth before our problems become completely insurmountable. It is up to the United States and other developed countries to take the leadership. I suggest the following:

1) The appointment of a special assistant to the President of the United States whose sole responsibility would be to identify ways and means of solving the growth of world population and increasing the world food supply.

2) Set up world-wide institutions in which family planning and population control advice is intimately coupled with maternal care services.

3) Change completely our farm policy so that the farmer can move toward maximum production. This will allow us to extend our Food for Freedom program in order to provide emergency food assistance to stave off disaster while hungry countries build up their own food production capability. At a time when people all over the world are starving it will be decidedly

un-American for the United States to do nothing in the way of supplying some food. We must insist, however, that countries receiving food aid from the United States make vigorous efforts to improve their own food production.

4) We must make an all-out effort to supplement traditional land-based agriculture by the development and manufacture of a low cost protein from fish. It has been recommended on several occasions that we must develop the technology of farming the oceans, but little seems to be happening. This will take time, and the need for urgency is great if we are not to destroy this natural resource before we learn to manage it effectively.

5) Instruction in family planning and the principles of population dynamics should be an essential part of the curriculum of all secondary schools.

6) Finally, we must start a general discussion now, in the community, in the states, in the nation, and throughout the world on the merits of famliy planning versus population control. The possible consequences of the decision between these two alternatives must be carefully spelled out to the world at large.

The Present Position of the United States

We must soon reach a satisfactory ending of our struggles in Southeast Asia. We must continue our efforts to work out cooperative solutions of international problems relative to thermonuclear devices. We must work for a stable economic situation and continue our drive to solve the major domestic problems, particularly those in large urban centers. But the population and food problems of the world will not wait for a solution — they can only get worse, and, in the not too distant future, will make our other problems look insignificant by comparison.

Recently, the President made the following statement in his health message to Congress: "Two vital fields long neglected by research are population and human reproduction. Thousands of parents want help in determining how to plan their families. Thousands of others are unable to have the children they desire. Our lack of knowledge im-

pedes our effort to provide the help they need. Far too little is known about the physiology of reproduction and its effect on all aspects of human life. Searching studies are needed to determine the complex, emotional, sociological, physiological, and economic factors involved. A wide range of scientists must bring to these problems their specialized disciplines — biologists, behavioral scientists, biochemists, pharmacologists, demographers, experts in population dynamics.

"To launch this effort I have directed the Secretary of Health, Education and Welfare to establish a center for population studies and human reproduction in the National Institute of Child Health and Human Development. The center will serve to give new energy and direction to the research activities of all federal departments and agencies in these fields.

"I am asking the Congress to appropriate $12 million to support the research activities of the center during its first year of operation.

"As we move to expand our knowledge of population and human reproduction, we must make that knowledge available to those who want it. Last year the federal government helped to bring information and counseling on a voluntary basis to more than 500,-000 women. But there are millions more who want help.

"I recommend that the Congress provide for an increase in funds from $25 million in fiscal 1968 to $61 million in fiscal 1969 so that 3 million women can have access to family planning help if they so desire."

Although these proposals are major steps forward for family planning and the medical health of the nation, they will do little to slow the growth of the U.S. population and will have little or no effect on the total world population. I am not arguing, however, against these recommendations and as chairman of the Population Committee of the National Academy of Sciences I have always supported recommendations concerning additional research. However, we cannot wait for new solutions. We must start now with what knowledge we already possess and continue to find better ways to approach

an ultimate solution as we move into the future. The appropriation and distribution of funds for population control in the United States or developing countries has not kept pace with the superlative statements made by national and responsible individuals on the importance of this problem.

AID Population Policy

Recently, Mr. William S. Gaud, the administrator of the U.S. Agency for International Development, made the following statement relative to the U.S. position concerning population policy. ". . . the government of every nation with a population problem, whether developed or developing, should do its utmost to increase the knowledge and practice of family planning among its citizens. Our role is to encourage and help the developing nations with this task." He went on to say that the United States must "respect the sovereignty and sensibilities of the nations we assist. The population question is as delicate as it is urgent. Over half the people in the developing world now live under governments that have policies of reducing birth rates. But some countries, even though they are aware of the seriousness of the problem and are working on it, either do not welcome outside help in this field or do not want it on a large scale. Our work in the population field must be carried on in such a way as not to raise political problems. The family planning programs we assist must be the host nation's programs — not our programs. They should avoid labels marked "Made in the United States." Mr. Gaud went on to say that "AID will support no family planning or population program unless it is voluntary. . . . We will assist only those programs in which individuals are free to participate or not as they see fit and where they have a choice of means. . . . We want no part of either international coercion or individual coercion. We do not make family planning a condition of aid."

It may be that we have reached a point where our policies, although admirable as first glance, must give way to a more vigorous program. It is quite clear that during the past 10 years our indirect efforts have had very little effect in slowing down the growth of world population. Furthermore, if the problem of population growth and food supply is the number two problem of the world, then it most certainly must be placed alongside the number one problem, namely, the search for lasting peace. It needs the same status and it needs the same amount of money. Most of all, it needs the leadership of the United States in convincing the world that something must be done, and done now, to decrease the growth of the world population and to increase food production dramatically and immediately. It is for these reasons that I encourage the President to appoint a special assistant who would be concerned exclusively with population and food problems.

Family Planning Programs

In 1963, the Committee on Science and Public Policy of the National Academy of Sciences issued a report on the "Growth of World Population" which emphasized in part that the governments of the world can no longer ignore the population problem. For the first time, a president of the United States made a positive statement concerning government programs and support for family planning programs. Until that time all government agencies were careful to avoid discussing this matter in open meetings. Both President Kennedy and President Johnson have repeatedly indicated that they recognized the seriousness of the problem and the need for intelligent and forthright action.

Much has been done in a number of areas and in a number of countries to deliver family planning services to individual families, but it is quite clear that only a minimal start has been made. A number of steps can be taken, but one area of particular promise is that which concerns family planning and maternity care.

Family Planning and Maternity Care

Much recent work has been done to couple family planning with maternity care. Drs. Howard Taylor and Bernard Berelson (1968) have summarized the effectiveness of providing family planning instruction in association with other aspects of maternity care. The results of the collaborative trial of the postpartem approach to family planning in 25 hospitals throughout the world have been reported by Dr. Gerald Zatuchni. Even in the underdeveloped countries, the data from these trials have been most encouraging. As Taylor and Berelson point out, there are some very compelling advantages of the association of family planning with maternity services. These may be indicated as follows: (1) *Physiological.* the use of the event of child birth for the identification of the physiologically most fertile women is especially important in countries where facilities are limited and efforts must be concentrated at points where they will have the most effect. Thus, the effort in India should be directed not to the 500 million people or to the 250 million females, but rather to the 20 million females who bear their first child in a given year and who have the greatest residual potential for adding to the population. It is well known that in the absence of birth control information, a second pregnancy is likely to occur very soon after delivery of the first child. In any case, an early decision has to be made with regard to family planning, and the delivery room or one close to it is an excellent classroom for transmitting this information. (2) *Educational.* The educational impact of a supervised obstetrical experience will be relatively greater where school systems are lacking and illiteracy is widespread. The education needed to convince people to reduce their family size is extremely difficult where literacy is low. Unfortunately, solution of the population problem cannot wait for the development of a general program of education. Thus one starts the educational process at the time of the first delivery. (3) *Accessibility.* Taylor and Berelson emphasize that a national program based on maternity care can in theory reach every eligible woman. In other words, it is much easier and more feasible to detect cases of pregnancy and to see to it that all pregnant women are provided with information about family planning than to educate the total female population. (4) *Acceptability.* It is felt, in general, that the pregnant population would accept family planning principles if these are presented at the time of the first birth. In this way family planning is built into the concept of maternal and infant care.

This whole concept of uniting family planning with maternity services, depends, of course, upon an organized effort to identify institutions where child delivery takes place. Unfortunately, in many underdeveloped countries, delivery of children is not concentrated in a few well-defined clinics or hospitals. In the United States, on the other hand, the proportion of all births that are professionally supervised is very large. However, much still needs to be done, particularly in the large cities, to educate the individual obstetricians in the techniques of providing adequate family planning advice. The amount of information on family planning given to the parent on delivery of the first child is less than adequate. This is particularly true in the poverty areas of large urban centers.

Taylor and Berelson have arrived at some approximate figures for cost of construction and of annual operation of a maternal help and associated family planning facility in a typical unit of 100,000 people involving 4000 annual deliveries. Construction costs would be about $100,000 and an annual operating budget of $40,000 or $10 for each delivery would be needed. To service completely a country like India, they estimate that at least $500 million would be needed for constructing hospital units for obstetrical and gynecological practice, and approximately $200 million for annual operation. For all of Latin America the figures would be approximately $250 million for construction and $100 million for annual operation. In a country of 5 million population it would cost approximately $2 million a year for operation and for a country of 25 million it would cost $10 million for operation. Using such calculations for the entire developing world, they estimate, with a population of about 2.2 billion, that the operating cost would be of the order of $880 million annually. It is of interest that the value of the foods which were shipped by the United States over the past few years to other countries has been about 1.5 billion dollars annually. Thus, to do the most effective job of trying to control the population growth in the underdeveloped world would cost approximately only one-half as much as we are currently spending in a stopgap manner to supply only food.

The Taylor-Berelson approach possesses, therefore, the great merit of reaching the most significant elements in a large population, and of dealing with them effectively and with dignity. Furthermore, the plan merits very serious consideration since it appears to be the one approach that could bring about a coordinated world effort.

I have emphasized this program for the developing countries because of the immediate and pressing need; however, much remains to be done in the United States along this same line. As Jaffe has pointed out "despite the vastly improved climate of the last decade, it remains true that in terms of systematic knowledge we know more about programing to meet community family planning needs in the developing countries than in the United States. In the U.S. many physicians, health officers, and researchers continue to be somewhat indifferent to the implementation of family planning services, although this is a field of health care with both immediate and long term medical, social and economic consequences of significance." Therefore we need the Taylor-Berelson plan even in the United States. In addition, we need to reach the nonpregnant but potentially fertile population. This means establishing family planning services in locations geographically accessible to the population in need. These services in most cases must be free or very heavily subsidized. Jaffe points out that "in most urban and suburban communities, this means establishment of a network of active, visible clinics in hospitals, health centers and other principal medical institutions, complemented by satellite clinics in poverty areas." We have ignored the needs of the poor too long. They want smaller families and therefore should be supplied with the necessary information to achieve a reduction in the number of offspring.

Education on the Problems of Family Planning and Population

The need for education at all levels is great; the earlier it is begun the more effective it will be. I believe that instruction in family planning and the principles of population dynamics should be an essential part of the curriculum of secondary schools. A successful program can lead to a lower incidence of unwanted pregnancies in the United States among both married and unmarried couples. In addition, it would greatly enhance America's sense of public urgency about helping nations everywhere that want and need to solve their problems of population growth.

A number of school systems have made an initial attack on this important problem and have worked up detailed outlines and supplied materials to the appropriate teachers for their use. In Baltimore we start the instruction in the elementary grades and give detailed information on family planning and population growth to the high school student. By placing the discussion of population growth and birth control in the same matter-of-fact setting as the teaching of social studies and biology, schools can help greatly to educate not only the students but also their parents as well. Someone must take the leadership to work with national organizations who are concerned with curriculum development. It is clear that a way must be found where this kind of information can be introduced systematically into the curriculum, either in social studies during the early stages of training or the biology courses at the high school level. One of the major problems is the identification of personnel who can present adequately these concepts to the students. It may well be necessary to establish summer institutes, with the appropriate fellowship support, for the training of teachers on the various topics that should be discussed in relation to family planning, population growth, and birth control. It is evident that secondary schools also face problems of community relations which tend to limit the extent to which they can deal with these so-called sensitive issues, and it may well be that initially other kinds

of institutional frameworks must be provided where birth control education can be given to unmarried students.

There are many other important matters that might be discussed under this heading, but probably one of the most important is that of *motivation*. Even though contraceptive technology has greatly improved, which makes it possible for families to lower their family size, the fact remains that there are many large *planned* families. Reduction of family size from 4 to 3 to 2 is essential if we are going to solve our population problem in the long run. At the present time there is some disagreement on the long range effectiveness of the family planning program and population control.

Population Control versus Family Planning

Some time in the not too distant future it is, of course, essential that the growth of the world population approach zero, i.e., where the deaths equal the births. Multiplication of the human population cannot be allowed to increase to a point where it would be greater than the mass of the earth. We can, to be sure, slow down on our medical research and let the natural epidemiological controls take over, or we can limit our food production and thus limit the population through famines and starvation. Wars provide another way of reducing the size of the population. It is evident that both morally and psychologically most people in the world would like to think that sometime in the not too distant future we will have peace, that sometime in the not too distant future we would be able to control disease and famine throughout the world so that all would live a meaningful, humane existence to a ripe old age. Under these circumstances, however, a large number of people will be capable of multiple births, and this would inevitably lead to an astronomical world population. It is under these conditions that we must gradually approach the population growth rate of approximately zero.

Recently, Kingsley Davis (1967) has criticized the family planning concept of population control because the basis of population planning has always been that of giving the family the "right to have the number of children that they want when they want them." Although he is perfectly correct in indicating that this is not population control but really population planning, it is the feeling of many of us that at least this is where one has to start.

Family Planning Is Not Population Control

I do not believe that anyone I know who has thought about the problems carefully would claim that family planning programs will, by themselves, achieve population control. Furthermore, Dr. Davis feels that the very existence of family planning programs creates "the illusion that it is solving the population problem" and "obscures potentially effective methods." On this basic point I disagree. What other *effective methods* can Dr. Davis suggest *at this time*? It seems to me that most governments that have considered this problem have been doing a part-time job in trying to stabilize the population by spreading the knowledge of the pill and other contraceptive devices. An inadequate job is being done in promoting the reduction of the birth rate. We need an all-out effort from all countries concerned to see if we can solve this problem. We have not had this effort to date.

Family planning, as I understand it, is not a program just for the distribution of contraceptive devices. Where knowledgeable personnel are available, they try to point out the broad social problems resulting from large families. They try to influence the *behavior* of the individual couples with regard to the size of the family. Unfortunately, even in the United States we have inadequate personnel to carry out this large educational program. But it could be done if adequate funds were available and family planning was intimately associated with maternal care. Therefore, I say we have not given family planning and the social education associated with it a fair chance in the United States.

Davis may be correct in emphasizing that this is not a *long-range* solution, The real question, then, is what can be done, and what should we be discussing and researching in terms of the long-range problems and true population control.

I agree with Dr. Davis that one of the first things that could be initiated immediately is alteration of the abortion laws state by state or even nationally so as to liberalize and promote free abortions. It is perfectly true that even in families that practice family planning through the use of current contraceptive technology mistakes are made, and the wife becomes pregnant even though she had no desire to be. The logical extension of the concept of a baby "only when you want it and if you want it" would allow the person to make the decision to have an abortion. It is not possible to determine the exact figure on how many abortions would be sought if they were legalized. But one can comment on the fact that Japan has effectively used this as a method of lowering its population growth. In some states it is now possible to obtain a legalized abortion for mental reasons and in cases of rape, but unfortunately this is not true in most of our states.

A type of research which would have a great effect on population control would be that related to the discovery of methods for sex determination. It has been suggested that if one could predetermine that the first offspring would be a male, it would have a great effect on the size of the family. In some, if not most societies, male babies are more desirable than females, and if the male was the first offspring, the motivation for having additional offspring would be reduced.

There have been a number of interesting incentive suggestions that might be made part of a national policy which would encourage a reduction in the size of the family group. In a positive way the federal government, for example, could pay a fee to a couple if they delayed their marriage beyond a given age. For example, if they did not marry until they were 24, they would receive a $500 fee from the government; if they waited until they were 30, they might even get a $4000 or $5000 fee. In this way one would tend to reduce the size of the family. It is evident that in the countries where late marriage is usual, the rate of population growth is considerably lessened. Unfortunately, this may not work in underdeveloped countries where education is at a low level and early marriage is customary. Even if marriage occurred early, it has been suggested that if pregnancy is delayed for 3 years, the couple would receive a government fee. If there is an additional 5-year delay between the first and second baby, the fee might be higher. All of these suggestions are interesting ones and should be further discussed by competent groups.

In the negative way, it has been suggested that the tax burden should be increased when a family has gone beyond a certain size. For example, there might be a tax exemption for the first two children, none for the third, and with the tax actually increased for any number above three. One might even add educational benefits for the first child, but decrease these for the second and eliminate them for the third, etc.

It has also been suggested that marriage fees be greatly increased, and that low cost public housing not be related to family size. In addition, a number of investigators have stimulated us to think about the possibilities of increasing female participation in the labor force and of promoting equal treatment for male and female. Of course, this trend has been greatly increased in recent years, but if it were fostered to an even greater extent for jobs that were most appropriate for females, it could be a decisive factor in delaying a marriage. It has also been suggested that when we are in a peace-time economy, we might promote a domestic peace corps program for all men between the ages of 18 and 20 which, in effect, would delay the age of marriage and inculcate changes of attitudes of family size.

Whatever the circumstances, however, it is clear that we must agree with Davis that the zero growth-rate concept must be explored, and that we must try to find ways to make it acceptable as one of our national goals.

It is possible that the U.S. Government itself could set some national goals and try to educate the people to accept them; but this would be no more than a certification of a *good* family planning program. It is one thing to idealize about policies which would bring about zero growth rate in the population but it is another thing to find a way to achieve this. Certainly broad-based family planning can reduce family sizes from 10, 8, 6 down to 4. This is the problem in many if not in most of the developing countries and in part of our own society. Having achieved this, then one is in a much better position to educate the population about the long-range desirability of having smaller families.

What Can a Biologist Do?

There is a lot that biologists can do individually and collectively. Probably the most important is to educate the public with regard to the urgency of the problem. We seem to be talking to ourselves. For example, during the summer of 1968 the Gallup poll asked a national sample of adults the following question: "What do you think is the most important problem facing this country today?" Less than 1% mentioned population. If the population problem is not too important in the minds of the public, there will not be an all-out effort by elected officials to institute new programs and support existing ones aimed at a solution.

Biologists understand what a logarithmic growth phase is and the consequences if it is allowed to continue for long periods of time. I urge you therefore to take every opportunity offered to speak about this subject. The undergraduate premedical students should be thoroughly trained in the subject before they get to medical school because they will not get this information in our present medical curriculum. Every course in biology, including biochemistry and molecular biology, should devote at least one lecture to the subject. Every college, university, and high school should organize at least one pub-

lic session on this subject every year. The biologists must take the leadership — now is the time to stop talking to ourselves and "speak out" to the rest of the population. An informed public will demand action.

References

Davis, Kingsley. 1967. Population policy: Will current programs succeed? *Science,* **158:** 730.

Markert, C. L. 1966. Biological limits on population growth. *BioScience,* **12:** 859-863.

Taylor, Howard C., Jr., and Bernard Berelson. 1968. Maternity care and family planning as a world problem. *Am. J. Obstet. Gyn.,* **100:** 885.

A review of the world population problems and references to "teaching projects, new curriculum ideas, resources and materials, program tools, books, articles, seminars and conferences and other important educational developments" can be obtained from *Intercom,* Vol. 10, July-August 1968. Single issue is $1.00 from Foreign Policy Association, Inc., 345 E. 46th Street, New York, N.Y. 10017.

Dimensions of the World Food Crisis

H. F. Robinson

The nature of the world food problem, including its scope, and some indications of methods and procedures that may be followed in effecting solutions were outlined in the President's Science Advisory Committee panel which produced the three-volume report entitled, The World Food Problem. *This is a synthesis of that report.* (BioScience 19, no. 1, p. 29-34)

At the September, 1967, Plenary Session the Honorable Henry M. Jackson, Senator from the State of Washington, spoke on the topic, "Public Policy and Environmental Administration," and began with r lating a fable written by James C. Rettie, which seems most appropriate to begin our discussion of the world food problem. I will not give that fable in detail but will relate only its general theme. As the story goes, a film had been made to represent a record of the earth's life history during the past 750 million years. The film, scaled in time and length to the total time span of the earth's history, required one full year to show and with the life span of an individual man taking only 30 seconds. The complexities of man in his interaction with environment were pointed out in the fable which ended with the statement and a question saying, "Man has just arrived on this earth. How long will he stay?"

We have heard this question raised in connection with ecological discussions and the emphasis placed on control of the environment with the plea to remove the pollution from the air and from the water and to restore these two to their once desirable characteristics. The same question regarding man and his ability to exist on this planet, coupled with fears of his possible ex-

The author is Vice Chancellor of the University System of Georgia, Atlanta.

tinction, may be more appropriate when the balance of the population growth with the available food supply is considered.

Seriousness of the Problem

The problem of feeding the people of the world is as old as civilization itself. The crisis between population growth and food supply has been variously predicted for the past 200 years, and I suppose we would say that the only new feature of the problem is its dimensions. Possibly another new and distressing feature of the problem is the disproportionality in the economic development, population density, and food supply throughout the world. This is really basic to the total problem. It is most important that we be reminded of our fortunate position in this nation as compared to that in the less developed countries. We must be prepared to assume our obligations and responsibilities to insure a proper diet and a decent existence for the less fortunate. The following excerpt from a recent issue of the Eli Lilly Company News Letter gives emphasis to our economic advantages and minority in numbers:

If all the people in the world could be reduced proportionately into a theoretical town of 1,000 people, the picture would look something like this: In this town there would be 60 Americans, with the remainder of the world represented by 940 persons. This is the proportion of the population of the

United States to the population of the world, 60 to 940. The 60 Americans would have half the income of the entire town with the other 940 dividing the other half. About 350 of these would be practicing Communists, and 370 others would be under Communistic domination. White people would total 303, with 697 being non-white. The 60 Americans would have 15 times as many possessions per person as all the rest of the world. The Americans would produce 60 percent of the town's food supply although they eat 72 percent above the maximum food requirements. They would either eat most of what they grow or store it for their own future use at an enormous cost. Since most of the 940 non-Americans in the town would be hungry most of the time, it would create ill feelings toward the 60 Americans, who would appear to be enormously rich and fed to the point of sheer disbelief by the great majority of the townspeople. The Americans would also have a disproportionate share of the electric power, fuel, steel, and general equipment. Of the 940 non-Americans, 200 would have malaria, cholera, typhus, and malnutrition. None of the 60 Americans would get these diseases or probably ever be worried about them.

There is reason for skepticism about the extent of assistance with the problems of food supply and economic development of the less fortunate by the more affluent nations. There is no doubt that people are more knowledgeable and have greater interest in solutions to problems of poverty, hunger, and malnutrition of the less fortunate than ever before. I do not know whether this concern is one of genuine interest in a better life for all mankind or whether it is based on fear. Unless effective steps are taken to improve economic conditions among the less fortunate, revolutionary tendencies and insecurity of governments may lead to a general chaotic condition throughout the world. It was this latter condition to which Dr. James Bonner, biologist at the California Institute of Technology, referred recently in a speech when he stated.

> We will, I suspect, begin to regard the starving population of the under developed nations as a race or species apart, people totally different from us as indeed they will be. "They are just animals," we will say, "and a serious reservoir of disease." The inevitable culmination of the two cultures will be that the one culture (the rich) will devour the other.

The PSAC Study

The deteriorating situation of the developing countries with respect to their food supply and balancing of the available food with the rapidly expanding populations prompted President Johnson's request to the President's Science Advisory Committee [1] in his

[1] The President's Science Advisory Committee Panel on World Food Supply was organized in the summer of 1966 with the following membership: Dr. Nyle C. Brady, Director of Research, Cornell University; Dr. Melvin Calvin, Professor of Chemistry, University of California at Berkeley; Dr. Milton S. Eisenhower, President, The Johns Hopkins University; Dr. Samuel A. Goldblith, Professor of Food Science, Massachusetts Institute of Technology; Dr. Grace A. Goldsmith, Dean, School of Public Health, Tulane University; Dr. Lowell S. Hardin, The Ford Foundation; Dr. J. George Harrar, President, The Rockefeller Foundation; Dr. James G. Horsfall, Director of the Connecticut Agricultural Experiment Station; Dr. A. T. Mosher, Executive Director, Agricultural Development Council; Dr. L. Dale Newsom, Professor of Entomology, Louisiana State University; Dr. William R. Pritchard, Dean, School of Veterinary Medicine, University of California at Davis; Dr. Roger Revelle, Director, Center for Population Studies, Harvard University; Dr. Thomas M. Ware, Chairman, International Minerals and Chemical Corporation; Dr. Stuart G. Younkin, Vice President, Agricultural Research, Campbell Soup Company; Dr. Ivan L. Bennett, Jr., Chairman, Deputy Director, Office of Science and Technology; Dr. Claire L. Schelske, Technical Assistant, Office of Science and Technology. I was appointed to serve as Executive Director of this panel. It is noted that Dr. Sterling Wortman, Director for Agricultural Sciences, The Rockefeller Foundation served for Dr. George Harrar during most of the study and Dr. John F. Kincaid, Vice President for Research and Development, and Mr. Charles Dennison, Vice President for Overseas Development, both of International Minerals and Chemical Corporation, served for Dr. Thomas Ware.

Food for Freedom message on February 10, 1966, to do the following:

Search out ways to:
1. ". . . develop inexpensive, high-quality, synthetic dietary supplements. . . .
2. ". . . improve the quality and nutritional content of food crops.
3. ". . . apply all of the resources and technology to increasing food production. . . ."

The study was organized around 14 subpanels whose membership consisted of a total of approximately 100 representatives from industry, universities, private foundations, and the Federal government. A wide range of the major issues were represented by the subpanels: population growth, nutrition, plant and animal production, fertilizers, pesticides, machinery, marketing and economic aspects of the food problem, and financial requirements needed to provide reasonable solutions. The report, including over 1200 pages, was prepared in three volumes at the conclusion of the study.

When the panel began its work, there was no general agreement as to the dimensions of the task and the approaches that should be taken in the study. As we began to examine the seriousness of the problem and the scope of the study, as well as to set objectives in examining food production in the developing nations, the importance and magnitude of the total economic development in relation to foreign technical assistance became increasingly apparent. The conception of the assignment was set forth in the following paragraph:

> The situation as the Panel now views it, after nearly a year of study, is that hunger and malnutrition are not primary 'diseases' of the last half of the twentieth century. Rather, along with the so-called population explosion, they are symptoms of a deeper malady — lagging economic development of the countries of Latin America, Asia, and Africa, in which nearly two-thirds of the people of the earth now live.

The seriousness of the world food problem and the predictions with respect to its most crucial hours have been described and discussed by many, and it is not the intention here to analyze

these predictions as to their validity and accuracy. It is clear that if present trends continue, the size and severity of the problem will become increasingly worse. The Panel surmised that within 10 to 15 years, when the serious consequences are readily apparent, it may then be too late to provide workable solutions.

The encouraging reports of increased production from various parts of the world due to the use of improved technology, including improved varieties, additional fertilizers, and modern cultural practices, have given new hope, at least on a temporary basis, and have further convinced us that certain programs can contribute toward the solution of the problem. However, the seriousness of the situation and the impending hunger resulting from the imbalance of available food with the population growth continues.

General Conclusions

The conclusions reached by the PSAC Panel in its report are as appropriate at this moment as at the time they were written and should serve as a guide in considering the global strategy that will be involved. These conclusions are as follows:

1) The scale, superiority, and duration of the world food problem is so great that a massive, long-range, innovative effort unprecedented in human history will be required to master it.

2) The solution of the problem, which will exist after about 1985, demands that programs of population control be initiated now. For the immediate future, the food supply is critical.

3) Food supply is directly related to agricultural development and, in turn, agricultural development and overall economic development are critically interdependent in hungry countries.

4) A strategy for attacking the world food problem will, of necessity, encompass the entire foreign economic assistance of the United States in concert with other developed countries, voluntary institutions, and international organizations.

There are two very basic factors in the food problem faced by the developing nations of the world. The problem can be stated clearly and succinctly, but it is often so obvious that we fail to comprehend the magnitude and scope. These factors are: (1) Population growth is occurring at a more rapid rate than the food to sustain the people, and (2) Increase in food production continues to lag behind expectations in many of the developing nations.

Another basic consideration in development of the report was the time period over which the findings were expected to be generally applicable and most appropriate in terms of solutions that were to be suggested. It was decided that the time period of two decades, namely 1965-1985, would likely be the most critical period of the problem to be experienced. One of two conditions will probably become apparent by the end of this 20-year span in the developing nations with which we are chiefly concerned: (1) Either the population growth will have been brought under control and a balance will have been developed between the population and the food supply, or (2) Some nations, possibly many, will have passed the crest and will be accelerating on a declining grade of malnutrition, economic deterioration, and political instability to the point where no reasonable solution to the problem can be found.

Requirements for Solution

Total economic development is required in these less developed nations where the food supply is critical and population growth most rapid if there is to be meaningful solutions for these less fortunate people in the world. It is obvious to all of those closely involved in technical assistance that the task is much more complicated now than was visualized at the time President Truman set forth his Point Four Program in the 1940's. We now know that the task involves building an entirely new economy of which agricultural development is only a part. Political stability and the general attitude by the recipient governments as well as the will and determination of the people to work for a higher standard of living are of critical importance. The disruptions, constraints, and disturbing political con-

ditions with which many of these nations try our patience, and the frustrations we meet in working with the governments are often so great as to threaten our withdrawal from any future involvement. However, we know that overcoming these difficulties will continue to require long periods of tolerance, and we must exercise the most astute management to avoid crises that may disrupt all of our foreign technical assistance programs. We cannot leave these responsibilities to others because of the frustrations and difficulties that may be encountered.

The PSAC Panel on World Food Supply indicated a strong belief for agricultural development and economic growth in the developing nations of the world as an absolute requirement if the people were to avoid starvation. We in the academic world must contribute in every possible and appropriate manner in these activities.

The Panel was in general agreement that the food problem would not be solved from our continuing the shipment of food abroad. We were most critical of that part of the foreign aid program which has relied on food aid to overcome the hunger problems in those nations experiencing the imbalance between food and population. The governments of those recipient nations have contributed to this problem, and many of them are continuing to impede domestic developments by appealing to outside sources for food aid rather than increase their own local production. However, shipments of food required to prevent starvation in a few cases where there are major problems with drought and other difficulties that have prevented normal production of the crops can be justified.

It is known that some government leaders in the nations receiving food aid have taken special advantage of this program to either discourage, or not encourage, increased agricultural production. It has been considered economically desirable to try and provide the deficit in food from outside sources through food aid rather than furnish financial aid and other resources required to encourage agricultural productivity within the developing nation.

Every possible means should be used to identify those who are exploiting for personal gain the assistance being provided from developed nations.

In accumulating data on total food requirements for the world, areas considered representative of major developing nations of the world where the food problem is either most urgent now or expected to become of increasing seriousness were selected for attention. These areas included India and Pakistan in the Far East and Brazil in South America. Little special attention was given to Africa since it is expected that problems of food supply in all of the African nations will become serious, but the critical period is expected to be beyond the time to which this study was focused.

One of the first requirements in considering solutions to the food problem of the future is to seek reliable estimates of the magnitude of the population within the range of time to which the study is intended to apply. The World Food Report by the President's Science Advisory Panel projected growths to year 2000, but, as indicated, basic emphasis was given to the period between now and 1985. In predicting population growth, two estimates were derived for each point in time. One was based on continued growth at the present rate and the second, designated "low estimate," was based on the assumption that family planning programs during the next two decades might lead to a progressive decrease to 30% in the probability that a woman of a given age would bear a child (fertility rate).

Projections indicated that the population would rise from the present possibility 3.6 billion people in the world to between 4.65 billion (low estimate) or 5.03 billion by 1985. By the year 2000, the population at its present rate of growth would be approximately 7.15 billion, compared to 6 billion from use of the low estimate, which gives the maximum amount of optimism to the effectiveness of family planning programs.

If populations continue to grow at the present rate, caloric requirements are expected to increase until, by 1985, 52% more calories will be required on a world-wide basis than at present. We would need 43% higher calories by the end of the next two decades if the population could be controlled to the extent indicated in the low estimates. Even the most effective family planning programs, which could be expected to be implemented in the rapidly growing nations, will provide only minor curbs on the populations to be fed during the immediate years ahead. By the year 1985, we are predicting more than 5 billion with normal population growth. The optimistic family planning program could result in only about 385 million fewer people. Thus, we recognize the urgency of the problem. While our family planning programs are expected to have long-term effect, they will have relatively little impact on the food needs of the world during the next two or three decades.

In seeking the food that is required to meet present deficiencies and provide for the population growth of the future, we gave consideration to all known sources. This included the food from the sea, bacteria, petroleum, as well as synthetic and all traditional sources. We came to the definite conclusion that there is *no panacea to this global problem.* Assuming that the marine sources of food might be greatly increased, possibly expanding to 10 to 20 times the present food from the sea, it is not expected that this source will have a major impact on the solution of the problem. The same can be said for other unique sources. Although we do not offer these as potential reservoirs expected to meet the major demands, research should be continued and expanded on all new and novel sources of food in order to achieve greater productivity in the future. All possible avenues of food production will be needed and must be exploited in the years ahead.

If the world food problems are to be solved and catastrophic conditions prevented that are likely to result from population growth, then the increased production of food in the less developed nations must come from improved basic agricultural practices and a generally better economic condition within those nations. This will include the increased use of proper fertilizers, pesticides, improved varieties of seeds, additional machinery appropriate to the various conditions within these nations, the proper use of available water, and most emphatically — generally improved economic conditions. Parallel with these needs, attention must be given to transportation. These nations must develop roads needed to move food from farms to the markets and to enable the farmer to move his requirements from markets back to his producing lands. Markets, both domestic and foreign, must be improved and emphasis given to preservation of the food being produced, marketed, and utilized by the people. Arrangements must be made to provide the farmer with the necessary incentive to increase his production. If these modern inputs, which are generally known by all, cannot be supplied to those nations needing increased food supply, then all other efforts to reach meaningful solutions are likely to fail.

Land

In considering requirements for increasing food on a world-wide basis, first attention was given to the question of availability of land. While this study did reveal approximately double the amount of potentially arable land ever reported in any previous study, the requirements for clearing, draining, irrigating, and other needs for putting it into production are likely to prevent its availability for crop and animal production during the most critical period of this problem.

The conclusion is obvious — we must give major attention to increasing the productivity of the presently arable land and not expect to increase the food supply by expanding onto lands not previously arable. This is especially true in Asia and in Europe. There is also relatively little additional land to be cultivated in the Soviet Union. Further, the great potential for increased productivity of the available land is in the tropics where yields are not only generally low but the requirements for additional food are the greatest. More than half of the potentially arable land, which amounts to more than 4 billion acres, is in the tropics, and about one-sixth is in the humid tropics. The difficulties in increasing productivity in this part of the world are largely associated with a lack of research results that are applicable to this geographical area. Increased attention should be given to tropical soils and climates in order to provide for manifold increases in the productivity of the lands in the tropical and subtropical areas.

Manufactured Inputs

The subpanel concerned with fertilizers estimated that approximately 61 million metric tons of plant nutrients would be required, in addition to the present roughly 6 million metric tons now being applied, in the developing nations if their food production is to be increased 100% above present levels. Such fertilizer use would necessitate a capital outlay in the neighborhood of $30.5 billion for the production of raw material, mixing plants, distribution, and other requirements. Even the 25% increase in food yields which we urge should be provided by the early 1970's would require a total additional investment cost of approximately $2.5 billion.

The fertilizer component needed for increasing food production, while considered to be the most important component, is not the only one necessary for good crop production. It is only with adequate water, improved seeds, appropriate machinery, and adequate cultivation that the farmer can be expected to realize optimum returns from increased fertilizer applications.

Recent emphasis that has been placed on fertilizer requirements has led to some difficulties in depressing prices for fertilizers on the world market. Many of the major fertilizer manufacturing industries have attempted to respond to the request for greatly increased use of fertilizers by providing the materials to the people of less developed nations. There is not an overproduction of needed fertilizers, but a lack of their distribution. The developing nations are unable to purchase the needed fertilizers with the financial resources they have at their disposal. This apparent surplus of fertilizers due to last year's increased production must not be considered as indicative that we have met the needs of this important component in the food production program. Rather, it is an indication of the complexity of the problem and of the need to take all possible measures to increase economic development in those nations that need to purchase the manufactured inputs required for increasing food supplies.

Varieties, Pesticides, Machinery, and Irrigation

Effective breeding programs must be developed within the nations needing improved crops. The national programs should be applied because their principle objective should be the production of high yielding strains of adapted and desired crops. Emphasis may also be placed on producing crops, particularly cereals, with improved nutritional characteristics. Following the procedures developed in basic research in the United States, genes for high quality protein may be incorporated into crops, such as corn, that are developed within a developing nation's breeding program.

The importance of improved crop varieties in solving the world food problem is indicated in the higher yields of rice from the International Rice Institute in the Philippines and the high-yielding, short, stiff stalk wheats from the International Maize and Wheat Center in Mexico.

However, shipping in new varieties and strains from research centers abroad is not the final answer. Lack of complete adaptation to climates, the need for quality to satisfy the appetites and customs of the people, and resistance to diseases and insects peculiar to the area are some important factors dictating that adaptive research be conducted to provide crop varieties and strains specifically for the needs of a country.

The use of pesticides will have to be increased at least sixfold if the insects and diseases are to be controlled in the developing nations. Adequate farm machinery must provide at least one-half horsepower per hectare for the absolute minimum power needs to achieve a reasonable level of agricultural productivity. The need for new irrigation projects to yield the required water was recognized in those nations where moisture supply is a problem. Many nations can provide the needed water from underground wells, while others will have to resort to major impounding projects in order to obtain an adequate supply for crop production. Irrigation cannot be fully effective unless the total program of improved practices by the various farming programs is rigidly followed.

Education and Research

Those who have participated in technical assistance in the developing nations have emphasized from the outset the importance of education and research appropriate to the needs of the people of these less developed nations. The tremendous magnitude of the problem assumes even greater dimensions when we consider the time scale which must be used in solving it and the great difficulties encountered because of lack of education. Traditional procedures followed by the Western nations must meet the needs of the less developed areas if we are to make rapid progress in the immediate future. Approaches must be used that will educate people of all ages. Ways must be found to communicate with the people if the recommendations made are to be adopted on a wide scale and at a rapid pace. This pace is needed to achieve economic and social development. Technical assistance will have to move at a more rapid rate than the normal educational procedures. Universities of developed nations will have to lead in the innovations needed in the educational processes. Individuals will be expected to work with people of the hungry nations to provide effective communication as one of the most important components of the educational program.

The rate of progress toward improving the educational development of the people is quite slow. Vice-President Humphrey in an address of February 9, 1968, entitled "Nation Building and Peace Building" stated: "Since 1960, despite enormous investments in education, world illiteracy has grown by some 200 million people. Of 373 million children in developing nations, 115 million (or 30%) are in school and about 250 million (or 70%) are not in school."

Not only education itself but the type of training needed among the people must be considered. Efforts must be redirected if the food requirements are to be met in the future. Vocational education, particularly education relating to agricultural careers, must be emphasized. Statistics indicate that only about 4 to 5% of the some 85,000 foreign students studying in the United States are pursuing academic programs that will lead to careers in agriculture and closely related fields. Dr. Roger Revelle, reporting on the special study on "Education in India," found that less than 10,000 agricultural graduates were among the 273,000 who had degrees from universities as of 1961. The manpower requirements are likely to be at least ten- to twentyfold above the presently available number and will tax to capacity the institutional facilities of not only the developed but the developing nations.

Research requirements are in many ways as great and even more demanding than those in education. Errors in approaches and judgment have been made in attempting to help the needy nations. Suggested programs that are essentially a transfer of knowledge of one country to another without the needed adapted research to insure success of the technology in the new environment do not help. The PSAC Report is specific in its recommendations that the misconceptions of the "know-how"-"show-how" approach must be erased. Developing nations cannot be "shown how" until the "know how" is available and specific for the needs of the social structure, the physical environment, the economic conditions, and general agricultural development of the nation. Adaptive research is needed, basic research should be carried out by the affluent nations until the economic development of the needy nations has reached a point where they can afford to allocate their resources to these problems.

Economic Implications and Financial Requirements

The Panel in its analysis of the overall problem indicated required compound growth rates during the next two decades for the developing countries would probably be in aggregate about as indicated below:

	Per cent	
	Present	Required
Increase in Food Demand	3.0	4.0
Increase in Food Production	2.7	4.0
Increase in Gross National Income	4.5	5.5

Such growth rates would require massive efforts and progress which have never before been achieved in any 20-year period. Only Mexico and Taiwan are at the present realizing growth rates of the order considered necessary.

The total financial requirements for technical assistance is staggering and the likelihood of our meeting the needs is most discouraging when we consider the resources being allocated by the developed and more affluent nations. Although the Panel had serious doubts that the financial requirements could be met, they did decide that it was still economically possible when considered on a multi-lateral basis. These needs were approximated to be in the range of $12 billion above the 1965 base of capital investments expended in the some 70 developing nations having food problems. This is the estimated present extent of the increase required to achieve the 4% annual growth rate in food demand and supply. These annual expenditures will be expected to increase to some $25 billion by about 1985. The report concluded on this point with the following statement: "to achieve such a feat would require capital and technical involvement of developing and developed nations alike on a scale unparalleled in peace time history of man."

The attitude of the present Congress toward providing the technical assistance needed is demonstrated in the foreign aid bill, which is at the lowest level in modern history. Unless the financial needs are made available at a much greater rate in the immediate future than in the past, not only will the requirements of the future be greatly amplified but there is a possibility that the rapidly deteriorating conditions of many of the hungry nations will have proceeded to the point where mass starvation and general chaos cannot be avoided.

Impact of the Report

An example of the possible impact of the PSAC Report is the interest expressed in the findings of this Panel by the officials of the Indonesian government and the scientists of that nation. Dr. Sarwono Prawirohardjo, who heads the Indonesian Institute of Sciences, asked the National Academy of Sciences to arrange a panel of experts from the United States and other nations to come to Indonesia to study its food problems with the possibility of developing solutions along the lines that were outlined in the PSAC World Food Report. A 27-man delegation did conduct a Workshop of Food, headquartered in Djarkarta, Indonesia, during the period May 27-June 1, 1968. We had the able assistance and cooperation of approximately 80 Indonesian scientists and technical workers from the various islands of that nation. A report was developed following the intensive study of problems of a nation experiencing a major food crisis. Major recommendations of that study have already been incorporated into the revised agricultural program presently being developed for immediate implementation in Indonesia. Indications are that other nations may be interested in similar intensive studies utilizing this PSAC Report as a basis for these investigations. This is rewarding to those who gave so generously of their valuable and limited time to the study. Many biological scientists may be called to participate in increased efforts in technical assistance. This must happen if hungry people are to be fed and if nations are to experience the forward thrust in economic development needed to bring some equitable balance in living conditions.

Tropical Agriculture
A Key to the World Food Crises

H. David Thurston

The world food crisis is most serious in the tropics. Tropical agriculture has concentrated on cash and plantation crops, neglecting food crops. Tropical food production can be increased through conventional agriculture by overseas technical programs, but training the young people of developing countries is the best method. (BioScience 19, no. 1, p. 29-34)

After reading the papers by Drs. McElroy and Robinson, little additional discussion seems necessary on whether or not the world faces a food crisis. President Lyndon B. Johnson (Hornig, 1967), reflecting our government's judgment, has stated "The world food problem is one of the foremost challenges of mankind today." This challenge is an especially strong one for all biologists. If one is interested in making the world a better place in which to live, or, for more selfish reasons, is interested in lessening the prospects for international conflicts, one concrete way of making a real contribution is to alleviate the gravity of the world food situation.

Where is the food crisis? Martin E. Abel and Anthony S. Rojko (1967) have stated, "Two-thirds of the world's people live in countries with national average diets that are nutritionally inadequate. A country is classified as diet-deficient if the average annual per capita consumption of food results in a deficiency of calories, proteins, or fat below minimum levels recommended by nutritionists. The diet-deficient areas include all of Asia, except Japan, Israel, and the Asian part of USSR, all but the southern tip of Africa, part of South America, and almost all of Central

America and the Caribbean." In other words the problem is largely in the tropics, subtropics, and contiguous areas. Failure to recognize the world food crisis as a tropical problem often deludes people into thinking that our temperate zone agricultural technology can be transplanted directly. The principles and methods from temperate zones often work, but there must be adaptive research to make them work under tropical conditions.

The tropics consist of the zone bounded on the north by the tropic of Cancer and on the south by the tropic of Capricorn. The latitude at these points is 23°27'. Some would extend the tropics to include the area between 30° North and 30° South latitude. A few minutes of study with a globe will show that most "developing" countries are in or on the border of the tropics. Uruguay, for example, is the only country of Latin America with its boundaries entirely within the temperate zone. In Africa, only Morocco and Tunisia are entirely within the temperate zone.

Because of the effect of altitude, many crops grown in temperate zones are also grown in the tropics. Seasonality exists with respect to rainfall, but the extremes and seasonality of temperature we experience in temperate zones does not. Daylength also has a striking effect on crops and animals in the tropics, but changes in length of day and in solar radiation are small in

comparison with the corresponding changes in temperate zones. Thus, even when working with crop plants which are common in temperate zones, adaptive research is necessary when working with them in the tropics. The tropics should not be thought of as a single unit, however, since a wide diversity of ecological and climatic regions can be found within them.

George Harrar (1961) has stated "Rice, wheat, maize, sorghum, the millets, rye, and barley are principal foods in cereal-producing areas, but elsewhere cassava, the sweet potato, potatoes, coconuts, and bananas are basic foods. Although over 3000 plant species have been used for food and over 300 are widely grown, only about 12 furnish nearly 90% of the world's food." Many more of these crop plants are grown in the tropics than in the temperate zones, and we of the temperate zone often do not know much about these plants.

Agricultural research in tropical areas in the past has been primarily on cash and plantation crops while food crops — the plants that people eat, especially in the hot, humid tropics — have been largely ignored by research workers. The Food and Agricultural Organization of the United Nations (FAO) (1966) renders a valuable service by compiling statistics on food production throughout the world. If one studies the 1966 figures for world food produc-

The author is affiliated with the Department of Plant Pathology, New York State College of Agriculture, Cornell University, Ithaca, New York.

tion, one finds that such crops as sweet potatoes, yams, and cassava are ranked after rice and maize as important food sources in the tropics. Plantains (cooking bananas) are also of great importance as a food crop in tropical areas.

These crops, with the possible exception of sweet potatoes which grow well in temperate zones, have been largely ignored by agricultural researchers. Perhaps I can illustrate this point with research on cassava in my field, plant pathology. *The Review of Applied Mycology (R.A.M.)* is probably the best abstracting journal for information on plant diseases throughout the world. From 1945 to 1965 there were 119 references to cassava in the *R.A.M.* or six references per year. Carnations were on the same page and I noted 350 references to carnations during the same period or 17 references per year. In 1966 the *R.A.M.* had two references to cassava diseases and 17 to carnation diseases. There were 234 references to research on tobacco diseases in 1966 in the *R.A.M.* These figures illustrate how research (on a world-wide basis) is not giving some of the important food crops in the tropics the attention they need.

I do not wish to imply that research on important plants such as carnations and tobacco is not valuable, but I do wish to make clear the point that research on some of man's basic food crops such as cassava and plantains is insignificant in comparison. Lack of research on cassava is not due to lack of disease problems. Chevangeon (1956) has listed 73 species of fungi that have been found associated with cassava. In addition, many destructive diseases caused by bacteria, viruses, nematodes, and various abiotic factors are reported in the literature. In 1956 G. W. Padwick brought together the available information on losses caused by one virus disease, cassava mosaic, and estimated that the yearly loss in yield due to the disease was equivalent to 11% of the yearly production of cassava in Africa.

The starchy crops such as cassava, sweet potatoes, yams, and plantains hardly enter into world commerce when compared to the cereals. One of the reasons is that they can seldom be stored for any appreciable time, but they are probably far more important as food in the tropics than available figures indicate.

Nutritionists generally dislike these crops because they are primarily carbohydrate and have a low protein content, yet varieties exist with an appreciable protein content and much might be done in a breeding program to increase it. These crops also can be converted to protein when used as feeds for livestock. Yields of cassava in Brazil, expressed as calories per hectare, are about three times those from corn or rice (Jones, 1959). The starchy root and tuber crops and plantains have a real potential for rapidly reducing food shortages in tropical countries.

Numerous books and references can be found on the cash and plantation crops of the tropics such as sugar cane, rubber, coffee, tea, cacao, citrus fruits, and bananas for fruit, but there is a paucity of information on tropical food crops as they grow in the tropics. Before World War II, most of the research done by the Dutch, English, French, Belgians, and Americans in the tropics was done on cash or plantation crops. Since World War II, other entities such as US-AID (United States Agency for International Development), universities, private foundations, the UN-FAO (United Nations Food and Agricultural Organization), and the Inter-American Institute of Agricultural Science of the OAS (Organization of American States), have entered the field of research in agriculture in the tropics, but even so a great enough emphasis has not been focused on tropical food crops. Outstanding contributions have been made in research on rice, corn, wheat, and potatoes, research which has had and will continue to have an impact on alleviating food shortages, but opportunities for research on other tropical food crops are now largely ignored.

Most of our success stories about agricultural research in developing countries pertain to the subtropics or the semi-temperate border of the tropics. Success stories about agricultural research in the hot, humid tropics are hard to find. The development of IR-8 and IR-5 rice by the International Rice Research Institute in the Philippines is an outstanding exception. Vicente-Chandler (1967) has noted that there are 2 billion acres in the hot-humid area of tropical Latin America, almost as much as the entire United States. In the entire Amazon Basin (half the size of the USA) there are only 10 experiment stations, some with only one researcher with the equivalent of a high school education. From 1960-62 the U.S. Government and international and regional agencies together spent less than 8 million dollars on agricultural research in all of Latin America and only a small part of this in the hot-humid tropics. Two billion dollars were spent on agricultural research during the same period in the United States by the government and agricultural industries. This does not mean that agricultural research in Latin America is the responsibility of the government of the United States, but these observations do bring into focus the relative emphasis on agricultural research in the two areas.

Most of the students from developing countries who come to the United States to study come from tropical countries. Yet few courses are available at most U.S. universities on tropical agriculture. Furthermore, only a superficial introduction to tropical agriculture can be given in one course. In addition, very few students from developing countries study agriculture, and few of these take courses related to tropical agriculture. To quote William C. Paddock (1967) "in 1962, Central America had only 187 university students out of 10,546 studying agriculture." He also adds "In nearly all Latin American countries, for example, the percentage of university students studying agriculture has decreased during the past decade. For instance, Mexico has declined from 3 to 1 percent; Panama from 4 to 2 percent; Dominican Republic from 2 to 1 percent. Of 105,000 Latin American students enrolled in the United States during the decade 1956 to 1965, only 5% studied agriculture." It should be pointed out, to put this situation into proper perspective, that the U.S. government and the other agencies which send students from developing countries to the United States to study give high priority to agriculture.

In plant pathology, I know of no course in the United States (including Hawaii and Puerto Rico) in tropical plant pathology. Little or no emphasis is given in existing courses to tropical problems. In other words, students from developing countries trained in plant pathology in the United States return with a training consisting almost entirely of a study of temperate crop plants and their problems. I suspect the situation is similar in other biological disciplines.

Let us return to the world food crisis. What are the possible solutions for the world food crisis?

1) Atomic war is one solution. We as biologists can do much to see that this is not the solution.

2) Birth Control. Dr. McElroy has covered the many ramifications of this solution. The food crisis may be upon us, however, before this solution is able to bring about real change or slow down the population increase.

3) Massive food shipments. At present, only a very small percentage of the world's total food supply consists of food shipments to developing countries. In 1966 the United States shipped over 15 million tons of grain to developing countries (Abel & Rojko 1967). However, according to FAO statistics (1966), the world production of cereals in 1966 was over 1 billion tons. In addition to the unfortunate side effects of this type of solution, which allows developing countries to delay facing their food problems realistically and thus undertaking to solve their agricultural problems, it appears that in a decade the United States, Canada, and Australia may not be able to continue this type of aid. As recently as 1966, A. H. Moseman stated that "the estimated 42 million ton gap ten years hence exceeds the total of one annual U.S. wheat crop, and the 88 million ton shortfall in 1968 will be beyond U.S. cropping capacity, even if we were to put into production the 55 to 60 million acres now in reserve. It is abundantly clear that the U.S. cannot feed the world." Don Paarlberg who was the U.S. gov-

ernment's Food for Peace coordinator, stated in 1968, "If we were to remove all acreage restrictions, our grain production might increase the world total by some four percent." A recent study by Martin E. Abel and Anthony S. Rojko (1967) of the Economic Research Service of the United States Department of Agriculture gives a less pessimistic prediction: "the results of this study imply that the world probably will continue to have excess production capacity by 1980." Massive food shipments can be of help but they are not the solution to the world food crisis.

4) Increased food production. Some of this may come from fresh and salt water fish, from desalinization of sea water for the deserts, from synthetic foods, and from microorganisms and other nonagricultural food sources. These are extremely important and promising areas of endeavor for biologists. Breakthroughs may occur, but it is doubtful that these sources will produce food fast enough to solve the world food crisis. They are, however, long-range solutions that in several decades may be the key to mankind's food problem.

For the short-range solution, most of the food needed will have to come from more efficient conventional agriculture in tropical countries.

How can food production be increased in developing countries which, as I have pointed out, are primarily tropical? Part of the solution is massive overseas technical programs. Another aspect of the solution is to train the young people of developing nations both in their home countries and abroad so that they can increase food production.

First, let us examine the concept of massive overseas technical programs. By "massive" is meant a commitment by the people of the United States and their government large enough to make reasonable progress in reducing the gravity of the world food crisis. However, we must keep in mind that the United States cannot possibly do the job alone. Other favored countries of the temperate zones should make similar commitments. England, France, Holland, Germany, Russia, Canada, Japan, and many others have much to

offer and should join this effort.

Since World War II, many agencies such as U.S.-AID, U.S. universities, the UN-FAO, the Peace Corps, private foundations such as the Rockefeller Foundation and the Ford Foundation, and many other entities have had overseas technical programs with some commitment in agriculture. An expansion, with modifications, of the activities of these agencies could have an ever-increasing impact on the world food crisis.

Those who have studied the phenomenal success story of U.S. agriculture know that much of the credit is due to the combination of research, education, and extension in our land-grant system of colleges and universities. Unfortunately, this combination and cooperation is seldom found in developing nations. Successful extension is complicated by the sheer numbers of farmers in many tropical countries where as many as 50-80% of the population may be actively engaged in farming versus 4-5% in the United States. The level of education is also a problem in an effective extension of new agricultural technology since largely illiterate populations cannot easily assimilate new knowledge. Lester Brown (1965) has clearly shown the importance of this and other basic factors in obtaining a "yield take-off" in an agricultural country. This does not mean that the job cannot be done, but that experimentation and innovation in extension in developing countries must find methods of accomplishing the task.

Even in the fields of education and research in agriculture in developing countries a poor record of cooperation is more often the rule than the exception. Agencies, both national and international, often duplicate efforts, facilities, and manpower even to the point of interagency animosity. Cooperation and coordination of efforts between agencies should be studied and encouraged. As in taxonomy, splitters usually win in the long run over the lumpers, but the effort should be made to focus these massive efforts on common goals.

During the past two decades, a number of guidelines or principles have been observed which can be very useful for overseas technical programs. There seems to be general agreement on most of these points, but seldom is this agreement translated into action. I would like to give a few examples.

1) When sending people to developing countries it is absolutely essential to send the very best people available. Second raters cannot do the job. The added difficulty of language problems, cultural adjustments, and working in a new and different climate with new crops and technical problems means that only the very best are able to make significant progress. It is necessary to send men who are not only technically competent but by temperament and interest have the patience to work under commonly frustrating circumstances.

2) Continuity of effort is absolutely essential. One- or two-year stints are unfair to the agency, to the individual, and to the developing country. Far too often, about the time an investigator arrives at the point where he can begin to produce he returns home or goes to another country. Few research programs or universities in the United States would have such an impossible and self-defeating personnel policy. Scientists need to be trained and hired to spend decades, not years, in the tropics. To do this, the agencies, such as universities, need long-term commitments of funds for continuity of personnel on overseas assignments.

3) Far too many scientists go to tropical countries as advisors. If one cannot go as a working partner or colleague it may be better to stay home. Few problems in agricultural science exist on which all the advice possible cannot be given in a few weeks. Frequent short visits over a period of many years would be better than a stay of a year or two if one's only function is to give advice.

4) Human relationships are of primary importance. Customs and traditions in tropical lands are often strange and different to people of temperate zones. It is not only important, but essential, to learn as much as possible about the culture, customs, traditions, history, and sociology of the tropical country where one will work in order to be able to partially understand its reason for existence before one can

hope to bring about change, if indeed change is necessary for progress.

The ability to meet one's hosts and treat them as equals and coworkers often is more important than one's scientific knowledge. Jose Nolla (1962) has pointed out that even the poorest farmer and laborer often has great pride and human dignity. The least suggestion of inferiority will be resented and may ruin all one's future work. On the other hand, when treated as equals, the poor farmers can become the warmest of friends and loyal supporters. We in the United States can learn much from them about how to live and enjoy life without losing our much prized reputation for "getting the job done."

5) Any worth-while research effort to increase food production in a developing country should have as one of its aims a training program for local personnel. This enables a tropical country to develop the competent leadership necessary to assume the direction of its own food production efforts. Too often in overseas technical assistance programs several years of intelligent and productive effort by an outside scientist may be essentially lost because no local personnel were assigned to work and learn at his side in the development of a program which will continue on after he leaves.

The United Nations, the United States, and many other nations have been sending thousands of technical personnel overseas during the past two decades to work in increasing food production. Seldom have these personnel received more than a short orientation program to prepare them for their assignments. They may be well prepared in their field of specialization as regards the temperate regions, but they do not have a sound understanding of how to most effectively work in an overseas tropical environment. Professional State Department personnel usually spend many years preparing for their assignments. It should be no less important for young people interested in international agriculture to receive several years of special education and training in preparation for an overseas career. This education should include not only a sound professional

training but also language competence, courses and seminars dealing with the tropics as related to their subject matter field, and an opportunity to work and live in a developing country before graduation. Thesis research (especially at the Ph.D. level) should be done overseas in a tropical environment. This type of training should produce men with a real background of competence, training, and aptitude for working abroad in the tropics.

One of the best and most lasting solutions to the world food crisis is to train the young people of developing nations so that they can help to increase food production. This should be done both in their own countries and abroad.

We have been training students from foreign countries in the United States for probably more than 100 years and in ever-increasing numbers since World War II. The question I wish to ask is, "Have we been doing a good job of training them to return home to increase food production?" I don't think we have for many reasons. If we examine some of the reasons why we have not been doing a good job, perhaps we can improve our future performance.

In agriculture, the great majority of foreign students from tropical countries are "asphalt" farmers. Students from Latin America, Africa, and Asia usually come from a stratem of society in which people do not actually till the soil with their hands. Many departments in U.S. colleges of agriculture require their undergraduates to give proof of farm experience or obtain such experience before or during their time in college as a prerequisite for graduation. We should do the same for foreign graduate students who plan to major in an agricultural science. There is no classroom substitute for practical farm experience.

The foreign students that do manage to come to the United States are usually a highly selected group. When they return home, they often end up as administrators. Poor administration is one of the facts of life in most tropical countries. Yet we make no attempt to give even passing reference to this important aspect in our training programs.

Increasing numbers of tropical countries are setting up graduate and undergraduate schools to train the people their countries need for increasing agricultural production. Foreign students seldom, if ever, are exposed to a study of teaching methods or given practical experience in teaching, yet they may return to a teaching position or may be expected to set up a graduate program. We have given almost no attention to this aspect of training.

Increasing specialization and fragmentation of biological sciences is the rule in the United States at the present time. Students from developing countries need a far broader training than we are now generally able or willing to give.

At present in the United States, the emphasis in most fields of biology is on basic research. Applied or practical research has somehow developed a connotation of being "second class." Considerable basic research is needed if breakthroughs are to be made in tropical agriculture, but there is a far more pressing need for practical and applied research. Students from foreign countries, and U.S. students interested in international agriculture, soon find out that the prestige and the challenging forefront of human knowledge is in basic research, and the best of them frequently seek training and do their thesis in "basic" research. What they need, however, is training in how to apply the methods and principles they learn here in solving the problems of increased food production in a tropical environment.

Frequently, a well-trained scientist may return to his country with glowing letters of recommendation from his department and advisor after a brilliant academic career and after completing a thesis which is a real contribution in his field. He insists on, and gets, a fine laboratory, expensive equipment, and technical assistants. After a few years his superiors begin to ask embarrassing questions on practical applications and expect him to give them figures in dollars, rupees, or pesos on how his research has increased food production. When they are not forthcoming, administrators become gun-shy of future brilliant returnees and it becomes in-

creasingly difficult to support good research.

I have previously mentioned the lack of training with a tropical emphasis. Much could be done here to at least expose students from tropical countries to the pertinent literature in their field of specialization as regards the tropics. In addition, a few universities now encourage students from developing countries to do their thesis in a tropical environment. This type of training should be far more effective than that which most students receive at present.

Every major university department in the agricultural sciences in the United States turns down large numbers of qualified students from developing countries every year. At present, there is no method of helping these students, no central clearinghouse to help them find the type of training they need, with the result that there is an obvious duplication of effort and seeming chaos in placing students from foreign countries. Selection of students is equally confused. The present process is similar to a lottery since the information available about the students is usually not sufficient for an adequate judgment. A study of these problems by our organization and other similar bodies should result in worthwhile recommendations which could improve this chaotic situation. Only the most highly qualified and motivated students, those who plan to return to the tropics and work in increasing food production there should be given priority. This may be asking the impossible, but we certainly could do a far better job than we are doing at present. Our resources, and those of tropical countries, are not so great that an essentially hit and miss system of student training and selection will meet the challenge of increasing food production in these critical days.

There is a tremendous ferment in our society today. Our youth are confused and unhappy with the world as it is. There is a great backlog of youth in our nation who want to make the world a better place in which to live. Unfortunately, they don't know how, and they have few skills. Love of humanity and the best of intentions will not make a better life for others. You cannot will it. Our society, and biologists in

general, have a challenging task — namely, to interest our best young people in biological science and show them a way whereby they can have a real impact on making the world a better place in which to live. To do this job, however, I believe we have to go outside of our profession and enlist the aid of professionals in communication. We can help, but we cannot do it alone. Once we have students in the classroom or laboratory we can do much to show them the opportunities, but we have to get them into the classroom first. If their high school biology is deadly dull and no connection is made between frog eggs and a better world, we will not be doing our job.

International activities, especially those in the biological sciences, are often thought of as an activity which universities should engage in as a philanthropic cause. As Charles Frankel (1968) has pointed out "it is that; but it is also a commitment that can sustain universities in their honesty and their honor. It is through the shock of new perspectives that people can veraciously look at themselves. It is through the exchange of ideas across the frontiers that people come to look at their own traditions objectively. International education involves the simple practical business of keeping universities true to their own vocation.

"It is from this point of view that one can speak of international education not only as a duty but as an opportunity, not only as a service to the world but as a way of learning from the world. Properly conceived and organized, international education can represent precisely the sort of marriage of self-interest and social purpose, of social influence and emancipated intelligence, which should characterize all relationships between the university and the world."

Summary

The world faces a food crisis and much of the problem is in the tropics and subtropics. Tropical agricultural research in the past has concentrated primarily on cash and plantation crops, and the food crops have been largely neglected. Great opportunities exist for biologists interested in tropical food crops to make significant contributions to solving some of the problems of food shortages in developing countries.

The most realistic short-range method of solving the world's food crisis is to increase food production through conventional agriculture in the tropics. This can be done in part by overseas technical programs originating in developed countries, but training the young people of developing nations to do the job of increasing food production themselves is the better and more lasting method.

The efficiency of overseas technical programs can be greatly increased by stimulating closer cooperation among overseas technical agencies, by sending only the most competent personnel overseas, by establishing continuity of effort and personnel for decades and not months or years, and by greater cognizance of the importance of human relationships when working in developing countries.

Much can be done to improve the education and training that we of the temperate zones give young people from developing countries, both in their own countries and abroad. This training has usually been deficient in practical or farm level experience, training in administration, training with a tropical emphasis, and in giving too much emphasis on basic rather than applied or practical research.

The young people of our society, and those of most developing countries are seriously disturbed, if not in open revolt, about the world as it is. They want to make the world a better place in which to live. Biologists have an exciting challenge — namely, to interest young people in biological science and show them a way whereby they can have a real impact on two of the world's most serious problems — hunger and malnutrition.

References

Abel, M. E., and A. S. Rojko. 1967. World food situation. Prospects for world grain production, consumption, and trade. Foreign Agr. Econ. Rept. No. 35. USDA, Washington, D.C.

Brown, Lester R. 1965. Increasing world food output. Foreign Agricultural Economic Report No. 25. USDA, Econ. Res. Serv.

Chevangeon, Jean. 1956. Les maladies cryptogamiques du manioc en Afrique occidentale. *Encycl. Mycologique*, **28**: 1-205.

Food and Agriculture Organization of the United Nations. 1966. FAO, *Production Yearbook*. Vol. 20.

Frankel, Charles. 1968. The university and the world. *Univ. Rev.*, **1**: 8-11. State University of New York.

Harrar, J. G. 1961. Socio-economic factors that limit needed food production and consumption. *Fed. Proc.*, **20**: 381-383.

Hornig, D. F. (Chairman). 1967. *The world food problem. Report of the Panel on the World Food Supply.* A report of the Presidents' Science Advisory Committee. Vol. 1. The White House, Washington, D.C.

Jones, William O. 1959. *Manioc in Africa.* Stanford University Press, Stanford, Calif. 315 p.

Moseman, A. H. 1966. National systems of science and technology for agricultural development. Proceedings of the St. Paul Conference. University Directors of International Agricultural Programs. University of Minnesota, St. Paul, Minn.

Nolla, Jose A. B. 1962. The necessarily broad view in studying tropical plant diseases. *Phytopathology*, **52**: 946-947.

Paarlberg, Don. 1968. World food: Present situation and future prospects. In: World Markets and the New York Farmer.

Paddock, W. C. 1967. Phytopathology in a hungry world. Ann. Rev. *Phytopathology*, **5**: 375-390.

Padwick, G. W. 1956. *Losses Caused by Plant Diseases in the Colonies.* Phytopathological papers No. 1. Commonwealth Mycol. Inst., Kew, Surrey, England.

Vicente-Chandler, Jose. 1967. A prospectus of natural resource use and research programs for semitropic regions. The Southeastern area meeting of the National Association of Conservation Districts, San Juan, Puerto Rico.

The Population
Crisis Is Here *Now*

Walter E. Howard

If babies of the future are to live, there must be fewer of them. No matter how much food there is, the birth rate cannot continue to exceed the death rate. It can no longer be a basic human right to have as many children as one wants, for such action clearly dooms others to an involuntary premature death. (BioScience *19*, no. 9, p. 779-784)

Preface

At the present world rate of population growth of 2% per year, a mere dozen people a thousand years ago could have produced the present world population, and in another thousand years each one of us could have 300 million living descendants. Obviously, that cannot be—something must be done. Either the birth rate must be significantly curtailed or the death rate drastically increased.

The world's overpopulation crisis is of a magnitude beyond human comprehension, yet the government and the public remain seemingly indifferent. Better awareness and a more forthright leadership are obviously needed, from biologists and politicians alike. Will you help? A vastly increased rate of involuntary premature deaths can be prevented only by an informed public, here and abroad, following dynamic leadership. No population can continue to increase indefinitely, no matter how much food there is. If civilization is to be viable, we must end the arrogant assumption that there are unlimited resources and infinite air and water. People must develop much greater voluntary restraint in reproduction—or conception itself will have to come under government control.

This earth does not have the resources necessary to provide even the present world population with the degree of af-

The author is a professor of wildlife biology in the Department of Animal Physiology and a vertebrate ecologist in the Experiment Station, University of California, Davis.

fluence that the middle-class citizen enjoys. Even though the average birth rate in the United States has declined during the past decade from about seven children per family to fewer than three, the population density has been growing much more rapidly than before. The reason is the high population base level; there are now so many more women that their "small" families add a greater number of new people to the population each year than did their grandmothers, even with much larger families.

No population can continue to grow beyond certain limits; eventually, involuntary self-limitation—in the form of premature deaths from starvation, pestilence, and wars—will prevent any further increase in density. Since all finite space is limited, it is an indisputable fact that birth rates and death rates must someday be balanced. Already the rich are devouring the poor—the survival of the fittest.

Introduction

The intent of this article is not to alarm the reader unnecessarily. But how is that possible? Alarm is called for; man should be alarmed. Man must be aware of his dilemma, for if he attempts to feed the world without effective control of the birth rate, he actually is only deferring the starvation of an even greater number of people to a later date.

The world is facing this acute overpopulation situation specifically because of advances in agriculture and health, through science and technology, and a

lack of similar progress in the field of sensible birth control. Families are not having more babies, it is just that more now survive.

Passion between the sexes must, of course, remain a basic human right, but it cannot include the having of children at will. While intercourse remains an individual and private matter, procreation must become of public concern. Conception should not be a euphemism for sexual relations. The obvious goal for all societies wishing an abundant life and freedom from want should be a low-birth-rate, low-death-rate culture. Man's responsibility to the next generation includes a primary duty of limiting the size of that generation.

Our problem is uncontrolled human fertility—not underproduction and maldistribution—and corrective action is being dangerously delayed by wishful thinking that some miracle will solve the problem. There is a prodigious need for immediate public awareness of the current critical situation, since overpopulation is intimately involved with political, economic, and sociological problems—in fact, with everyone's peace, security, and general well-being. All of the world's desperate needs—ample food, permanent peace, good health, and high-quality living—are unattainable for all human beings both now and in the foreseeable future for one obvious reason: there are too many people. A soaring population means a shrinking of man's space on this earth.

Not only is population growth the most

basic conservation problem of today, but its dominating influence will affect the ultimate survival of mankind. Man can no longer be indifferent to this basic population problem. Its severity behooves all to act now. Hunger and overpopulation will not go away if we do not discuss them, and the bringing of too many babies into this world is not just someone else's problem; it is everyone's concern. The destiny of overpopulation is erosion of civilized life.

The World's Population

To appreciate the recent rapidity with which the world's population has grown—it took from the beginning of man until 1850 to reach a population of one billion people, only 80 years more (1930) to reach two billion, then only 30 years (1960) to reach the three billion mark, and in less than 15 years after 1960 we expect four billion. In the next 25 years after that, the population is expected to increase by another three and one-half billion people. If there have been about 77 billion births since the Stone Age, then about 1 out of every 22 persons born since then is alive today; but in only 30 or 40 years from now, if current rates of increase continue, 1 out of every 10 people ever born will be living at that time. The youth of today might see the United States with a population equal to what India has now.

Only a small proportion of the world's population has made the demographic transition of attaining both a lower fertility and a lower mortality; most have decreased only the premature death rate. The population has continued to increase rapidly because reductions in fertility have not been sufficient to offset the effects of current reductions in mortality produced by technological sanitation, disease control, and pesticide use.

The reproductive potential of the world is grim, for 40 to 45% of the people alive today are under 15 years old. How can this tremendous number of babies soon be fed solid foods? And look how soon those who survive will be breeding.

Even though technology exists that could manufacture enough intrauterine devices for every woman, the problems of distribution and the shortage of doctors make it impossible for the devices to be inserted fast enough to control the world's population growth. Within a few years

the number of people dying each year from causes related to poor nutrition will equal what is now the entire population of the United States.

In the United States if the fertility and mortality trends of 1950-60 should be re-established, replacing the 1968 low birth rate, in only 150 years our country alone could exceed the current world population of over 3.3 billion, and in 650 years there would be about one person per square foot. This will not happen, of course, because either the birth rate will decline, or more likely, the death rate will increase.

Rate of Population Increase

The basic factor is the difference between birth and death rates, not what the levels of births and deaths happen to be. Continued doubling of a population soon leads to astronomical numbers. If the world population increase continued at the low rate of only 2%, the weight of human bodies would equal the weight of the earth in about 1500 years.

The world population is reported to be currently growing by 180,000 a day, more than a million a week, or about 65 million a year, and each year it increases in greater amounts. If current trends continue, the population will reach about 25 billion in only 100 years.

Prior to Christ, it took about 40,000 years to double the population, but the current growth rate of about 2% would require only 35 years to double the present population. Populations that grow by 3% per year double within a generation and increase eighteen-fold in 100 years.

Population Dynamics

If 90% of a population survives long enough to reproduce, an average of 2.3 children per family will keep the population stable. Only a very slight increase to 2.5 children would produce an increase of 10% per generation, and 3.0 children per family would cause an increase of 31% per generation. If child-bearing families averaged 3.0 children, about one woman in four would need to be childless for the population to remain stable.

A sustained geometric increase in human beings is, of course, impossible; once the population's base level of density is high, as it now is, birth rates cannot continue much above the death rates for long

without a truly impossible density being produced. As the base population density rises, even a lower birth rate can still mean that there will be a greater absolute increase in total numbers than was occurring before, when population was less and birth rates were higher.

Obviously, if input (natality) continues to exceed outgo (mortality), any finite space must eventually fill up and overflow. Populations increase geometrically, whereas food and subsistence increase arithmetically. The geometric ratio of population growth is also known as the ever-accelerating growth rate, the logistic curve, the well-known S-shaped or sigmoid growth curve, and compound interest.

When populations of people are exposed to stressing pressures, including those due to overpopulation, they may respond in a strange way of breeding earlier and more prolifically, further aggravating the situation. The principal way in which man differs from other animals is in his intellect, his ability to read and communicate, to learn, to use tools, and his society; and he also differs from other species in that he attempts to protect the unfit and all "surplus" births.

Predisposition to Overpopulate

Nature has seen to it that all organisms are obsessed with a breeding urge and provided with the biological capacity to overproduce, thereby ensuring survival of the species. Since man now exercises considerable control over so many of the natural factors which once controlled his population, he must also learn to control his innate trait to reproduce excessively.

It is not a question of whether this earth has the resources for feeding a much greater population than is now present—of course, it has. The point is that the human population is now growing too fast for food production ever to catch up without stringent birth control.

Carrying Capacity and Self-Limitation

No matter how far science and technology raise the carrying capacity of the earth for people, involuntary self-limiting forces will continue to determine man's upper population density. Surplus populations do not just quietly fade away—quite the contrary. Before surplus individuals die, they consume resources and contribute in general to other population stresses, all of which make the environment less suitable, thus lowering its carrying capacity. Man needs space to live as much as do plants and animals.

The balance of nature is governed primarily by the suitability of the habitat and species-specific self-limitation, where members of each species involuntarily prevent any further increase in their kind. This self-limitation consists of undesirable stresses which cause individual births in a family to be unwanted or cause a compensating increase in death rates. Members of the population become their own worst enemy in the sense that they are responsible for the increased rates of mortality and, perhaps, also some reduction in natality.

Nearly all organisms that are well-adapted to their environment have built-in mechanisms for checking population growth before the necessary food and cover are permanently destroyed. But nature's population control processes are unemotional, impartial, and truly ruthless, a set of conditions that educated men will surely wish to avoid.

Instead of man learning how to conquer nature, he may annihilate it, destroying himself in the process. In current times at least, there is no hope that man as a species will voluntarily limit his birth rate to the low level (zero or even minus replacement) that the overall population must have. Also, unfortunately, when a population level is below carrying capacity the innate desire to have larger families then becomes very strong, making human husbandry difficult to practice.

Nature does not practice good husbandry—all its components are predisposed to overpopulate and, in fact, attempt to do so, thus causing a high rate of premature deaths. If food supply alone were the principal factor limiting the number of people, man would long ago have increased to a density where all of the food would have been consumed and he would have become an extinct species.

When other organisms follow a population growth curve similar to what man is currently experiencing—and they do this only in disturbed (usually man-modified) environments—they can then become so destructive to their habitat that the subsequent carrying capacity may be dramatically reduced if not completely

destroyed, thus causing not only mass individual suffering and a high rate of premature deaths but also a permanent destruction of the ecosystem.

Whenever man's population density has been markedly reduced through some catastrophe, or his technology has appreciably increased the carrying capacity of his habitat (environment), the growth rate of his population increases. The population then tends to overcompensate, temporarily growing beyond the upper limits of the carrying capacity of the environment. The excess growth is eventually checked, however, by the interaction of a number of different kinds of self-limiting population stress factors. These include such forces as inadequate food and shelter, social stress factors, competition for space, wars, an increase in pestilence, or any of many other subtle vicissitudes of life that either increase the death rate, reduce successful births, or cause individuals to move elsewhere. Unfortunately, in the developed countries, science and technology are developing at an exponential rate, so the population growth may not again be sufficiently halted by self-limitation until the earth's resources are largely exploited or a world famine or other drastic mortality factor appears.

Although nature practices survival of the fittest, man believes that all who are born should be given every opportunity to live to an old age. If this is to be our objective, and I am sure it will, then we have only one other alternative, i.e., to restrict the number of births. And to accomplish this, it seems better to reduce conception rather than to rely on abortions. Abortions are a solution, however, when other means of preventing conceptions have broken down. Surprising to most people, abortions induced by a doctor are safer than childbearing.

There is a need too for man to establish a stable relationship with the environment. Man must recognize that he also responds to many, in fact, most of the laws of nature. And his population checks are largely famine, pestilence, and war. Man has transferred himself from being just a member of the ecosystem to a dominant position, where he now mistakenly assumes that the ecosystem is his to control at will. He forgets that he is part of nature. To see his true place in the world he must not attempt to trans-

cend too much over nature, but to discover and assimilate all he can about the truth of nature and his own role in nature.

Only self-limitation can stem the population tide, and the only voice man has in the matter is whether it will be done involuntarily by nature's undesirable stresses, as witnessed by the history of civilization, or will be done consciously by not allowing his kind to exceed an optimum carrying capacity.

Socio-Economic Situations

It is incongruous that student unrest is so great and race problems so much in the front, yet almost everyone seems unaware that the basic cause of most of these socio-economic stresses is overpopulation, about which almost nothing is said by all of these energetic and sometimes vociferous groups. The daily economic pressures of individuals attempting to provide a decent civilization, especially for themselves, may lead to the ultimate destruction of all ecosystems. Surplus individuals do not quietly fade away.

In spite of man's power of conscious thought, the only species so endowed, he seldom thinks beyond his lifetime or his own family's particular needs. The great desire of most people to provide their children and themselves with all of today's advantages is an important factor in reducing family size. That is not enough, however, for these families are still raising the population level.

At the same time that the world's population is increasing, both the number and the percentage of the "have-nots" increase and, in addition, the gap widens between the "haves" and "have-nots." As tragic as it may sound, when an underdeveloped country's population density is growing rapidly, both health and agricultural aid from the United States may not only be wasted but may severely aggravate the already deplorable social and economic situation in that country.

In industrially developed countries, middle-class couples often have fewer children than they would like (if they only had more money, domestic help, etc.), whereas in underdeveloped countries and ghettos the reverse is too frequently true. High birth rates tend to nullify national efforts to raise average per capita income since there is less money for savings and developmental investments. Neither families nor a nation can escape when life is held close to the margin of subsistence.

Overpopulation inevitably commits too many people to poverty and despair. With perpetual pregnancies the bonds of welfare become inescapable, for unskilled parents cannot feed a large family from the wages they can earn. No matter how you look at it, families of more than two or three children intensify the problem of national development, and this happens whether the parents are poor, middle class, or wealthy.

A complete reorientation of social values and attitudes regarding births is urgently needed now. We need new baby ethics, an awareness of the tragedies associated with too many babies. Bringing births and deaths into balance will demand great social, economic, and political changes.

With reference to our affluence, we cannot turn back—if for no other reason than the fact that there are now too many people to permit going back—to a less materialistic existence without cars, pesticides, diesel exhaust, sewage and garbage disposal, etc. The stork has passed the plow. Food prices in developing nations are rising faster than the purchasing power.

Economic Interests

Man seems to be governed by economic self-interest. Societies become conditioned to the tenets of the economists—that money can buy anything. Without the basic resources there can be no wealth and affluence; but, unfortunately, the exploitation of resources seems to be considered the very foundation of all "progress."

"Progress" is the magic word. It means to increase property values and returns on one's investment; it is the deity of modern civilization. Yet, do any of us really know what we are progressing toward? Too often, the chamber-of-commerce form of "progress" is the next man's destruction.

Man seems to be more concerned with the quality of his goals than with the quantity of his goods. The more slowly a population increases the more rapid is the growth of both its gross and per capita income.

The harmful consequences of overpopulation are blindly overlooked by those who favor an expanding population for reasons of military strength, economic progress, scientific and agricultural development, and eugenics.

Man's economic dreams, his selfishness, and his materialism interfere with his awareness of the fate of the unborn. He is too busy in the United States in covering two acres per minute with houses, factories, and stores. His highways are now equivalent to paving the entire state of Indiana. Every day, California loses 300 acres of agricultural land.

Unfortunately, little planning has been done on how the socio-economic problems can be handled once the population growth is stopped. If the rush of today's living and industrial development or defense spending just slows down, a painful recession is upon us. We have no government study on how the nation could exist without a growing population.

Resource Management

Insidious economic pressures seem to prevent any effective management of resources in a manner that would provide for their utilization in perpetuity. Concrete and pavement surely are not the epitome of the human species' fulfillment. An ecological appreciation of resource management is needed, and ecological ethics must replace ecological atrocities.

Man is rapidly depleting the nonreplenishable resources. Half of the energy used by man during the past 2000 years was used in the last century. Man is reported to have mined more in the past 100 years than during all previous time. But, every barrel has a bottom; unbridled technology promises to speed us faster toward that bottom. Our planet's resources diminish faster as society's affluence is increased. Our qualitative sense of appreciation of our environment seems to be replaced by mere quantitative values. Why cannot civilization fulfill its obligation of being a competent steward of all resources?

It is inevitable that the limited legacy of natural resources must steadily yield in the face of the current explosion in the world population. As the population swells, open spaces are inundated by a flood of housing, and resources shrink faster. The United States and other developed nations are consuming a disproportionately large share of the world's

nonrenewable and other resources at an ever-accelerating rate, perhaps 20 to 30 times as much on a per capita basis as are individuals in undeveloped countries. In 1954, the United States was reported to be using about 50% of the raw-material resources consumed in the world each year, and by 1980 it might be 80%. But we do not have an endless earth of boundless bounty. Any finite resource is subject to eventual exhaustion.

Effect of Science and Technology

The world may have sufficient resources, but it has never provided enough food and other necessities of life for all people at any one time. As technology improved, enabling better utilization of resources, the population similarly increased, so that there have always been many who died prematurely, as Malthus predicted.

No one anticipated the scope and rapidity of the technological changes that have occurred in Western society. About one-third of the people now consume about two-thirds of the world's food production, while the other two-thirds go undernourished. But, unfortunately, these starving people reproduce at a high rate. As individual aspirations rise and per capita resources fall, the widening gap between the haves and the have-nots could well generate some serious social and political pressures.

In recent times spectacular gains have been made in controlling mass killers such as typhus, malaria, yellow fever, small pox, cholera, plague, and influenza; but no corresponding checks have been made on birth rates. It is ironic that the root of our overpopulation problem is technical advances brought about by our increasing intellect (the knowledge explosion of the last hundred years).

Technology can produce almost anything, but only at the usually recognized high price of resource consumption and waste accumulation. As our technology advances, the amount of resources utilized per person also increases, and the supply is not endless.

Technology and science can and do progress at an ever-increasing rate, but can social, political, and religious views change rapidly enough to cope with this "progress"? The fruits of all our scientific and technological advances will be ephemeral if the world's population continues to explode. Our intelligence is so powerful that it may destroy us because we lack the wisdom and insight to recognize and correct what we are doing to ourselves and, especially, to future generations. We are passing on an enormous population problem to the next generation.

Pollution and Waste Disposal

Affluent societies have also been labeled "effluent" societies. That man is a highly adaptable species that can live in polluted environments, in extremely crowded conditions, in situations of acute malnutrition, and in some of the most depressing of environments is well exemplified today. But why should he? And how much lower can he sink and still survive as a "successful" species?

Mushrooming with the population are pollution and litter. We produce 70% of the world's solid wastes but have only 10% of the world's population. There is a need to make the reuse and disposal of rubbish more economical.

Popular Solutions and Misconceptions

Hopeful but inadequate panaceas include synthetic foods (proteins and vitamins), hydroponics, desalinization of seawater, food from the ocean, more agricultural research, fertilizers, irrigation, the vast unused lands, land reforms, government regulation, price support, migrations, redistribution of food and wealth, and private enterprise.

Science and technology may find a way to produce more food and to accommodate more people, but in the end this, of course, will only make matters that much worse if birth control is not effective. It should be obvious that the only solution is a drastically reduced birth rate or a greatly increased death rate. The one inescapable fact about a country's population—about the world's population—is that the death rate must someday equal the birth rate, regardless of how plentiful food may be.

Unfortunately, a basic American philosophy is the belief that our free-enterprise system can produce anything that is necessary, a false cornucopian faith that our population growth is not a real threat. Our overpopulation-underdevelopment dilemma is not a matter of increasing

production to meet the demand for more food; rather, the only solution is to limit demand for food so that production may someday catch up to the population's needs.

Role of Family Planning

There is no question that family planning has made great progress. But today's society and religious groups must recognize the urgency for adopting the pill, IUD, other chemical and mechanical devices (both undependable), sterilization, abortion—in fact, any means of limiting childbirth. The promotion of some form of effective means of artificial birth control is the only moral, human, and political approach available to prevent the misery and suffering which will result if people are permitted to have as many "planned" children as they want.

Despite the great benefits of family planning programs, especially the benefits to the families concerned, family planning is not a euphemism for birth control. We need to develop a social and cultural philosophy that even a family of three children is too large and to overcome the fear of some ethic and religious sects that other groups may multiply faster, becoming more dominant. Family planning per se has little relevance to the underdeveloped countries of the world or to poverty groups in the more advanced countries. Therefore anything other than government control of conception may be self-defeating.

Sexual Desire and Love of Children

The basic conflict with the overpopulation problem is that of desires—actually drives—and the fact that most young women are fecund; without either the strong drives or the ability of women to conceive, there would be no problem. As with all organisms, man's potential fecundity and predisposition to overproduce are the basic causes for his excess fertility over deaths. Most babies are the consequence of passion, not love. But children are loved.

Motherhood must become a less significant role for women. We must forego some of our love for children and learn to be content with fewer numbers. What is needed in the way of governmental control of births is not control of an individual's behavior but control of the consequence of such behavior, the prevention of intemperate breeding.

There is no question that children make family ties more intimate, but man has already done too well toward "fathering" the country. Compassionate relations between spouses, not the having of children, must become the primary goal of marriages in the future. There is no need to find drugs that destroy sexual desire; the objective is to control the conception rate, not frequency of intercourse.

Is Having Children a Basic Right?

One price that society must be willing to pay for sustained world peace is a stringent universal birth-control program, which will require revolutionary revisions of modes of thought about our basic human rights with regard to family planning.

The increasing disparity between population density and food supply, by itself, justifies effective birth control regardless of the "morality" associated with depriving parents of the right to have as many planned children as they choose.

Having too many children can no longer be dismissed as an act of God, for it is now truly the consequence of a complacent society that is unwilling to take any of many steps available for preventing surplus births. Our primitive reproductive instincts cannot be condoned in the face of modern survival rates. The two are no longer in balance.

To say that the opportunity to decide the number and spacing of children is a basic human right is to say that man may do whatever he wants with nature without thought of its inevitable consequence to future generations. Our legal and ethical right should be to have only enough children to replace ourselves.

No longer can we consider procreation an individual and private matter. Intercourse, yes, but not unregulated numbers of conceptions since they affect the welfare of all other individuals living at that time plus those to be born in the future.

Religious Complications

It needs to be said over and over again that the bringing of surplus children into this world, whether from personal desire or from religious edicts, destines not only some of these children but many others to a premature death. Overproduction actually lowers the maximum density that can be sustained for normal life spans, thereby increasing the number of souls in need of salvation.

The "morality" of birth control in today's burgeoning human population has taken on an entirely new aspect. God clearly never meant for man to overpopulate this earth to the point where he would destroy many other forms of life and perhaps even himself. The religious doctrines we lean on today were established before science and technology had dramatically raised the carrying capacity for man.

The question of complete abstinence as the only acceptable means of family regulation is as ludicrous as compulsory euthanasia. The mortal sin, if there is one, in God's eyes surely would be associated with those who do *not* practice birth control, for to let babies come "as they naturally do" will prove to be a form of murder—through starvation, pestilence, and wars resulting from excess babies. It must be recognized that the number of children can no longer be left to "the will of God" or to our own desires and family plans, and if population controls are to be successful, they may have to be determined by government regulations.

Religious views that do not condone rigorous birth control must realize that every surplus birth their philosophy promotes will guarantee, on the average, a horrible death some day to more than one individual.

Although the Christian attitude implies that everything on this earth was created for man's use, in reality man is inescapably also part of nature.

Some form of compulsory control of birth rates is essential, although I see no reason why various religious groups cannot be permitted to achieve birth limitations in whatever manner they choose. If a woman or a couple exceeds the limit set by society, however, then they must be dealt with by law compelling them to be sterilized, to have an abortion, or by some other repayment to society.

Birth control is not murder, as some claim, but lack of it in today's overpopulated world most surely will be. For those who strongly oppose the setting of any limit on the number of children a family can have, I ask them to tell the rest of us just how they think the premature death rate should be increased to offset their extra births.

Wealth vs. Number of Children

Civilization can no longer endure a way of life in which people believe they have the right to have as many children as they can afford. This is hypocritical, for those who can "afford" luxurious living are already utilizing many times their share of the limited food and other resources, and also they are contributing much more pollution to the environment than are the have-nots. The affluent population needs to be made aware of the overpopulation problems, for they often desire to have more children per family than those who are in poverty.

Too much of today's religious climate makes birth control a politically sensitive area, thus constraining public officials. But, as citizens, are we not justified in asking why our governmental officials have not done more to make us aware of the urgency of population control—political sensitivities notwithstanding?

Governments should be guiding the development of a better life and world to live in, but if it does not recognize the need for human husbandry, then it will be fostering the ultimate destruction of the earth rather than the goals it seeks.

Man, in spite of his intellect, is so concerned with the present that he too often turns a deaf ear to alarming sounds of the future. Another difficulty in stabilizing the population is that our standard of living and our economy cannot survive in a static state.

Limiting Size of Families

We can no longer be prophets and philosophers; we must act. The biomagnification of births must be brought to an abrupt halt. Procreation must come under governmental control if no other way can be found. Perhaps what is needed is a system of permits for the privilege of conceiving, or compulsory vasectomies of all men and sterilization of all women who have been responsible for two births.

Since the taboo against birth control is inviolable to some, regardless of the dire consequences of overpopulation, laws must be passed to regulate conceptions and births. Each individual needs to have the right to produce or adopt only a replacement for himself or herself.

The general public must be made to realize that from now on, for a married couple to have more than two children or three at most, is a very socially irresponsible act. We must advocate small families. When business is good and living

has quality, marriages will naturally tend to be earlier and births more numerous; therefore, only through the development of new nonfamilial rewards can later marriages be made to appear attractive to people. Taxes now subsidize children, whereas we should be taxed for the privilege of having children.

A rising age at marriage is an effective way of reducing births, and, sociologically and economically, it gives women more time to become better educated, acquire nonfamily sorts of interests, and develop greater cautions toward pregnancy.

Up to now, only death has been of public concern; procreation has remained an individual and highly cherished private matter. But this privilege cannot continue, and regulation of the number of conceptions, or at least births, must also become a government function.

Population Control or Premature Deaths

Man must decide whether the future growth of populations will be governed by famine, pestilence, and war, on whether he will use his intellect to control birth rates artificially. If the population growth is not controlled by lower birth rates, hundreds of millions of people must soon die prematurely each year.

Man must use his intellect to counteract his excessive fertility, for all species have been endowed by nature to be overfecund. If he does not, the extra individuals will be eliminated by the natural process of "struggle for existence—survival of the fittest," which causes all surplus individuals to die prematurely as a result of nature's ruthless laws of involuntary "self-limitation" whenever the carrying capacity has been exceeded. That territoriality and aggression are life-preserving functions of the social order of animals is frightening when man applies these same principles to his own species.

There have always been hungry people in the world, but both the total number of individuals and the percentage of the total population that are destined to go hungry in the future will be dramatically increased if birth rates are not drastically checked. Many like to think that nature will somehow take care of things. They fail to remember how nature has taken care of many species that were no longer adaptable to existence on this earth—they are now preserved as fossils.

Modern public-health methods and medical technology have lessened the chronic hunger, general economic misery, and other vicissitudes that once caused high mortality rates. But, sooner or later, any increase in births over deaths will be balanced by an increase in the rate of premature deaths.

Human Husbandry and Quality Living

Human husbandry implies that we regulate the population density before the natural self-limiting demographic and societal stress factors do it for us. But human motivation will always work against good human husbandry, because to each individual who has quality living, a large family will seem desirable.

The population of the world is so great that what used to be a ripple when it doubled now means catastrophic effects because of the great numbers involved and the lack of this earth's ability to support them. Man is not practicing good husbandy when he lets his population density expand beyond the carrying capacity.

The most important thesis regarding the need for human husbandry is that human beings will not voluntarily restrict their number of children to just two when economic, social, and political conditions appear to be personally favorable. A quality society with quality existence is now unattainable in many parts of the world, and may soon be unattainable any place in the world. The "economic" struggle of overpopulation is the world's greatest threat to quality living, enriched leisure, and even man's ultimate existence.

Conclusion

The ultimate goal must be a zero population growth. To achieve "quality living" instead of nature's "survival of the fittest," as has persisted throughout the history of mankind, the birth rate must not continue to exceed the death rate. If the birth rate of nations and the world are not greatly reduced, an ever-increasing amount of starvation and other types of premature deaths are inevitable. There is a prodigious need for mankind to practice human husbandry (Human Husbandry, a guest editorial in *BioScience,* **18:** 372-373, 1968, by Walter E. Howard).

A conscientious regulation of fertility is needed, or a calamitous rise in premature mortality rates is inevitable. Without this tremendous voluntary restraint or the development of a strong social stigma against bearing more than two or three children, the rate of conceptions must come under some form of governmental control. It can no longer be a basic human right to have as many children as one wants, especially if such action dooms others to a premature death.

Even though the above picture is bleak, the world is not going to come to an end. In fact, none of the people who read this article are going to starve, but their very existence is going to cause others who are less well off to perish. As overpopulation becomes worse, the percentage of the people who will fall into this nonsurviving unfit category must obviously increase. If babies of the future are to live, there must be fewer of them now.

The Impact of Disease on Wildlife Populations

Carlton M. Herman

Disease is defined broadly as a result of attributes disadvantageous to a species. Chief factor is adverse conditions of habitat. Ecological aspects of several diseases are discussed in relation to habitat dependency. It is emphasized that any ultimate control of disease in wildlife populations must be developed through habitat manipulation. (BioScience 19, no. 4, p. 321-325)

It is well known that wild animal populations exhibit fluctuations, sometimes cyclic, and that some species become extinct. Many government agencies and private groups are increasingly aware of this phenomenon and are conducting studies to determine causes, developing methods to preserve endangered species, and instigating operations to combat causes of population reductions while the world is faced with the problem of overpopulation by man.

We must be aware of other ecological factors before we attempt to interpret the impact of disease on wildlife populations. Particular attention is being given currently to studies on species threatened with extinction. The United States Department of the Interior, through the Bureau of Sport Fisheries and Wildlife, recently established a program for research on rare and endangered wildlife. This program was reviewed by Erickson (1968). Various other groups are engaged in related programs: Nature Conservancy, Ducks Unlimited, World Wildlife Fund, Audubon Society, and the International Union for the Conservation of Nature and Natural Resources are a few of them.

The author is Chief of the Section of Wildlife Disease and Parasite Studies at the Patuxent Wildlife Research Center, Bureau of Sport Fisheries and Wildlife, Department of the Interior, Laurel, Md.
This is the eighth paper from the symposium "Ecosystems — Evolution and Revolution."

Man has had direct impact on wild animal populations, primarily by using animals as a source of food. For example, hunting has been implicated directly in the demise of the passenger pigeon and the reduction of the American bison. Many other examples could be cited. In a similar manner, hunters have brought wild animal species to the brink of extinction by practices such as trophy collecting and the sale of feathers, furs, and ivory. In addition, man has had a direct impact on some animal populations that are in conflict with his own well-being. He has destroyed predators that attack his domestic livestock — wolves, coyotes, and eagles; animals that attack food supplies — particularly rodents; and animals that serve as carriers of zoonotic diseases — again particularly rodents.

Natural phenomena and man's activities also contribute indirectly by destroying habitat or modifying it to such an extent that it becomes inadequate to support the species. Natural phenomena include such things as fire, plant successions, and floods. Man's activities include agricultural development, urban development, drainage, and others.

Definition of Disease

Before attempting to review the impact of disease on wildlife populations, it is necessary to accept a definition of "disease." Many definitions have been promulgated. I like best, for the present

discussion, one presented by Charlie Barron (1963) in some introductory remarks at the First International Conference on Diseases of Wildlife. "It is life outside of a zone of normalcy taking into consideration age, sex, race, geographical distribution, and any other attribute that is disadvantageous to the species." Using such a definition, I feel at liberty to interpret more fully ecological relationships in expressing a viewpoint on the impact of disease on wildlife populations.

Classically, survival is dependent on availability of shelter, food, and water. The summation of these factors may be considered the natural abode of animals, otherwise referred to as habitat. Other related factors include behavior and population density.

Disease is a product of adverse habitat. Even when all factors in the habitat are favorable to a species, disease still can become a controlling factor. Favorable habitat may develop an overpopulation out of proportion with the existing habitat and, unless controlled, again results in a situation disadvantageous to the species. Population and habitat must be kept in balance.

Habitat and Ecological Relationships

Lack (1954), in reviewing the influence of disease on bird numbers, emphasized the role of inadequate food supply as a predisposing factor when disease becomes evident in birds. He cited the report by the Committee of Inquiry on Grouse Disease as a prime example. As he pointed out, every few years the numbers of red grouse in northern England and Scotland have been heavily reduced, apparently by disease. The etiologic agent is a nematode of the genus *Trichostrongylus* that infects the intestinal tract. Nearly every grouse is infected, with no evident harm except when the nematodes are present in large numbers. At that time the grouse are usually in poor condition and often die. The eggs of the parasite are passed in the bird's feces. The larvae hatch and climb to the tips of the heather (*Calluna vulgaris*), which is the staple food of red grouse, and enter another bird when it eats infected heather-tips. The denser the grouse population the greater the proportion of infected heather-tips and, hence, the greater the number of parasites which enter each grouse. The infection intensifies as the number of grouse rises until eventually the birds are killed in large numbers and become scarce again, with a consequent reduction in the number of the parasites available. Lack further points out that the practice of burning the heather reduces the population of the infective nematode larvae thus permitting an increase in the grouse population far above the level at which strongylosis formerly brought it down. He summarizes the evidence by pointing out that the onset of grouse disease is due not merely to the population density of the birds, but rather to their numbers in relation to food supply, and that the strongylosis sets in when the birds are weakened by food shortage.

We (Herman and Wehr, 1954; Herman et al., 1955) have found a similar condition in a Canada goose population at the Pea Island National Wildlife Refuge on the coast of North Carolina. *Amidostomum* is a common nematode in the gizzards of Canada geese throughout their range, usually present with no evident harm in every bird examined. In birds from Pea Island, these worms occur in greater numbers and often with evidence of severe tissue damage to the host gizzards. Such heavily infected birds exhibit severe weight loss — often weighing only half as much as healthy birds — and usually are infected also

with large numbers of other parasites. The main food supply of these geese is the roots of water plants growing in the sound on the west side of Pea Island from ½ to 5 miles off shore. However, at times adverse weather conditions keep the birds away from these favorite feeding grounds and force them to obtain much of their food on the island itself. This secondary food source is much lower in protein and is in too short a supply to adequately maintain the population. Thus, as with the grouse, the geese, on an insufficient and inadequate diet, are more susceptible to the ravages of the parasite.

A possible relationship between the intensity of coccidian infection of California quail and food habits was observed some years ago by Herman et al. (1943). During the dry summer months, when intensity of coccidian oocyst output was at its lowest, the birds subsisted mainly on seeds. During the months of heaviest rainfall, the birds fed mainly on leafy plants and had many more coccidial oocysts in their feces. Another interesting ecological relationship of coccidian infection to habitat was reported to me by Van Haaften (1964, personal communication). In studies on wild rabbits in newly established polters in Holland, he found that rabbits on sandy soils were free of coccidia while rabbits living on clay soils had a high incidence.

The relationship of food habits to disease and its impact on mammal populations probably is best exemplified by the occurrence of direct life cycle nematodes in deer. My remarks here are based on observations I made on deer in California some years ago (Herman, 1945). Eggs of the worms are passed out onto the soil with the droppings of the host, which may be cattle or sheep as well as deer, for many of these parasites are common to all these species. A period of time for development outside the host is required, differing somewhat with the species of parasite, temperature, and humidity. The infective larvae climb up blades of grass where they become available to grazing animals. To maintain the cycle, infected animals must be present on grassy areas

to deposit the worm eggs, and the deer must feed on the grass in such areas. Another point to bear in mind is that a few worms may do little harm; it is the heavy infections that are fatal. The number of parasites in an individual deer depends on both the concentration of infective stages in the grass and the amount of grazing done by the animal. However, mild infections may lower the resistance of an infected animal and thus make it more vulnerable to other diseases. Deer seem to thrive better on browse than on a grass diet. It is possible that deer subsisting almost exclusively on grass have a lowered resistance due to nutritional deficiencies, which, in turn, make them more vulnerable to the ravages of the worm infections.

In California, the infected deer were mostly small ones or yearlings, and losses seemed largely confined to these smaller animals. Over a period of years, the greatest losses in yearlings occurred when there was an early spring and green grass was available over a longer period of time. The greatest mortality of young deer occurred in areas where there was little or no browse available to the smaller animals. Such a situation can occur when no browse is available or when, because of overpopulation, the fresh shoots of browse plants have been harvested to a point where only larger animals can reach this food supply.

Fluctuations of North American deer populations have been reported frequently by many investigators. A good review of some of the outstanding changes is presented by Lack (1954). Since the beginning of the present century, deer populations have exhibited dramatic increases in numbers of individuals. This has been attributed partly to protection from man, first by the universal establishment of a buck law (making it unlawful to kill does), and further by complete protection in some areas (such as the Kaibab National Forest and other Government preserves). Forestry and agricultural practices have made the habitat much more suitable for deer and the numbers of natural predators have been much reduced. Consequently, overpopulations, far beyond the food capacity of the habitat, occur in many areas. Malnutrition, often starvation, and fatality result. These conditions are accentuated during winter months. Often these losses are associated with disease-causing organisms, parasites as well as bacterial and viral agents. Here is a good example of the ecological interdependency of overpopulation and disease in the broad sense of my definition. Disease thus is an expression of lowered resistance that results from malnutrition. Under these circumstances, there may be a population crash — a decline at a much more rapid rate than the previous population increase. Perhaps more data are available on the balance between habitat and population density for Cervidae than for any other group of animals. These data point out the necessity for ecological balance of all factors involved in population control. While changes in habitat can increase or decrease the potential of population density, healthy populations must keep within the limitations of their habitat or adverse factors (disease) will come into play to establish the balance.

Man can enter the picture by his activities. A classic example occurred in California in the early twenties, when an estimated 22,000 deer were slaughtered in a limited area as a measure toward confining an outbreak of viral foot-and-mouth disease (Keane, 1927). Leopold et al. (1951) reported that the population in this area had recovered to approximately its original density within 10 years, and within 20-25 years overpopulation had developed, with the characteristic signs of malnutrition and overutilization of food supply.

Of course deer are not the only animals in which dramatic population changes have been noted. Elton's (1942) views on voles, mice, and lemmings have become classic, although he did not believe disease, at least in the narrow sense, was involved. Studies of a severe mouse outbreak in eastern Oregon and parts of Nevada, California, Washington, and Idaho brought out some pertinent factors. A collection of reports from several agencies was published by the Federal Cooperative Extention Service (Beck et al., 1959). As other species of animals, the meadow mouse (Microtus) fluctuates in num-

bers. During 1957, the population increased to such an extent that local farmers called upon government authorities for assistance. The mild winter of 1957-58 provided a higher survival rate than usual. Populations were estimated at 200 to 4000 mice per acre, with newspapers reporting as many as 10,000 mice per acre in some areas. With such tremendous population growth, these rodents extended their food intake beyond their normal food supply to the point of causing extensive damage to agricultural crops, fruit, and forest trees. Concurrent with the increase in the mouse population, there was an increase in predators, particularly hawks, owls, and gulls. Whether predation by these birds played an important role in the subsequent decline of the Microtus population is not at all clear. They certainly played a role along with other natural control mechanisms such as disease, lack of food, climatic factors, reduced and retarded reproduction, and adrenal exhaustion. A program of poisoning also was initiated.

The first isolation of an infectious agent was on 17 November 1957. By December, many dead Microtus were becoming evident in certain infested areas. A mortality of about 31% was noted on a 20-acre study plot supporting a population estimated at 506 mice per acre. Thus, all indications pointed to an epizootic in the highly overpopulated habitats. Laboratory tests showed that the Microtus were infected with Francisella tularensis. A number of other infectious agents were isolated during the course of subsequent studies, but tularemia appeared to be the only one which reached epizootic proportions. Death rates from this cause ran as high as 42%. F. tularensis also was isolated from water samples, and, in view of experiences with water-borne epidemics in southeastern Europe and in the USSR, the possible hazard to humans was investigated. However, it soon became clear that the threat was minimal. Tularemia was the only disease capable of causing human illness that could be correlated with the same disease in the animals. Only 12 confirmed human cases were reported, and none of these was traced to direct asso-

ciation with the Microtus.

The data amassed on this mouse irruption and its regression show no direct association between malnutrition and losses from tularemia, but the association was definitely a part of the overall picture. The studies emphasize that there are many ecological interrelationships playing a part in population fluctuations.

In human populations, the relation of food supply to disease has been even more evident. Malnutrition is one of the prime problems facing many of the poorer nations of the world today. Even when malnutrition is not ordinarily considered widespread, lack of a single food staple can provide a severe problem. Lack (1954) tells of the situation in Ireland during the last century. When the potato was introduced to Ireland near the end of the 16th century, the people numbered just under a million, by 1790 they had increased to 4 million, and by 1845 to 8 million, the cultivation of potatoes apparently being the main, though probably not the only, cause. Around 1847, the potato crop failed. Starvation, with resultant disease and emigration, caused the population to drop during the next few years to about 2 million or one-quarter of what it had been. One shudders to project what might happen to the world population today should there be a complete failure of the rice crop.

Perhaps the most dramatic impact of any disease on wildlife populations is that of type C botulism on our western waterfowl. Botulism has been most evident in the marshes north of Salt Lake in Utah, but has also caused drastic losses in California and Oregon and has been prevalent to a lesser extent in other areas of North America. At first known as western duck sickness (Wetmore, 1918), the disease causing the die-offs was finally recognized as a form of botulism (Kalmbach and Gunderson, 1934). In Utah alone, in 1912, conservative estimates indicated that well over 100,000 ducks died from this malady. Botulism has continued to recur in waterfowl almost every summer and fall in most areas where it has become established. Losses may be mild or even absent in some years because of weather conditions unfavorable to the botulism organism. This disease, as it occurs in ducks and other wildlife, is a perfect example of my premise that disease is a product of the habitat. Its occurrence has nothing to do with the density of the duck population. The clinical signs and fatalities that occur in the waterfowl result from the effect of consumed toxin. A bacterium (*Clostridium botulinum*) which thrives on decaying matter in an anaerobic environment produces the toxin as an excretory product. Ducks, feeding on animal or plant matter contaminated with the toxin or drinking water saturated with it, suffer a debilitating paralysis from the action of this toxin on the nervous system. The bacteria flourish in an environment conducive to death of shallow-water inhabiting invertebrates, a condition which can be brought about by lowering water levels to create a feather edge. The plankton die under such circumstances, and the resulting oxygen reduction presents an ideal condition for the growth of the *Clostridium*. A similar condition may be produced by temporary flooding.

A few years ago, type E botulism was found in fish from Lake Michigan and several human deaths were traced to this source. Not only has this had an economic effect on the fishery industry but extensive losses also have been noted among gulls and loons (Herman, 1964; Fay, 1966). It has been difficult to evaluate the impact of the losses because of our limited knowledge of the birds involved. For several years, it was calculated that approximately 3000 loons died each summer, although prior reports estimated a total population of only approximately 1200 of these fish-eating birds living on the lake at the season of the outbreaks. An additional ecological factor is suggested by results of experimental studies by Jensen and Gritman (1966) who demonstrated an adjuvant effect between botulism types C and E in the mallard duck. Type C also has been reported from ducks in the Great Lakes area.

During the past century, the activities of man have greatly changed the ecology of the Great Lakes both by overfertilization and by pollution from agricultural, animal, and industrial wastes. The utilization of the water by shore cities and development of the St. Lawrence Waterway have also contributed to some of the changes that have occurred. The predominant biota of this water habitat are considerably different today than in the past. In fact, no type E botulism was known from Lake Michigan a decade ago nor had there been any episode suggestive that it had been a problem.

Another bacterial agent that has caused extensive epizootics among waterfowl is the *Pasteurella* associated with avian cholera. This hemorrhage-producing bacteria was first recognized in 1944, where it was associated with extensive losses in California and Texas (Rosen and Bischoff, 1949, 1950). This infection has occurred primarily in coots, a variety of ducks, and some gulls in these two locations nearly every winter since then, killing hundreds of birds. Sporadic losses have been reported from other areas in the United States involving Canada geese, Eider ducks, and other species of waterfowl.

Lead poisoning is an important mortality factor in waterfowl populations (Bellrose, 1959). This condition is a result of man's activities. For many decades, waterfowl have been shot at, to the point where much of their habitat is saturated with spent lead shot. As a result of their feeding habits, the birds consume sufficient quantities of these shot to produce lead poisoning and death. Many birds die as a direct result, while others with only a sublethal dose have a lowered resistance to other infections.

The waterfowl population in North America has been decreasing, at least since the beginning of the present century. Man has been a contributing factor, although he has done much to try to stem the tide. In years past, large numbers of birds were shot for market, and the take by individual hunters was in excess of the capability of the populations to recover from the slaughter. To counteract this condition, government agencies have established legal bag limits and seasons, and both government and private agencies have established refuges and habitat management procedures. The refuge system, by providing resting sites along the migration routes and in wintering areas, has had a tremendous effect and has undoubtedly retrieved some species, such as the snow goose, which were threatened with extinction. Many land uses developed by man as a consequence of his population increase have reduced the amount of favorable habitat available to the waterfowl population. Perhaps the most significant of these practices is drainage for agricultural purposes. The Canadian prairie provinces and the northern prairie States of the United States are often referred to as the breeding basket of many of our wild duck species. Here so-called prairie potholes serve as the primary breeding areas, and in years of drought many of them became untenable for the birds, thus greatly reducing production. Crissey (1968) has emphasized that the changes in proportion of birds nesting in the prairie potholes is caused by the amount and pattern of precipitation, which materially increases and decreases the number of potholes. It has been known for some time that when the potholes go dry, the North American duck population decreases.

There are many ecological factors involved in attaining a favorable balance between waterfowl and their habitat. Shelter, food supply, cropping pressures, and disease all play a part. Survival depends on the balance of these factors in the winter habitat with the potential of recovery of population levels in the breeding habitat.

Disease may enter the picture during the breeding season as well. O'Roke (1934) indicated that losses to ducklings from the blood parasite *Leucocytozoon* in early summer in Michigan sometimes approaches 100%. In more recent studies (Herman, 1968), we have observed extensive losses in Canada goose goslings in northern Michigan. Losses at the Seney National Wildlife Refuge appear to occur cyclically about every 4 years. In one year, about 80% of the goslings succumbed. The infection is transmitted by black flies (Simuliidae). Weather, both temperature and rainfall, as well as age of goslings at time of initial exposure appear to be among controlling factors.

Another type of ecological relationship exists in the occurrence of trichomoniasis in doves (Stabler and Herman, 1951). Here we have an infection of the oral cavity in which a protozoan parasite is transmitted directly from infected parent to offspring in the normal feeding process. In addition to this cycle of transmission which kills many nestling birds, a further die-off occurs during fall and winter when the wild doves congregate at feeding sites such as back yards or feed lots. Once again, the activities of man contribute to population fluctuations. It has been suggested also that disease, along with man's slaughter of the passenger pigeon for economic gains may have contributed to the demise of this bird (Stabler and Herman, 1951; Schorger, 1955). Trichomoniasis is an ideal suspect. These birds were believed to have produced only one offspring per year per breeding pair. An epidemic of throat trichomoniasis 2 or 3 years in succession could have had a drastic effect on such a population.

The disease whose impact on a wildlife population is best known is the virus-caused myxomatosis of rabbits. Knowledge of this disease has been summarized in a book by Fenner and Ratcliffe (1965) devoted entirely to the subject. The etiologic agent is a myxoma virus, one of a subgroup of the poxvirus group which also includes fibroma viruses from rabbits, hares, and squirrels. These viruses demonstrate varying degrees of cross-protection in experimental animals.

Myxomatosis was first recognized in the European rabbit, *Oryctolagus cuniculus,* in a laboratory strain in South America in 1897. Subsequent studies have demonstrated that the disease produces prominent external lesions and a high rate of mortality in this host. A carrier state exists in several species of *Sylvilagus* rabbits (cottontails) in the western hemisphere, with rare evidence of lesions and no reported fatalities. Susceptibility tests have been performed on a wide variety of animals with no resultant visible signs of lesions or antibody response. The myxoma virus is, thus, a disease-causing agent with a very narrow host specificity.

The European rabbit was introduced into Australia with the first arriving white settlers in 1788, and many more were brought during subsequent decades. Concurrently, changes in the environment from agricultural developments and domestic stock proved unfavorable for much of the native flora and fauna but ideal for the rabbits. Not only did the rabbits compete with the stock for forage, but their habits as burrowing animals were detrimental to growth of forage. The rabbit population increased to a point where it became untenable. Fencing, poisoning, and other techniques were initiated to combat the rabbit problem. The pastoral nature of the land, requiring large holdings to make operations economically feasible, made intensive control efforts uneconomical because of the low intrinsic value of the land. In the years immediately following World War II, some 100 million rabbits passed through human hands annually in Australia, in the form of carcasses or skins for export, with unknown but certainly considerable additional numbers finding their way to local markets or being killed but not recovered; this toll had no marked effect on overall rabbit abundance.

Intermittently over the years there was much discussion and pressure, both political and scientific, to release a potent disease into the population. Abortive attempts were made in isolated areas. The successful establishment of myxomatosis in Australia in 1950 was the culmination of a series of laboratory and field tests extending over more than a decade. The method of transmission was not known at the time. Ultimately it was found that, in Australia, mosquitoes served as vectors, although extensive studies there and elsewhere have since shown that a wide range of arthropods can act as vectors, transmitting by contamination, and acting as "flying pins." Although slow to establish itself, myxomatosis ultimately spread throughout the rabbit range. It is hardly necessary to state that myxomatosis has brought, and is still bringing, almost incalculable benefit to Australia. It has made a substantial contribution to the solution of the country's rabbit problem; and although the problem that remains is still challenging, it now appears to be manageable. In many areas, sheep production has again increased. Thus far, there is no evidence of an increase in native marsupial herbivores. By far the most important effect has been botanical, resulting from an easing of grazing and browsing pressure on pasture plants and seedlings of shrubs and trees.

The rabbit was considered an agricultural pest in many parts of its native Europe, and, in the late '30's, several abortive attempts were made to establish myxomatosis in the population. In June, 1952, a French doctor, in an effort to control the rabbits on his private estate, introduced the virus into the population. Within a month all the wild rabbits on his estate had died. Subsequently, the disease has spread throughout France and portions of the neighboring countries, as well as Great Britain. Not only has the disease greatly reduced the wild rabbit population, with economic gains to agriculture and losses to the hunting public, but it has also created a severe problem in the domestic rabbit production industry where many retired workers were largely dependent upon rabbit raising for their livelihood.

Of course there are many other facets to the European rabbit problem. Immune responses, development of resistant hosts, and density of rabbit and vector populations will all contribute to the ultimate achievement of a balance. Space has permitted me to reiterate only a few of the facts included in the book. It should be required reading for every student of the ecology of disease and its impact on a population.

In my presentation, I have, of necessity, left out many references I might have included. There is much literature on the impact of disease on aquatic animals; temperature and salinity, along with some of the factors reported above, are important in the aquatic environment.

My main thesis has been to emphasize the dependency of disease on habitat and ecological relationships. While there is limited documentation that disease, as an individual factor, can drastically affect population fluctuations, it is certainly evident that, acting with other ecological phenomena, disease can have extensive impact. It is imperative that we recognize the dependency of the occurrence of disease in wildlife on habitat conditions. Methods of therapy and immunization developed during the past 5 to 8 decades for combating disease in man and his domestic stock are usually not feasible as approaches to wildlife disease. It therefore behooves us to give close attention to habitat relationships in an effort to uncover ways in which we can develop management of habitat as a tool in controlling wildlife disease losses.

References

Barron, C. N. 1963. Introduction to section on pathology. *Proc. 1st Intern. Conf. Wildlife Dis.*, p. 310.

Beck, J. R., S. B. Osgood, and M. D. Smith. 1959. The Oregon meadow mouse irruption of 1957-1958. *Fed. Coop. Ext. Serv.*, Oregon State College, Corvallis. 88 p.

Bellrose, F. C. 1959. Lead poisoning as a mortality factor in waterfowl populations. *Bull. Illinois Nat. Hist. Survey,* **27**: 235-286.

Crissey, W. F. 1968. Small water areas in the Prairie Pothole region. Transactions of a seminar held Feb. 20-22, 1967, to mark the opening of the Prairie Waterfowl Research Centre, *Can. Wildlife Serv. Rept.*, Series 6, 1968. In press.

Elton, C. 1942. *Voles, Mice and Lemmings—Problems in Population Dynamics.* Clarendon Press. Oxford. 496 p.

Erickson, R. C. 1968. A Federal research program for endangered wildlife. *Trans. 33rd N. Am. Wildlife Conf.*, p. 418-433.

Fay, L. D. 1966. Type E botulism in Great Lakes water birds. *Trans. 31st N. Am. Wildlife Conf.*, p. 139-149.

Fenner, F., and F. N. Ratcliffe. 1965. *Myxomatosis.* Cambridge University Press, Cambridge. 379 p.

Herman, C. M. 1945. Deer management problems as related to diseases and parasites of domestic range livestock. *Trans. 10th N. Am. Wildlife Conf.*, p. 242-246.

——. 1964. Significance of bird losses on Lake Michigan during November and December 1963. Publ. 11, Great Lakes Res. Div., University of Michigan. p. 84-87.

——. 1968. Blood parasites of North American waterfowl. *Trans. 33rd N. Am. Wildlife Conf.*, p. 348-359.

Herman, C. M., J. E. Chattin, and R. W. Saarni. 1943. Food habits and intensity of coccidian infection in native valley quail in California. *J. Parasitol.,* **29**: 206-208.

Herman, C. M., J. H. Steenis, and E. E. Wehr. 1955. Causes of winter losses among Canada geese. *Trans. 20th N. Am. Wildlife Conf.*, p. 161-165.

Herman, C. M., and E. E. Wehr. 1954. The occurrence of gizzard worms in Canada geese. *J. Wildlife Management,* **18**: 509-513.

Jensen, W. I., and R. B. Gritman. 1967. An adjuvant effect between *Clostridium botulinum* types C and E in the mallard duck (*Anas platyrhynchos*). Botulism 1966. *Proc. 5th Intern. Symp. on Food Microbiol.* Barnes and Noble, New York, p. 407-441.

Kalmbach, E. R., and M. F. Gunderson. 1934. Western duck sickness, a form of botulism. *U.S. Dept. Agr. Tech. Bull. 411,* 81 p.

Population and Panaceas
A Technological Perspective

Paul R. Ehrlich and John P. Holdren

The proposition that technology can solve the problems posed by the sheer size of present and projected world populations is examined in detail. The probable potential for short- and long-term gains in agricultural technology, ocean fisheries, desalination of seawater, nuclear power production, and related areas is evaluated in the framework of known and predicted requirements. It is concluded that in the absence of effective population control measures any imaginable technological effort will fall short. (BioScience *19,* no. 12, p. 1065-1071)

Today more than one billion human beings are either undernourished or malnourished, and the human population is growing at a rate of 2% per year. The existing and impending crises in human nutrition and living conditions are well-documented but not widely understood. In particular, there is a tendency among the public, nurtured on Sunday-supplement conceptions of technology, to believe that science has the situation well in hand—that farming the sea and the tropics, irrigating the deserts, and generating cheap nuclear power in abundance hold the key to swift and certain solution of the problem. To espouse this belief is to misjudge the present severity of the situation, the disparate time scales on which technological progress and population growth operate, and the vast complexity of the problems beyond mere food production posed by population pressures. Unfortunately, scientists and engineers have themselves often added to the confusion by failing to distinguish between that which is merely theoretically feasible, and that which is economically and logistically practical.

As we will show here, man's present technology is inadequate to the task of maintaining the world's burgeoning billions, even under the most optimistic assumptions. Furthermore, technology is

The co-authors are affiliated, respectively, with the department of biological sciences, and with the Institute for Plasma Research and department of aeronautics and astronautics, Stanford University. This article is reprinted with the permission of Paul R. Ehrlich and John P. Holdren.

likely to remain inadequate until such time as the population growth rate is drastically reduced. This is not to assert that present efforts to "revolutionize" tropical argiculture, increase yields of fisheries, desalt water for irrigation, exploit new power sources, and implement related projects are not worthwhile. They may be. They could also easily produce the ultimate disaster for mankind if they are not applied with careful attention to their effects on the ecological systems necessary for our survival (Woodwell, 1967; Cole, 1968). And even if such projects are initiated with unprecedented levels of staffing and expenditures, without population control they are doomed to fall far short. No effort to expand the carrying capacity of the Earth can keep pace with unbridled population growth.

To support these contentions, we summarize briefly the present lopsided balance sheet in the population/food accounting. We then examine the logistics, economics, and possible consequences of some technological schemes which have been proposed to help restore the balance, or, more ambitiously, to permit the maintenance of human populations much larger than today's. The most pertinent aspects of the balance are:

1) The world population reached 3.5 billion in mid-1968, with an annual increment of approximately 70 million people (itself increasing) and a doubling time on the order of 35 years (Population Reference Bureau, 1968).

2) Of this number of people, at least one-half billion are undernourished (defi-

cient in calories or, more succinctly, slowly starving), and approximately an additional billion are malnourished (deficient in particular nutrients, mostly protein) (Borgstrom, 1965; Sukhatme, 1966). Estimates of the number actually perishing annually from starvation begin at 4 million and go up (Ehrlich, 1968) and depend in part on official definitions of starvation which conceal the true magnitude of hunger's contribution to the death rate (Lelyveld, 1968).

3) Merely to maintain present inadequate nutrition levels, the food requirements of Asia, Africa, and Latin America will, conservatively, increase by 26% in the 10-year period measured from 1965 to 1975 (Paddock and Paddock, 1967). World food production must double in the period 1965-2000 to stay even; it must triple if nutrition is to be brought up to minimum requirements.

Food Production

That there is insufficient additional, good quality agricultural land available in the world to meet these needs is so well documented (Borgstrom, 1965) that we will not belabor the point here. What hope there is must rest with increasing yields on land presently cultivated, bringing marginal land into production, more efficiently exploiting the sea, and bringing less conventional methods of food production to fruition. In all these areas, science and technology play a dominant role. While space does not permit even a cursory look at all the proposals on these topics which have been advanced in recent years, a few representative examples illustrate our points.

Conventional Agriculture. Probably the most widely recommended means of increasing agricultural yields is through the more intensive use of fertilizers. Their production is straightforward, and a good deal is known about their effective application, although, as with many technologies we consider here, the environmental consequences of heavy fertilizer use are ill understood and potentially dangerous[1] (Wadleigh, 1968). But even ignoring such problems, we find staggering difficulties barring the implementation of fertilizer technology on the scale required. In this regard the accomplishments of countries such as Japan and the Netherlands are often cited as offering hope to the underdeveloped world. Some perspective on this point is afforded by noting that if India were to apply fertilizer at the per capita level employed by the Netherlands, her fertilizer needs would be nearly half the present world output (United Nations, 1968).

On a more realistic plane, we note that although the goal for nitrogen fertilizer production in 1971 under India's fourth 5-year plan is 2.4 million metric tons (Anonymous, 1968a), Raymond Ewell (who has served as fertilizer production adviser to the Indian government for the past 12 years) suggests that less than 1.1 million metric tons is a more probable figure for that date.[2] Ewell cites poor plant maintenance, raw materials shortages, and power and transportation breakdowns as contributing to continued low production by existing Indian plants. Moreover, even when fertilizer is available, increases in productivity do not necessarily follow. In parts of the underdeveloped world lack of farm credit is limiting fertilizer distribution; elsewhere, internal transportation systems are inadequate to the task. Nor can the problem of educating farmers on the advantages and techniques of fertilizer use be ignored. A recent study (Parikh et al., 1968) of the Intensive Agriculture District Program in the Surat district of Gujarat, India (in which scientific fertilizer use

was to have been a major ingredient) notes that "on the whole, the performance of adjoining districts which have similar climate but did not enjoy relative preference of input supply was as good as, if not better than, the programme district. . . . A particularly disheartening feature is that the farm production plans, as yet, do not carry any educative value and have largely failed to convince farmers to use improved practices in their proper combinations."

As a second example of a panacea in the realm of conventional agriculture, mention must be given to the development of new high-yield or high-protein strains of food crops. That such strains have the potential of making a major contribution to the food supply of the world is beyond doubt, but this potential is limited in contrast to the potential for population growth, and will be realized too slowly to have anything but a small impact on the immediate crisis. There are major difficulties impeding the widespread use of new high-yield grain varieties. Typically, the new grains require high fertilizer inputs to realize their full potential, and thus are subject to all the difficulties mentioned above. Some other problems were identified in a recent address by Lester R. Brown, administrator of the International Agricultural Development Service: the limited amount of irrigated land suitable for the new varieties, the fact that a farmer's willingness to innovate fluctuates with the market prices (which may be driven down by high-yield crops), and the possibility of tieups at market facilities inadequate for handling increased yields.[3]

Perhaps even more important, the new grain varieties are being rushed into production without adequate field testing, so that we are unsure of how resistant they will be to the attacks of insects and plant diseases. William Paddock has presented a plant pathologist's view of the crash programs to shift to new varieties (Paddock, 1967). He describes India's dramatic program of planting improved Mexican wheat, and continues: "Such a rapid switch to a new variety is clearly understandable in a country that tottered on the brink of famine. Yet with such limited

testing, one wonders what unknown pathogens await a climatic change which will give the environmental conditions needed for their growth." Introduction of the new varieties creates enlarged monocultures of plants with essentially unknown levels of resistance to disaster. Clearly, one of the prices that is paid for higher yield is a higher risk of widespread catastrophe. And the risks are far from local: since the new varieties require more "input" of pesticides (with all their deleterious ecological side effects), these crops may ultimately contribute to the defeat of other environment-related panaceas, such as extracting larger amounts of food from the sea.

A final problem must be mentioned in connection with these strains of food crops. In general, the hungriest people in the world are also those with the most conservative food habits. Even rather minor changes, such as that from a rice variety in which the cooked grains stick together to one in which the grains fall apart, may make new foods unacceptable. It seems to be an unhappy fact of human existence that people would rather starve than eat a nutritious substance which they do not recognize as food.[4]

Beyond the economic, ecological, and sociological problems already mentioned in connection with high-yield agriculture, there is the overall problem of time. We need time to breed the desired characteristics of yield and hardiness into a vast array of new strains (a tedious process indeed), time to convince farmers that it is necessary that they change their time-honored ways of cultivation, and time to convince hungry people to change the staples of their diet. The Paddocks give 20 years as the "rule of thumb" for a new technique or plant variety to progress from conception to substantial impact on farming (Paddock and Paddock, 1967). They write: "It is true that a *massive* research attack on the problem could bring some striking results in less than 20 years. But I do not find such an attack remotely contemplated in the thinking of those officials capable of initiating it." Promising as high-yield agriculture may be, the funds, the personnel, the ecological ex-

[1]Barry Commoner, address to 135th Meeting of the AAAS, Dallas, Texas (28 December 1968).

[2]Raymond Ewell, private communication (1 December 1968).

[3]Lester R. Brown, address to the Second International Conference on the War on Hunger, Washington, D.C. (February 1968).

[4]For a more detailed discussion of the psychological problems in persuading people to change their dietary habits, see McKenzie, 1968.

pertise, and the necessary years are unfortunately not at our disposal. Fulfillment of the promise will come too late for many of the world's starving millions, if it comes at all.

Bringing More Land Under Cultivation. The most frequently mentioned means of bringing new land into agricultural production are farming the tropics and irrigating arid and semiarid regions. The former, although widely discussed in optimistic terms, has been tried for years with incredibly poor results, and even recent experiments have not been encouraging. One essential difficulty is the unsuitability of tropical soils for supporting typical foodstuffs instead of jungles (McNeil, 1964; Paddock and Paddock, 1964). Also, "the tropics" are a biologically more diverse area than the temperate zones, so that farming technology developed for one area will all too often prove useless in others. We shall see that irrigating the deserts, while more promising, has serious limitations in terms of scale, cost, and lead time.

The feasible approaches to irrigation of arid lands appear to be limited to large-scale water projects involving dams and transport in canals, and desalination of ocean and brackish water. Supplies of usable ground water are already badly depleted in most areas where they are accessible, and natural recharge is low enough in most arid regions that such supplies do not offer a long-term solution in any case. Some recent statistics will give perspective to the discussion of water projects and desalting which follows. In 1966, the United States was using about 300 billion gal of water per day, of which 135 billion gal were consumed by agriculture and 165 billion gal by municipal and industrial users (Sporn, 1966). The bulk of the agricultural water cost the farmer from 5 to 10 cents/1000 gal; the highest price paid for agricultural water was 15 cents/1000 gal. For small industrial and municipal supplies, prices as high as 50 to 70 cents/1000 gal were prevalent in the U.S. arid regions, and some communities in the Southwest were paying on the order of $1.00/1000 gal for "project" water. The extremely high cost of the latter stems largely from transportation costs, which have been estimated at 5 to 15 cents/1000 gal per 100 miles (International Atomic Energy Agency, 1964).

We now examine briefly the implications of such numbers in considering the irrigation of the deserts. The most ambitious water project yet conceived in this country is the North American Water and Power Alliance, which proposes to distribute water from the great rivers of Canada to thirsty locations all over the United States. Formidable political problems aside (some based on the certainty that in the face of expanding populations, demands for water will eventually arise at the source), this project would involve the expenditure of $100 billion in construction costs over a 20-year completion period. At the end of this time, the yield to the United States would be 69 million acre feet of water annually (Kelly, 1966), or 63 billion gal per day. If past experience with massive water projects is any guide, these figures are overoptimistic; but if we assume they are not, it is instructive to note that this monumental undertaking would provide for an increase of only 21% in the water consumption of the United States, during a period in which the population is expected to increase by between 25 and 43% (U.S. Dept. of Commerce, 1966). To assess the possible contribution to the *world* food situation, we assume that all this water could be devoted to agriculture, although extrapolation of present consumption patterns indicates that only about one-half would be. Then using the rather optimistic figure of 500 gal per day to grow the food to feed one person, we find that this project could feed 126 million additional people. Since this is less than 8% of the projected world population growth during the construction period (say 1970 to 1990), it should be clear that even the most massive water projects can make but a token contribution to the solution of the world food problem in the long term. And in the crucial short term—the years preceding 1980—*no* additional people will be fed by projects still on the drawing board today.

In summary, the cost is staggering, the scale insufficient, and the lead time too long. Nor need we resort to such speculation about the future for proof of the failure of technological "solutions" in the absence of population control. The highly touted and very expensive Aswan Dam project, now nearing completion, will ultimately supply food (at the present

miserable diet level) for less than Egypt's population growth during the time of construction (Borgstrom, 1965; Cole, 1968). Furthermore, its effect on the fertility of the Nile Delta may be disastrous, and, as with all water projects of this nature, silting of the reservoir will destroy the gains in the long term (perhaps in 100 years).

Desalting for irrigation suffers somewhat similar limitations. The desalting plants operational in the world today produce water at individual rates of 7.5 million gal/day and less, at a cost of 75 cents/1000 gal and up, the cost increasing as the plant size decreases (Bender, 1969). The most optimistic firm proposal which anyone seems to have made for desalting with present or soon-to-be available technology is a 150 million gal per day nuclear-powered installation studied by the Bechtel Corp. for the Los Angeles Metropolitan Water District. Bechtel's early figures indicated that water from this complex would be available at the site for 27-28 cents/1000 gal (Galstann and Currier, 1967). However, skepticism regarding the economic assumptions leading to these figures (Milliman, 1966) has since proven justified— the project was shelved after spiraling construction cost estimates indicated an actual water cost of 40-50 cents/1000 gal. Use of even the original figures, however, bears out our contention that the *most* optimistic assumptions do not alter the verdict that technology is losing the food/population battle. For 28 cents/ 1000 gal is still approximately twice the cost which farmers have hitherto been willing or able to pay for irrigation water. If the Bechtel plant had been intended to supply agricultural needs, which it was not, one would have had to add to an already unacceptable price the very substantial cost of transporting the water inland.

Significantly, studies have shown that the economies of scale in the distillation process are essentially exhausted by a 150 million gal per day plant (International Atomic Energy Agency, 1964). Hence, merely increasing desalting capacity further will not substantially lower the cost of the water. On purely economic grounds, then, it is unlikely that desalting will play a major role in food production by conventional agriculture in the short term.[5] Technological "break-throughs" will presumably improve this outlook with the passage of time, but world population growth will not wait.

Desalting becomes more promising if the high cost of the water can be offset by increased agricultural yields per gallon and, perhaps, use of a single nuclear installation to provide power for both the desalting and profitable on-site industrial processes. This prospect has been investigated in a thorough and well-documented study headed by E. S. Mason (Oak Ridge National Laboratory, 1968). The result is a set of preliminary figures and recommendations regarding nuclear-powered "agro-industrial complexes" for arid and semiarid regions, in which desalted water and fertilizer would be produced for use on an adjacent, highly efficient farm. In underdeveloped countries incapable of using the full excess power output of the reactor, this energy would be consumed in on-site production of industrial materials for sale on the world market. Both near-term (10 years hence) and far-term (20 years hence) technologies are considered, as are various mixes of farm and industrial products. The representative near-term case for which a detailed cost breakdown is given involves a seaside facility with a desalting capacity of 1 billion gal/day, a farm size of 320,000 acres, and an industrial electric power consumption of 1585 Mw. The initial investment for this complex is estimated at $1.8 billion, and annual operating costs at $236 million. If both the food and the industrial materials produced were sold (as opposed to giving the food, at least, to those in need who could not pay),[6] the estimated profit for such a complex, before subtracting financing costs, would be 14.6%.

The authors of the study are commendably cautious in outlining the assumptions and uncertainties upon which these figures rest. The key assumption is that 200 gal/day of water will grow the 2500 calories required to feed one person. Water/calorie ratios of this order or

less have been achieved by the top 20% of farmers specializing in such crops as wheat, potatoes, and tomatoes; but more water is required for needed protein-rich crops such as peanuts and soybeans. The authors identify the uncertainty that crops usually raised separately can be grown together in tight rotation on the same piece of land. Problems of water storage between periods of peak irrigation demand, optimal patterns of crop rotation, and seasonal acreage variations are also mentioned. These "ifs" and assumptions, and those associated with the other technologies involved, are unfortunately often omitted when the results of such painstaking studies are summarized for more popular consumption (Anonymous, 1968b, 1968c). The result is the perpetuation of the public's tendency to confuse feasible and available, to see panaceas where scientists in the field concerned see only potential, realizable with massive infusions of time and money.

It is instructive, nevertheless, to examine the impact on the world food problem which the Oak Ridge complexes might have if construction were to begin today, and if all the assumptions about technology 10 years hence were valid *now*. At the industrial-agricultural mix pertinent to the sample case described above, the food produced would be adequate for just under 3 million people. This means that 23 such plants per year, at a cost of $41 billion, would have to be put in operation merely to keep pace with world population growth, to say nothing of improving the substandard diets of between one and two billion members of the present population. (Fertilizer production beyond that required for the on-site farm is of course a contribution in the latter regard, but the substantial additional costs of transporting it to where it is needed must then be accounted for.) Since approximately 5 years from the start of construction would be required to put such a complex into operation, we should commence work on at least 125 units post-haste, and begin at least 25 per year thereafter. If the technology *were* available now, the investment in construction over the next 5 years, prior to operation of the first plants, would be $315 billion—about 20 times the total U.S. foreign aid expenditure during the past 5 years. By the time the technology *is* available the bill will be

much higher, if famine has not "solved" the problem for us.

This example again illustrates that scale, time, and cost are all working against technology in the short term. And if population growth is not decelerated, the increasing severity of population-related crises will surely neutralize the technological improvements of the middle and long terms.

Other Food Panaceas. "Food from the sea" is the most prevalent "answer" to the world food shortage in the view of the general public. This is not surprising, since estimates of the theoretical fisheries productivity of the sea run up to some 50-100 times current yields (Schmitt, 1965; Christy and Scott, 1965). Many practical and economic difficulties, however, make it clear that such a figure will never be reached, and that it will not even be approached in the foreseeable future. In 1966, the annual fisheries harvest was some 57 million metric tons (United Nations, 1968). A careful analysis (Meseck, 1961) indicates that this might be increased to a world production of 70 million metric tons by 1980. If this gain were realized, it would represent (assuming no violent change in population growth patterns) a small per capita *loss* in fisheries yield.

Both the short- and long-term outlooks for taking food from the sea are clouded by the problems of overexploitation, pollution (which is generally ignored by those calculating potential yields), and economics. Solving these problems will require more than technological legerdemain; it will also require unprecedented changes in human behavior, especially in the area of international cooperation. The unlikelihood that such cooperation will come about is reflected in the recent news (Anonymous, 1968d) that Norway has dropped out of the whaling industry because overfishing has depleted the stock below the level at which it may economically be harvested. In that industry, international controls were tried—and failed. The sea is, unfortunately, a "commons" (Hardin, 1968), and the resultant management problems exacerbate the biological and technical problems of greatly increasing our "take." One suspects that the return per dollar poured into the sea will be much less than the corresponding return from the land for many years, and the return from the

[5]An identical conclusion was reached in a recent study (Clawson et al., 1969) in which the foregoing points and numerous other aspects of desalting were treated in far more detail than was possible here.

[6]Confusing statements often are made about the possibility that food supply will outrun food demand in the future. In these statements, "demand" is used in the economic sense, and in this context many millions of starving people may generate no demand whatsoever. Indeed, one concern of those engaged in increasing food production is to find ways of increasing demand.

land has already been found wanting.

Synthetic foods, protein culture with petroleum, saline agriculture, and weather modification all may hold promise for the future, but all are at present expensive and available only on an extremely limited scale. The research to improve this situation will also be expensive, and, of course, time-consuming. In the absence of funding, it will not occur at all, a fact which occasionally eludes the public and the Congress.

Domestic and Industrial Water Supplies

The world has water problems, even exclusive of the situation in agriculture. Although total precipitation should in theory be adequate in quantity for several further doublings of population, serious shortages arising from problems of quality, irregularity, and distribution already plague much of the world. Underdeveloped countries will find the water needs of industrialization staggering: 240,000 gal of water are required to produce a ton of newsprint; 650,000 gal, to produce a ton of steel (International Atomic Energy Agency, 1964). Since maximum acceptable water costs for domestic and industrial use are higher than for agriculture, those who can afford it are or soon will be using desalination (40-100 + cents/1000 gal) and used-water renovation (54-57 cents/1000 gal [Ennis, 1967]). Those who cannot afford it are faced with allocating existing supplies between industry and agriculture, and as we have seen, they must choose the latter. In this circumstance, the standard of living remains pitifully low. Technology's only present answer is massive externally-financed complexes of the sort considered above, and we have already suggested there the improbability that we are prepared to pay the bill rung up by present population growth.

The widespread use of desalted water by those who *can* afford it brings up another problem only rarely mentioned to date, the disposal of the salts. The product of the distillation processes in present use is a hot brine with salt concentration several times that of seawater. Both the temperature and the salinity of this effluent will prove fatal to local marine life if it is simply exhausted to the ocean. The most optimistic statement we have seen on this problem is that

"*smaller plants* (our emphasis) at seaside locations may return the concentrated brine to the ocean if proper attention is paid to the design of the outfall, and to the effect on the local marine ecology." (McIlhenny, 1966) The same writer identifies the major economic uncertainties connected with extracting the salts for sale (to do so is straightforward, but often not profitable). Nor can one simply evaporate the brine and leave the residue in a pile—the 150 million gal/day plant mentioned above would produce brine bearing 90 million lb. of salts daily (based on figures by Parker, 1966). This amount of salt would cover over 15 acres to a depth of one foot. Thus, every year a plant of the billion gallon per day, agro-industrial complex size would produce a pile of salt over 52 ft deep and covering a square mile. The high winds typical of coastal deserts would seriously aggravate the associated soil contamination problem.

Energy

Man's problems with energy supply are more subtle than those with food and water: we are not yet running out of energy, but we are being forced to use it faster than is probably healthy. The rapacious depletion of our fossil fuels is already forcing us to consider more expensive mining techniques to gain access to lower-grade deposits, such as the oil shales, and even the status of our high-grade uranium ore reserves is not clear-cut (Anonymous, 1968e).

A widely held misconception in this connection is that nuclear power is "dirt cheap," and as such represents a panacea for developed and underdeveloped nations alike. To the contrary, the largest nuclear-generating stations now in operation are just competitive with or marginally superior to modern coal-fired plants of comparable size (where coal is not scarce); at best, both produce power for on the order of 4-5 mills (tenths of a cent) per kilowatt-hour. Smaller nuclear units remain less economical than their fossil-fueled counterparts. Underdeveloped countries can rarely use the power of the larger plants. Simply speaking, there are not enough industries, appliances, and light bulbs to absorb the output, and the cost of industrialization and modernization exceeds the cost of the power required to sustain it by orders of magnitude, regardless of the source of the

power. (For example, one study noted that the capital requirement to consume the output of a 70,000 kilowatt plant—about $1.2 million worth of electricity per year at 40% utilization and 5 mills/kwh—is $111 million per year if the power is consumed by metals industries, $270 million per year for petroleum product industries [E. A. Mason, 1957].) Hence, at least at present, only those underdeveloped countries which are short of fossil fuels or inexpensive means to transport them are in particular need of nuclear power.

Prospects for major reductions in the cost of nuclear power in the future hinge on the long-awaited breeder reactor and the still further distant thermonuclear reactor. In neither case is the time scale or the ultimate cost of energy a matter of any certainty. The breeder reactor, which converts more nonfissile uranium (^{238}U) or thorium to fissionable material than it consumes as fuel for itself, effectively extends our nuclear fuel supply by a factor of approximately 400 (Cloud, 1968). It is not expected to become competitive economically with conventional reactors until the 1980's (Bump, 1967). Reductions in the unit energy cost beyond this date are not guaranteed, due both to the probable continued high capital cost of breeder reactors and to increasing costs for the ore which the breeders will convert to fuel. In the latter regard, we mention that although crushing granite for its few parts per million of uranium and thorium is possible in theory, the problems and cost of doing so are far from resolved.[7] It is too soon to predict the costs associated with a fusion reactor (few who work in the field will predict whether such a device will work at all within the next 15-20 years). One guess puts the unit energy cost at something over half that for a coal or fission power station of comparable size (Mills, 1967), but this is pure speculation. Quite possibly the major benefit of controlled fusion will again be to extend the energy supply rather than to cheapen it.

A second misconception about nuclear power is that it can reduce our dependence on fossil fuels to zero as soon as that becomes necessary or desirable. In fact, nuclear power plants contribute only to the electrical portion of the energy bud-

---

[7]A general discussion of extracting metals from common rock is given by Cloud, 1968.

get; and in 1960 in the United States, for example, electrical energy comprised only 19% of the total energy consumed (Sporn, 1963). The degree to which nuclear fuels can postpone the exhaustion of our coal and oil depends on the extent to which that 19% is enlarged. The task is far from a trivial one, and will involve transitions to electric or fuel-cell powered transportation, electric heating, and electrically powered industries. It will be extremely expensive.

Nuclear energy, then, is a panacea neither for us nor for the underdeveloped world. It relieves, but does not remove, the pressure on fossil fuel supplies; it provides reasonably-priced power where these fuels are not abundant; it has substantial (but expensive) potential in intelligent applications such as that suggested in the Oak Ridge study discussed above; and it shares the propensity of fast-growing technology to unpleasant side effects (Novick, 1969). We mention in the last connection that, while nuclear power stations do not produce conventional air pollutants, their radioactive waste problems may in the long run prove a poor trade. Although the AEC seems to have made a good case for solidification and storage in salt mines of the bulk of the radioactive fission products (Blanko et al., 1967), a number of radioactive isotopes are released to the air, and in some areas such isotopes have already turned up in potentially harmful concentrations (Curtis and Hogan, 1969). Projected order of magnitude increases in nuclear power generation will seriously aggravate this situation. Although it has frequently been stated that the eventual advent of fusion reactors will free us from such difficulties, at least one authority, F. L. Parker, takes a more cautious view. He contends that losses of radioactive tritium from fusion power plants may prove even more hazardous than the analogous problems of fission reactors (Parker, 1968).

A more easily evaluated problem is the tremendous quantity of waste heat generated at nuclear installations (to say nothing of the usable power output, which, as with power from whatever source, must also ultimately be dissipated as heat). Both have potentially disastrous effects on the local and world ecological and climatological balance. There is no simple solution to this problem, for, in general, "cooling" only moves heat; it does not *remove* it from the environment viewed as a whole. Moreover, the Second Law of Thermodynamics puts a ceiling on the efficiency with which we can do even this much, i.e., concentrate and transport heat. In effect, the Second Law condemns us to aggravate the total problem by generating still *more* heat in any machinery we devise for local cooling (consider, for example, refrigerators and air conditioners).

The only heat which actually leaves the whole system, the Earth, is that which can be radiated back into space. This amount steadily is being diminished as combustion of hydrocarbon fuels increases the atmospheric percentage of CO_2 which has strong absorption bands in the infrared spectrum of the outbound heat energy. (Hubbert, 1962, puts the increase in the CO_2 content of the atmosphere at 10% since 1900.) There is, of course, a competing effect in the Earth's energy balance, which is the increased reflectivity of the upper atmosphere to incoming sunlight due to other forms of air pollution. It has been estimated, ignoring both these effects, that man risks drastic (and perhaps catastrophic) climatological change if the amount of heat he dissipates in the environment on a global scale reaches 1% of the incident solar energy at the Earth's surface (Rose and Clark, 1961). At the present 5% rate of increase in world energy consumption,[8] this level will be reached in less than a century, and in the immediate future the direct contribution of man's power consumption will create serious local problems. If we may safely rule out circumvention of the Second Law or the divorce of energy requirements from population size, this suggests that, whatever science and technology may accomplish, population growth must be stopped.

Transportation

We would be remiss in our offer of a technological perspective on population problems without some mention of the difficulties associated with transporting large quantities of food, material, or

[8]The rate of growth of world energy consumption fluctuates strongly about some mean on a time scale of only a few years, and the figures are not known with great accuracy in any case. A discussion of predicting the mean and a defense of the figure of 5% are given in Gúeron et al., 1957.

people across the face of the Earth. While our grain exports have not begun to satisfy the hunger of the underdeveloped world, they already have taxed our ability to transport food in bulk over large distances. The total amount of goods of *all* kinds loaded at U.S. ports for external trade was 158 million metric tons in 1965 (United Nations, 1968). This is coincidentally the approximate amount of grain which would have been required to make up the dietary shortages of the underdeveloped world in the same year (Sukhatme, 1966). Thus, if the United States *had* such an amount of grain to ship, it could be handled only by displacing the entirety of our export trade. In a similar vein, the gross weight of the fertilizer, in excess of present consumption, required in the underdeveloped world to feed the additional population there in 1980 will amount to approximately the same figure —150 million metric tons (Sukhatme, 1966). Assuming that a substantial fraction of this fertilizer, should it be available at all, will have to be shipped about, we had best start building freighters! These problems, and the even more discouraging one of internal transportation in the hungry countries, coupled with the complexities of international finance and marketing which have hobbled even present aid programs, complete a dismal picture of the prospects for "external" solutions to ballooning food requirements in much of the world.

Those who envision migration as a solution to problems of food, land, and water distribution not only ignore the fact that the world has no promising place to put more people, they simply have not looked at the numbers of the transportation game. Neglecting the fact that migration and relocation costs would probably amount to a minimum of several thousand dollars per person, we find, for example, that the entire long-range jet transport fleet of the United States (about 600 planes [Molloy, 1968] with an average capacity of 150), averaging two round trips per week, could transport only about 9 million people per year from India to the United States. This amounts to about 75% of that country's annual population *growth* (Population Reference Bureau, 1968). Ocean liners and transports, while larger, are less numerous and much slower, and over long distances could not do as well. Does anyone believe, then, that we are going to compensate for the world's population growth by sending the excess to the planets? If there were a place to go on Earth, financially and logistically we could not send our surplus there.

Conclusion

We have not attempted to be comprehensive in our treatment of population pressures and the prospects of coping with them technologically; rather, we hope simply to have given enough illustrations to make plausible our contention that technology, without population control, cannot meet the challenge. It may be argued that we have shown only that any one technological scheme taken individually is insufficient to the task at hand, whereas *all* such schemes applied in parallel might well be enough. We would reply that neither the commitment nor the resources to implement them all exists, and indeed that many may prove mutually exclusive (e.g., harvesting algae may diminish fish production).

Certainly, an optimum combination of efforts exists in theory, but we assert that no organized attempt to find it is being made, and that our examination of its probable eventual constituents permits little hope that even the optimum will suffice. Indeed, after a far more thorough survey of the prospects than we have attempted here, the President's Science Advisory Committee Panel on the world food supply concluded (PSAC, 1967): "The solution of the problem that will exist after about 1985 *demands* that programs of population control be initiated now." We most emphatically agree, noting that "now" was 2 years ago!

Of the problems arising out of population growth in the short, middle, and long terms, we have emphasized the first group. For mankind must pass the first hurdles—food and water for the next 20 years—to be granted the privilege of confronting such dilemmas as the exhaustion of mineral resources and physical space later.[9] Furthermore, we have not con-

veyed the extent of our concern for the environmental deterioration which has accompanied the population explosion, and for the catastrophic ecological consequences which would attend many of the proposed technological "solutions" to the population/food crisis. Nor have we treated the point that "development" of the rest of the world to the standards of the West probably would be lethal ecologically (Ehrlich and Ehrlich, 1970). For even if such grim prospects are ignored, it is abundantly clear that in terms of cost, lead time, and implementation on the scale required, technology without population control will be too little and too late.

What hope there is lies not, of course, in abandoning attempts at technological solutions; on the contrary, they must be pursued at unprecedented levels, with unprecedented judgment, and above all with unprecedented attention to their ecological consequences. We need dramatic programs now to find ways of ameliorating the food crisis—to buy time for humanity until the inevitable delay accompanying population control efforts has passed. But it cannot be emphasized enough that if the population control measures are *not* initiated immediately and effectively, all the technology man can bring to bear will not fend off the misery to come.[10] Therefore, confronted as we are with limited resources of time and money, we must consider carefully what fraction of our effort should be applied to the cure of the disease itself instead of to the temporary relief of the symptoms. We should ask, for example, how many vasectomies could be performed by a program funded with the 1.8 billion dollars required to build a single nuclear agro-industrial complex, and what the relative impact on the problem would be in both the short and long terms.

The decision for population control will be opposed by growth-minded economists and businessmen, by nationalistic statesmen, by zealous religious leaders, and by the myopic and well-fed of every description. It is therefore incumbent on all who sense the limitations of technol-

ogy and the fragility of the environmental balance to make themselves heard above the hollow, optimistic chorus—to convince society and its leaders that there is no alternative but the cessation of our irresponsible, all-demanding, and all-consuming population growth.

Acknowledgments

We thank the following individuals for reading and commenting on the manuscript: J. H. Brownell (Stanford University); P. A. Cantor (Aerojet General Corp.); P. E. Cloud (University of California, Santa Barbara); D. J. Eckstrom (Stanford University); R. Ewell (State University of New York at Buffalo); J. L. Fisher (Resources for the Future, Inc.); J. A. Hendrickson, Jr. (Stanford University); J. H. Hessel (Stanford University); R. W. Holm (Stanford University); S. C. McIntosh, Jr., (Stanford University); K. E. F. Watt (University of California, Davis). This work was supported in part by a grant from the Ford Foundation.

References

Anonymous. 1968a. India aims to remedy fertilizer shortage. *Chem. Eng. News,* **46** (November 25): 29.

———. 1968b. Scientists Studying Nuclear-Powered Agro-Industrial Complexes to Give Food and Jobs to Millions. *New York Times,* March 10, p. 74.

———. 1968c. Food from the atom. *Technol. Rev.,* January, p. 55.

———. 1968d. Norway—The end of the big blubber. *Time,* November 29, p. 98.

———. 1968e. Nuclear fuel cycle. *Nucl. News,* January, p. 30.

Bender, R. J. 1969. Why water desalting will expand. *Power,* **113** (August): 171.

Blanko, R. E., J. O. Blomeke, and J. T. Roberts. 1967. Solving the waste disposal problem. *Nucleonics,* **25**: 58.

Borgstrom, Georg. 1965. *The Hungry Planet.* Collier-Macmillan, New York.

Bump, T. R. 1967. A third generation of breeder reactors. *Sci. Amer.,* May, p. 25.

Christy, F. C., Jr., and A. Scott. 1965. *The Commonwealth in Ocean Fisheries.* Johns Hopkins Press, Baltimore.

Clawson, M., H. L. Landsberg, and L. T. Alexander. 1969. Desalted seawater for agriculture: Is it economic? *Science,* **164**: 1141.

Cloud, P. R. 1968. Realities of mineral distribution. *Texas Quart.,* Summer, p. 103.

Cole, LaMont C. 1968. Can the world be saved? *BioScience,* **18**: 679.

Curtis, R., and E. Hogan. 1969. *Perils of the Peaceful Atom.* Doubleday, New York. p. 135, 150-152.

---

[9]Since the first draft of this article was written, the authors have seen the manuscript of a timely and pertinent forthcoming book, *Resources and Man,* written under the auspices of the National Academy of Sciences and edited by Preston E. Cloud. The book reinforces many of our own conclusions in such areas as agriculture and fisheries and, in addition, treats both short- and long-term prospects in such areas as mineral resources and fossil fuels in great detail.

---

[10]This conclusion has also been reached within the specific context of aid to underdeveloped countries in a Ph.D. thesis by Douglas Daetz: "Energy Utilization and Aid Effectiveness in Nonmechanized Agriculture: A Computer Simulation of a Socioeconomic System" (University of California, Berkeley, May 1968).

Ennis, C. E. 1967. Desalted water as a competitive commodity. *Chem. Eng. Progr.*, **63:** (1): 64.

Ehrlich, P. R. 1968. *The Population Bomb.* Sierra Club/Ballantine, New York.

Ehrlich, P. R., and Anne H. Ehrlich. 1970. *Population, Resources, and Environment.* W. H. Freeman, San Francisco (In press).

Galstann, L. S., and E. L. Currier. 1967. The Metropolitan Water District desalting project. *Chem. Eng. Progr.,* **63,** (1): 64.

Gúeron, J., J. A. Lane, I. R. Maxwell, and J. R. Menke. 1957. *The Economics of Nuclear Power. Progress in Nuclear Energy.* McGraw-Hill Book Co., New York. Series VIII. p. 23.

Hardin, G. 1968. The tragedy of the commons. *Science,* **162:** 1243.

Hubbert, M. K. 1962. Energy resources, A report to the Committee on Natural Resources. National Research Council Report 1000-D, National Academy of Sciences.

International Atomic Energy Agency. 1964. Desalination of water using conventional and nuclear energy. Technical Report 24, Vienna.

Kelly, R. P. 1966. North American water and power alliance. In: *Water Production Using Nuclear Energy,* R. G. Post and R. L. Seale (eds.). University of Arizona Press, Tucson, p. 29.

Lelyveld, D. 1968. Can India survive Calcutta? *New York Times Magazine,* October 13, p. 58.

Mason, E. A. 1957. Economic growth and energy consumption. In: *The Economics of Nuclear Power. Progress in Nuclear Energy,* Series VIII, J. Gúeron et al. (eds.). McGraw-Hill Book Co., New York, p. 56.

McIlhenny, W. F. 1966. Problems and potentials of concentrated brines. In: *Water Production Using Nuclear Energy,* R. G. Post and R. L. Seale (eds.). University of Arizona Press, Tucson, p. 187.

McKenzie, John. 1968. Nutrition and the soft sell. *New Sci.,* **40:** 423.

McNeil, Mary. 1964. Lateritic soils. *Sci. Amer.,* November, p. 99.

Meseck, G. 1961. Importance of fish production and utilization in the food economy. Paper R11.3, presented at FAO Conference on Fish in Nutrition, Rome.

Milliman, J. W. 1966. Economics of water production using nuclear energy. In: *Water Production Using Nuclear Energy.* R. G. Post and R. L. Seale (eds.). University of Arizona Press, Tucson, p. 49.

Mills, R. G. 1967. Some engineering problems of thermonuclear fusion. *Nucl. Fusion,* 7: 223.

Molloy, J. F., Jr. 1968. The $12-billion financing problem of U.S. airlines. *Astronautics and Aeronautics,* October, p. 76.

Novick, S. 1969. *The Careless Atom.* Houghton Mifflin, Boston.

Oak Ridge National Laboratory. 1968. Nuclear energy centers, industrial and agro-industrial complexes, Summary Report. ORNL-4291, July.

Paddock, William. 1967. Phytopathology and a hungry world. *Ann. Rev. Phytopathol.,* **5:** 375.

Paddock, William, and Paul Paddock. 1964. *Hungry Nations.* Little, Brown & Co., Boston.

———. 1967. *Famine 1975!* Little, Brown & Co., Boston.

Parikh, G., S. Saxena, and M. Maharaja. 1968.

Agricultural extension and IADP, a study of Surat. *Econ. Polit. Weekly,* August 24, p. 1307.

Parker, F. L. 1968. Radioactive wastes from fusion reactors. *Science,* **159:** 83.

Parker, H. M. 1966. Environmental factors relating to large water plants. In: *Water Production Using Nuclear Energy,* R. G. Post and R. L. Seale (eds.). University of Arizona Press, Tucson, p. 209.

Population Reference Bureau. 1968. Population Reference Bureau Data Sheet. Pop. Ref. Bureau, Washington, D.C.

PSAC. 1967. *The World Food Problem.* Report of the President's Science Advisory Committee. Vols. 1-3. U.S. Govt. Printing Office, Washington, D.C.

Rose, D. J., and M. Clark, Jr. 1961. *Plasma and Controlled Fusion.* M.I.T. Press, Cambridge, Mass., p. 3.

Schmitt, W. R. 1965. The planetary food potential. *Ann. N.Y. Acad. Sci.,* **118:** 645.

Sporn, Philip. 1963. *Energy for Man.* Macmillan, New York.

———. 1966. *Fresh Water from Saline Waters.* Pergamon Press, New York.

Sukhatme, P. V. 1966. The world's food supplies. *Roy. Stat. Soc. J.,* **129A:** 222.

United Nations. 1968. *United Nations Statistical Yearbook for 1967.* Statistical Office of the U.N., New York.

U.S. Dept. of Commerce. 1966. *Statistical Abstract of the U.S.* U.S. Govt. Printing Office, Washington, D.C.

Wadleigh, C. H. 1968. Wastes in relation to agriculture and industry. USDA Miscellaneous Publication No. 1065. March.

Woodwell, George M. 1967. Toxic substances and ecological cycles. *Sci. Amer.,* March, p. 24.

Science, Birth Control, and the Roman Catholic Church

Jeffrey J. W. Baker

Despite the large number of writings dealing with the urgent need for meaningful birth control legislation, few, if any, have specifically named the Roman Catholic Church as a prime force in blocking such legislation. This article rectifies this omission and suggests that Pope Paul VI's 1968 birth control Encyclical, Humanae Vitae, *should remove the views of the Church on human reproduction from the realm of those deserving serious consideration. An appeal is made to the academic community for support of those Roman Catholic laymen and clergy who, often at great personal sacrifice, have spoken out against this Encyclical.* (BioScience 20, no. 3, p. 143-150)

Since it has long been a hobby, I have done quite a bit of research and writing on the history of the American Civil War. Before coming to the University of Puerto Rico, I was on the faculty of The George Washington University in Washington, D.C. While there, I took my wife to Ford's theater. We stood and looked at the balcony where, on the night of 14 April 1865, a man sat watching a popular play of the time, "Our American Cousin." At approximately 10:20 p.m., a tiny ball of lead, no more than one-half inch across, penetrated the man's skull, traversed his brain, and lodged behind his right eye. Nine hours later, President Abraham Lincoln was dead.

An autopsy was performed in the White House. The attending physicians were shocked to find that this one small bullet had shattered the president's skull. Two lines led from the point of impact and passed through the eye sockets until they met at the front. With very little else done, the top half of Lincoln's skull could have been separated from the bottom. Indeed, later it was, so that the brain could be removed and the bullet recovered.

The men performing the autopsy on Lincoln were surprised at the bone-shattering ability of the tiny bullet because they were practicing physicians, not scientists. Any good physicist, familiar with the

Adapted from a speech delivered March 1969, as part of a lecture series entitled "The Social Responsibility of the Scientist" commemorating the 66th anniversary of the founding of the University of Puerto Rico, where the author was a Visiting Professor of Biology. He is presently at Wesleyan University, in Middletown, Connecticut.

traversing of solid matter by shock waves, might have predicted the nature and extent of the damage with nearly complete accuracy. Indeed, many men killed in the Civil War with similar wounds had shown just such damage. Thus, what was a completely natural and predictable consequence to a 19th century scientist was a surprising phenomenon to his nonscientist counterpart.

In December 1968, I attended the meetings of the American Association for the Advancement of Science in Dallas, Texas. While there, I walked with a friend to Dealey Plaza. We stood on the curb a scant 4 feet from the spot where another president was murdered. I looked up at the Texas School Book Repository Building from which the fatal shot came and recall being surprised at how very easy it must have been. My mind flashed back to Wesleyan University in Middletown, Connecticut, where I was that terrible November 1963. I recalled discussing with a physicist the hopelessness of the case, once it was known what kind of rifle was used. For this was no 19th century pistol, but one of the most powerful rifles ever developed by man. When the mass and velocity of the bullet are fed into the proper equations, the result is inevitable—even a surface head wound might be sufficient to turn the entire brain to jelly. With penetration of the skull, the shock waves could explode a man's head and, in President Kennedy's case, they did. Thus, because of a particular bit of routine scientific knowledge, a scientist could know before

a nonscientist that Kennedy could not possibly survive.

The gap in terms of technological know-how between John Wilkes Booth's Derringer pistol and Lee Harvey Oswald's Mannlicher-Carcano rifle is a fantastically wide one. But, in terms of what has happened to our world in the past 100 years, the technological gap cannot begin to compare with the scientific one. And, again, the gap between scientist and nonscientist looms frighteningly large.

A Problem of Perception

In a speech delivered at Bard College in January 1967, Novel Laureate Albert Szent-Gyorgyi pointed out that the central nervous system of a living organism can be compared to a computer. In "lower" forms of animal life, the behavior seems largely instinctive. In other words, these animals are born with their computers already programmed. However, as we move to consider progressively "higher" forms of animal life, organisms seem less programmed and more amenable to environmental modifications of behavior, i.e., "learning." Man, who ranks himself the highest form of life, seems the least programmed, instinctively, among organisms. But through certain kinds of education, he may become very much so. In Szent-Gyorgyi's analogy, the aim of a liberal education is simply to program man's computer to play a fair game of life in what is now a rapidly changing environment. Thus we must be very careful not to program the computer too completely. We must program only to the point that the individual is free to choose his or her own circuits in the future, and thereby have the potential of leading a truly intellectual life. Too often, we have overprogrammed to the extent that the individual is no longer free to adapt or adjust to a changing society. In today's world, such an individual is doomed to intellectual extinction. *The same can apply to overprogrammed institutions made up of overprogrammed individuals.*

Szent-Gyorgyi went on to point out that while science has, almost overnight, drastically changed man's world, in the past 50,000 years his brain has not changed much at all. Instead, it evolved to fit the exceedingly primitive conditions under which early man lived. Biologically speaking, man's brain was not made to search for "truth," but to distinguish between enemy and friend—to tell a cave bear from a rock. Thus our brains were made for only short-range "truths"; those which permitted survival. Even at the heart of the so-called Christian era, most of those who deviated from short- to long-range "truths" were imprisoned or burned at the stake.

Again, Szent-Gyorgyi pointed out that the doorways from our brains to the environment—the senses—are not made so as to reveal the nature of things as science has revealed them to us. Our eyes do not see a chair or a table for what, to science, they really are—empty space, with here and there a particle with electrons buzzing around it. What modern science has done is to show man what, to that science, is the "real stuff" out of which the universe is made—the electrons, protons, neutrons, elementary nuclear particles, etc. In so doing, science has forced man into a world of dimensions which his brain was not made to detect or directly comprehend.

Consider temperature. Almost everyone knows what it is like to be burned with a match or boiling water at 100 C. But 15 million degrees, the temperature of the interior of the sun or a hydrogen bomb, means nothing to us—we simply have no machinery in our heads to even imagine it.

Consider force. As men, we can only conceive of force in terms of that which we can apply—the quantity of mass we can lift, the amount of physical work we can do, and so on. But when we are told that the explosive force of a 40-megaton atomic bomb landing in the center of 100 × 35-mile Puerto Rico will totally destroy all its villages, towns, and cities, we can only shake our heads. We are amazed—but we still cannot really conceive of such a force.

And so we remain unmoved.

Consider speed and velocity. We know how fast we can run and how fast our cars can go. But the speed of light and the supersonic speeds with which technology now deals routinely simply lie beyond the pale of our comprehension.

Most frightening of all is the fact that, even when dealing with life and death, our minds can only comprehend those situations dealing with low quantities. Thus the death of a child will sadden all of us, and the perishing of almost an entire family in a boating accident off Isla Verde beach fills us with horror and pity for the bereaved. But when we are told the same 40-megaton bomb that could destroy every Puerto Rican village, town, and city will also kill all of the island's almost 3 million inhabitants, the same emotional chords or feelings remain untouched. Our brains have simply not had time to evolve the capacity to feel grief and sadness in such huge dimensions. Indeed, we have actually become rather hardened to large-scale death, and scarcely notice that our news reports blithely and habitually report the military progress of the United States in Vietnam in terms of the number of counted enemy dead.

When one mentions temperature, force, velocity, etc., one is essentially talking about physical phenomena. But matters of life and death, although ultimately the expression of physical forces, must be dealt with in terms of biology. The Intercontinental Ballistic Missile systems being developed by the United States, the Soviet Union, and Red China, in terms of the physical forces involved, are frightening enough. But to the biologist, the situation is more than tense—it is perilous. Our ever-increasing ability to transmit death and destruction great distances has greatly lessened the factors which could prevent their ever being used.

An example is probably pertinent here. In certain species of animals, fighting among males is common during the breeding season. The observation of this fact was one of many that led Darwin to his "survival of the fittest" hypothesis. The idea of fighting for the female fits in well with the chivalrous views of manhood and womanhood fashionable in the Victorian Era, and was also harmonious with the later Freudian concept of sex as a primary drive. And thus the hypothesis survived for a very long time.

It is now fairly well established, however, that males will fight when no female is involved, and that more often than not it is food or territory, not fair womanhood, for which they fight. Further, and most important for the thesis being developed here, the loser of the fight is rarely, if ever, killed. For those few species who actually do engage in direct combat, each has its own built-in surrender signal. The rat and wolf present submissive postures to their rivals, who immediately cease being aggressive. Many other animals adopt the age-old technique of simply running away. Whatever the surrender behavior that has evolved, unnecessary slaughter is prevented by their presence.

Man, too, has surrender signals, and it is certainly no accident that they have been incorporated into our military systems. Thus the raised hands or the traditional white flag are familiar internationally and their violation is looked upon with vehement disapproval by most nations of the earth. But, here again, our evolution has been too slow. Within a scant 150 years—far too short a period for organic evolution by natural selection—we have gone from the ability to kill only a few men a few hundred feet away (where their surrender signals are plainly detectable) to our present-day potential of killing millions on the other side of the earth, where a surrender signal cannot be seen or, if transmitted, may come too late. A very real, essentially biological safety valve is gone.

It is, perhaps, their knowledge of these facts that accounts for the relatively recent extensive political activity on the part of scientists, not as politicians themselves (for which scientists seem remarkably unsuited) but as citizens whose special type of education necessarily makes them more aware of the very real perils mankind faces.

Having given several examples of essentially scientific but now political situations which our minds and senses are not really capable of fully grasping, it is necessary to proceed to another situation which many feel is by far the most serious facing mankind. This is the situation which Paul

Ehrlich (1968), Professor of Biology at Stanford University, aptly termed *The Population Bomb*.

The Statistics

In the year 1 A.D., the population of the earth was approximately 250 million persons. But even that number is hard to imagine in terms of individuals. It is easier, perhaps, if it is considered in terms of 500 San Juans, or if it is said that the population of the earth in the year 1 A.D. was just a little greater than that of the United States as it will be in 1972.

In the year 500 A.D., the population of the world was 300 million people. Note that the increase is only 50 million persons, or 100 San Juans, in five centuries.

By the year 1000, there were still only 450 million persons in the world—an increase of only 150 million. Of course, 150 million is three times as great an increase in five centuries as the 50 million in the previous five centuries. But then there were still whole vast areas of the rich earth's surface unexplored and uninhabited, and so there did not seem much to worry about. Nor was there much to be concerned about in the 16th century during the time of the Council of Trent, for the world was still inhabited by less than 600 million persons.

(The reader will perceive here an intentional point: the Council of Trent, a reactionary council establishing much of the basis of current Roman Catholic theology, was held in a world populated with far fewer persons than can be found today within the boundaries of mainland China alone.)

But this is still several hundred years ago. Moving closer, by 1900, the earth's population had become one and three-fourths billion persons.

Now we are truly in the realm of numbers that our minds cannot comprehend in terms of concrete realities. And so, as with the force of the atomic bomb, we talk about it as if it were something quite ordinary.

Or, we simply ignore it.

Note that with the first two 500-year time jumps, the population increase was only 50 and 150 million persons, respectively. The time jump from 1500 to 1900 is only 400 years. Yet, the population increase is 1 billion, 205 million persons.

Now we need jump only 60 years, not 400. And, in 1960, the earth was populated with 2 billion, 800 million people—an increase in less than a man's lifetime of over one billion persons.

There are more than enough figures available now to extrapolate a mere 31 years. In 1960 it was predicted that unless drastic population control measures were taken immediately, the population of the world would rise to 6 billion, 35 million people in the year 2000, an increase of 3 billion, 650 million. Now, in 1969, with very few really meaningful steps having been taken in the direction of population control programs, we can tell that this estimate has likely been too conservative and that the population increase may actually be far greater.

It is frustrating, but giving such statistics is usually quite futile, for one is forced to deal with figures that none of us can really comprehend—again, our brains were simply not designed to do so. It is possible that the present population growth rate becomes a bit more meaningful when it is realized that had it been going on at the same rate since the time of Christ there would be over 2000 persons per square foot on the surface of the earth.

Since this discourse deals at least partly with the Roman Catholic Church, perhaps it would help still more if the population growth rate is put in Professor Garrett Hardin's (1968) units of Vatican time.

June 1963. Giovanni Battista Montini became Pope Paul VI. In June 1964, just one year later, the Pope increased the size of the Vatican's own carefully selected Birth Control Commission to a total of 60 members. In the meantime, the world's population increased by 63 million people —a number roughly equal to the population of the entire nation of Nigeria.

October 1965. Pope Paul spoke before the United Nations and referred to birth control as "irrational." By this time, the world's population had increased by an amount equaling the population of East and West Germany combined.

March 1966. The Pope created a Commission of 16 bishops to review the 60-man Birth Control Commission Report. By this time, the world's population had increased by an amount equaling the population of the Phillipines.

June 1966. The 16-bishop Commission submitted its report to the Pope. In the meantime, a number of persons equal to the population of the Congo was added to the world. Now it seemed as if there would finally be some action. The reign of Pope John XXIII had given the world reason to hope that at last the Roman Catholic Church was ready to face reality.

But, no, in November 1966, Pope Paul said he needed more time to "study the matter." He selected a 20-man Commission for further investigation of the problem. In the meantime, the world's population had increased by an amount equal to the population of South Vietnam.

April 1967. An historic month. Members of the Birth Control Commission, realizing (it would be nice to believe) that every day's delay spelled tragedy for millions, leaked their recommendations to the press. Now Rome's hand was forced, for it became publicly known that the vast majority of the Birth Control Commission—all Roman Catholics, and including theologians and nontheologian advisors—favored any means of birth control other than abortion for Catholics. By this time, a number of persons equal to the entire population of Italy had been added to the earth.

December 1967. The 20-man Commission reported to the Pope. In the meantime, the world's population had grown by an amount equaling the population of Turkey.

25 July 1968. Pope Paul issued his birth control encyclical, *Humanae Vitae*.

To total this segment of Vatican time, from the time of Pope Paul's ascension to the throne to the issuance of this incredible encyclical, the population of the world had increased by an amount equal to *the entire population of six United Kingdoms*.

And, 20 million persons died of malnutrition.

But now we are back to those same inconceivable numbers again. And, while the San Juan newspaper *El Mundo* can print a truly excellent series of articles at Christmas time on the poverty and misery suffered by a few Puerto Rican families with more children than they can possibly feed properly, there seems to be no way man's emotions can be similarly stirred when he learns that there are literally millions of such families living in the same or worse conditions.

Rational Escapism

Faced with the reality of the inconceivable, we resort to simplistic explanations or solutions which our minds *can* compre-hend. We look to international politics and say that the problem is due to wealthy nations not sharing their wealth with the less fortunate. Most certainly, this is part of the problem. But this overlooks the fact that wealth of nations is measured in terms of gross national product or the standard of a nonedible substance—gold. Needed are vital macromolecules—pro-teins, lipids, and carbohydrates—produced most efficiently by living organisms within a *properly balanced* natural system.

We say that if nations behaved in a more "Christian" manner, and shared their riches, things would be better. Most certainly they would, but inasmuch as only in the movie *The Shoes of the Fisherman* has even the Vatican (itself wealthier than some nations of the earth) seen fit to do so in any meaningful way, is it realistic to sit by and watch people starve to death while we wait for this Christian action on the part of nations making less pretentious claims to righteousness?

We say that the agriculturists are going to save us, that new farming techniques, mining of the sea, and other get-rich food schemes are going to provide the solution. An effective rebuttal to this argument is provided by an analyst in the Puerto Rican Office of Economic Opportunity who writes: "Articles appear regularly in the press that the utilization of fertilizers, oceans, and solar energy can provide food for many more millions of people. These science-fiction possibilities do not, how-ever, make today's poor feel less hungry." Equally effective is the obvious fact that at our present population growth rate the space needed for this miraculous farming will have to be used by man to live on and pollute. There also remains the opinion of more than a few that, despite improve-ment in food production efficiency, if all the food available today were evenly dis-tributed among the world's peoples, everyone would go hungry. Further, even if we *were* able to give every man on earth enough to eat for an indefinite period into the future, there is substantial research evidence showing that an organism's be-havior patterns become decidedly abnor-mal when subjected to extended periods of high population density. Finally, in an overpopulated, unbalanced system, the overall quality of life is greatly decreased.

The overpopulation problem is bringing man face-to-face with the harsh realities

of the laws of thermodynamics, bioener-getics, and ecology which no scientist, Catholic or non-Catholic, can deny; and it is no accident that the scientific advisors to Pope Paul's Birth Control Commission were the ones most vocal in their support of birth control. In essence, we are faced with having to live on a planet which has only a certain input of useful potential energy. Additional energy is pumped into the earth every day by the sun, of course, but only at a rate which cannot keep up with the pace at which our expanding population must continue to use it in order to survive.

For the scientist, it is far easier to sit smugly in the laboratory and say that such matters lie in the political rather than the scientific realm. Often, far too often, this is what has been done. But three events in recent history have forced scientists to speak out and participate in problems of vast political and sociological significance. The first is the development of nuclear weapons. The second is the misuse and pollution of our natural environment. The third is a natural extension of the first two, and one that must first be solved before the others can be adequately handled. This is the checking of the human popula-tion growth rate.

This third event has also brought about an historical first; one foreshadowed, per-haps, by an editorial appearing in the highly respected journal, *New Scientist* (1 August 1968), just one week after the birth control Encyclical was released by Pope Paul VI:

> Bigotry, pedantry, and fanaticism can kill, maim, and agonize those upon whom they are visited just as surely as bombs, pogroms and the gas chamber. Pope Paul VI has now gently joined the company of tyrants, but the damage he has done may well outclass and out-last that of all earlier oppressors.

In the following months and continuing up to the present, it has become clear from articles appearing in other journals that a large portion of the scientific aca-demic community, particularly the biolo-gists, find themselves in direct conflict with a certain segment of the Roman Catholic Church hierarchy—unfortu-nately, by far the most powerful segment. It is a conflict that *Humanae Vitae* forces upon us. It is a conflict that science cannot lose. The only question is, *can it be won in time?*

Science vs. the Church

In the time that the reader has spent on this article thus far, a few things have happened. For one thing, many people have starved to death. For another, the perennial optimist in most of us tends to bring to the surface several points on which, hopefully, this article is incorrect or perhaps overly pessimistic.

Some of these points can be anticipated. For one, it was stated that this is the first time that science finds itself in conflict with the Roman Catholic Church, a state-ment that certainly seems incorrect on the basis of several other events, most notably the infamous case of Galileo. But the Galileo case has not been overlooked. In-deed, it is on the basis of that case that we can feel confident that science will win over *Humanae Vitae*.

A brief review of the Galileo case is highly pertinent here. In 1633, Galileo was summoned to Rome to face charges of teaching the Copernican-Kepler view of the universe rather than the Church-ap-proved Ptolemaic version. Basically at issue was whether the earth was the center of the universe and everything revolved around it, or whether the earth was in orbit itself around some other central body, notably, the sun. As everyone knows, under threat of torture and imprisonment, Galileo was forced to recant and refute his own scientific evidence supporting the latter hypothesis.[1]

But two points are important here. First of all, while in the Galileo case the Church made a very sharp attack upon science, in general, the attack was not returned. Nor has it ever been. Until *Humanae Vitae*, science has done little more than observe with detached interest the opinions of the Papacy on certain scientific hypotheses. Occasionally there would be some minor stir, as in the case of statements on Adam and Eve and human evolution made by Pope Pius XII which made a few biol-ogists, especially Catholic biologists, cringe. But after all, if some Roman Catholics, or all of them, for that matter, chose to take seriously what Pius XII had to say about evolution, that was certainly their own business, not science's.

---

[1]Often a new pope selects the name of a previous pope whose life and deeds he particularly admires. One wonders if there is any significance in the fact that Galileo was first checked by Rome during the reign of Pope Paul V.

In general, then, science ignores Roman Catholicism, and there are several good reasons for this. First, Roman Catholicism is easily the most dogmatic of the Christian religions and, of course, dogmatism has no legitimate place in science. In March 1954, Pope Pius XII decreed that the belief that Mary's body did not decay but was assumed into heaven, body and soul, was a necessary part of the Christian religion. In his encyclical announcing this, he finished by stating that, " . . . if anyone, which God forbid, should dare wilfully to deny or call into doubt that which we have defined, let him know that he has fallen away completely from the divine and Catholic faith." One can imagine what would happen to a scientist if he tacked anything like that onto one of his research papers (e.g., if anyone, God forbid, should dare deny or call into doubt that the degree of actinomycin D binding to chromatin is related to the degree of repression of the chromatin and that removal of histone increases the capacity of repressed, condensed chromatin to bind actinomycin D, let him know that he is no longer a biologist). But further, in the Galileo case, it really did not matter very much if the average man-in-the-street believed that the earth orbits the sun or vice versa—at the time, neither belief greatly affected the welfare of mankind.

The most important point is the second one. The Roman Catholic Church based a great deal of its theology on an earth-centered universe; at stake was an entire concept concerning the relationship of God and man. The argument went something like this: God made man in his own image and therefore man and the earth he inhabits must be at the center of things. Further, in the scriptures it says that Joshua made the sun stand still—he could hardly have done so if it was the earth that moved, and not the sun. Thus the Church crawled further and further out on a limb and lashed out more and more paranoically at Galileo, just as Pope Paul VI is now doing against those Roman Catholic priests and bishops who have had the courage to point out that *Humanae Vitae* puts the Church out on a limb even shakier than the one Galileo selected.

As everyone knows, the Church was wrong—dead wrong—and Galileo was right. And, slowly, the Church began to crawl back along the limb until the safety of the main trunk was reached and the theology could be readjusted to a non-homocentric universe, and a bit of history could be rewritten.

But it took the Church 189 years to admit it was wrong (on 11 September 1822). Even then, it did not admit Galileo was right. It merely said that it was no longer a serious sin against God to think that he *might* be right. Not until 203 years had passed were the works of Kepler, Copernicus, and Galileo removed from the Index of forbidden books. As far as I know, the Roman Catholic Church to this day has never publicly admitted that the earth really does go around the sun (possibly that is why the United States sent astronaut Borman to the Vatican). Professor Hardin has wagered that if the Church ever does retry Galileo (which has been seriously suggested), it will find him guilty again.[2]

As stated previously, it does not make much difference if the Roman Catholic Church chooses to believe that the sun orbits the earth, instead of *vice versa*. But it does greatly affect mankind if very many persons take seriously the idea that to use an artificial contraceptive is a grave sin against God. This, then, is certainly one reason why the scientific community, as well as the rest of the academic world, has been so shocked by *Humanae Vitae*. Mankind simply cannot afford to wait for two centuries for Rome to admit its error—the present population growth rate and the accompanying death rate by disease and starvation simply will not permit it.

On 29 December 1968, a strong protest statement against *Humanae Vitae*, instigated by the author, Professor Ehrlich, and Professor Ernst Mayr (Harvard University), was released to the press. At that time, over 2600 scientists, Roman Catholic and non-Roman Catholic, had signed this statement (the resulting publicity has greatly increased this number). In discussing this action, one priest told me he thought it to be a waste of time because those Roman Catholics who have had the benefit of a good education pay no attention to the Pope and use contraceptives anyway.

This is true enough. Indeed, recent surveys indicate that almost 80% of Roman Catholics in the United States practice means of birth control forbidden by the

Church. But the United States is not the world. It is the world's uneducated that will suffer the most from the fear of eternal punishment in the flames of Hell in the hereafter—and they are the ones who stand at the bottom of the economic ladder and who can least afford to have large numbers of children.

Another stock argument used in defense of the Pope is that the birth rate in many Catholic countries is often the same or even lower than birth rates in such non-Catholic countries as India, where the Pope has no authority. This is possibly true. But is it right to use the existence of poverty and misery in non-Catholic countries as an excuse to block attempts to correct slightly less miserable situations in Catholic countries? Further, do these birth rate statistics take into account the over 900,000 abortions a year in Catholic Italy, where contraceptives are outlawed? Does it account for the frequent use of infanticide by women in Catholic Columbia, where access to knowledge of any other means to limit family size has been denied by the Church and government? The same press release that gave out the comparative birth rates in Catholic and non-Catholic countries also pointed out that in Catholic Austria, Belgium, and France, it is estimated that there is at least one abortion for every live birth. According to Alvaro Garcia-Pena, Director of the Population Reference Bureau's Latin American Department, in Uruguay the ratio is three abortions to every live birth. In Latin America, 78% of the abortions performed (many of them fatal) are carried out on married women.

The Cause for Concern

Since it is evident that most Roman Catholics, even those who publicly defend *Humanae Vitae*, privately ignore it, and that even if the Pope reversed his stand tomorrow, it would have little immediate effect on the world's alarming birth rate, it is still reasonable to probe further to understand why there is such concern in the academic community about the birth control encyclical.

One does not have to look far. The great danger of *Humanae Vitae* lies in the support it gives to organized conservative Catholic resistance to the initiation of publicly financed population control programs. In the past, opposition by such

---

[2] In Scranton, Pennsylvania, a priest was reprimanded for five points in his writings, one of which was that he was too lenient in his interpretation of Galileo. The year? 1969.

groups has effectively prevented or slowed population control programs through the United Nations, *even to non-Catholic nations,* such as India. This, it will be seen, *does* give the Pope some authority in non-Catholic nations. In the United States, conservative Catholic opposition helped defeat Senator Gruening's efforts to pass a law promoting the dissemination of birth control information—just the *information,* mind you, not the contraceptives themselves—to those who wanted it. Some of the testimony delivered against this legislation makes pitiful reading indeed.

The President's Scientific Advisory Committee, in its massively documented three-volume report, *The World Food Crisis,* stated that, "The solution to the problem that will exist after about 1985 *demands* that programs of population control be initiated now." The "now" was 2 years ago, and no such programs have been initiated. *Section XXIII of Humanae Vitae specifically encourages renewed interference in governmental efforts to disseminate birth control information.* This fact renders ridiculous the charge that those non-Catholics who have protested against the Encylical are interfering in the private affairs of the Roman Catholic Church. I suspect that as far as most non-Roman Catholics are concerned, the Church could return to believing that the sun goes around the earth for all they care. But they are quite within their rights to protest when, through political activity, it attempts to limit their freedom to think and act otherwise.

Political Interference: A Case History

Except for a few regions, it is difficult for a person living in the United States to fully comprehend what Roman Catholic political interference means. But those who live in Puerto Rico are well aware of the extreme coercive tactics to which the Church has resorted in its fight against birth control by means that it does not find acceptable. Failing to convince the laymen of the "immorality" of contraception, the Church in Puerto Rico turned to "spiritual retreats" for government and civic leaders, doctors, nurses, social workers, etc. In reality, these retreats were mostly indoctrination courses in Catholic thinking on the subject of birth control. Associations were formed of Roman Catholic physicians, Roman Catholic nurses,

Roman Catholic lab technicians, etc., all opposed, of course, to birth control aid.

Despite repeated official statements by the then-in-power Popular Democratic Party (PDP) that the government was not promoting any birth control programs and that for strict health reasons only were contraceptive services being given, the Church continued its attack against the government, mainly because it wished the "Neo-Malthusian" laws of 1937 repealed.[3]

Partly because of the 1937 legislation and partly because of the tabling of a bill which would have authorized the release of public school children during school hours to receive religious instruction, the Society of the Holy Name initiated a movement for the formation of the "Christian Action Party." The movement was given the green light by Archbishop Davis, who saw this party as a means to "define the rights of the faithful." The reigning Popular Democratic Party was labeled by the bishops of Puerto Rico and others of the hierarchy as "Godless, immoral, antichristian, and against the Ten Commandments" . . . certainly a notable record for any political party. In a pastoral letter to the laity dated 18 October 1960 and read from the pulpit in all Roman Catholic Churches in Puerto Rico, Archbishop Davis and Bishops McManus and Aponti forbade Catholics from voting for the PDP because its philosophy was "antichristian, anticatholic, and based upon the modern heresy that the popular will and not Divine Law decides what is moral or immoral." (The "immoral" practices the good bishops had in mind were the birth control services provided at public hospitals, clinics, and health centers.)

The response of the PDP was simply and reasonably to point out that the birth control laws were not compulsory but simply allowed those individuals who wished birth control *information* to obtain it without breaking the law. As one PDP leader put it, "The government should not be subordinated to an exclusive creed or moral interpretation of a specific religious

---

[3]These laws simply made it no longer a felony to advertise contraceptive methods or provide contraceptive services and enabled the Commissioner of Health to regulate the teaching of birth control in health centers, maternal hospitals, and clinics to married couples or those living together publicly. Under government regulation, sterilization was also permitted on the advice of physicians. The fact that the Medical Association and the Association of Graduate Nurses, as well as many members of the University academic communities, backed this legislation led to the formation of the aforementioned Catholic organizations.

group which condemns or prohibits the moral beliefs of other groups, and should not interfere with purely moral questions, like the use of birth control devices, which pertain to the free will of the individual."

Governor Munoz Marín, founder of the PDP and a Roman Catholic, made his reply to the 18 October pastoral letter sharper and still more to the point:

The statement of the Catholic bishops is an incredible and unjust intervention in the rights and the political freedom of citizens in Puerto Rico. It has the characterists of medieval obscurantism.

We could not believe that in the modern world, nor in a country intimately associated with the United States, such a document could be issued. When the Popular Party states that it is not possible to sanction punitively those acts over which there is no general consensus, it is referring to the differences between Catholics and those of other Christian denominations.

The bishops' document assumes or pretends to assume that in Puerto Rico there is an established Church, and that that Church is theirs. Neither in Puerto Rico nor in any part of the U.S. democracy is there one church established, and we have the duty to respect the differences of opinion that exist between Christians.

The reaction of the hierarchy to these statements was typical. On 22 October, a few days before the election, a pastoral letter was read from the pulpit stating:

For a Catholic to vote in favor of the Popular Democratic Party is to vote in favor of the anti-Catholic morality proclaimed by the Popular Party, is to vote in favor of the destruction of the Ten Commandments of the Law of God, is to act against his own Catholic convictions and, whether the Bishops say it or not, it is a sin to act contrary to one's own convictions. If the faithful should not heed the warning of the Bishops, that is a matter for their consciences, but they . . . are committing a sin. With penalties or without penalties from the Bishops, they violate the Law of God which prohibits favoring a morality without God, which is clearly a disobedience against God and is evidently a sin.

The results of the elections were an anticlimax. The Popular Democratic Party was victorious, with the Christian Action Party receiving little more than 5% of the total vote cast. Proof of wholesale fraud connected with voter registration for the Christian Action Party—defended because of the overriding moral issues involved

(! ! !)—led to an investigation in which more than 3000 fraudulent registrations were uncovered. In 1964, two of the three bishops (with some urging) went elsewhere, and were replaced. The one remaining, Aponti, continues his fulminations against birth control, but one gets the impression that not even *he* takes anything he says on the matter very seriously anymore. But meaningful birth control programs in Puerto Rico are still being crippled by the political extortions of the Church.

The happy outcome of the Puerto Rican elections should in no way be used to justify lessened concern about the fact that *Humanae Vitae* specifically encourages such nonsense. The 1960 Puerto Rican elections were a very special case. Governor Marín was a very popular and powerful political leader. Further, while its quality varies widely, public education in Puerto Rico is widespread. Thus most Puerto Ricans have generally been educated beyond the stage of being frightened by threats of eternal hellfire and damnation. Such is not the case in much of Latin America or countries such as Spain or Italy. Even in liberal Puerto Rico, the Executive Director of the Family Planning Association, an intelligent and courageous woman, has been slandered, threatened, and attacked from the pulpit in the presence of her children. One priest told his congregation that "a woman with a Satanic purpose in mind has been visiting the community." Threats were made to bar any Catholic from the Church who attended birth control meetings. Even after the 1960 election debacle, the San Juan Chancery attempted to bar from the sacraments and church services those who had disobeyed the hierarchy's voting instructions.[4]

The Theology of *Humanae Vitae*

For a person trained in science to delve into theology, especially Roman Catholic theology, is a dangerous venture. Until very recently, orthodox theological research has been primarily apologetic; certain assumptions are never challenged, only supported. For example, the scriptural evidence which supports belief that

God really meant for Peter and his "successors" to be Popes is marshaled in full strength, while scriptural and historical evidence casting doubt upon this belief is downplayed or "explained" away. Days spent by this writer in the Library of Congress trying to wade through a vast entanglement of Roman Catholic theological literature in an attempt to understand how a *Humanae Vitae* could ever have happened were dismaying ones, and the complexities of the scientific research literature seemed like paradise in comparison. Only two thoughts prompted me to continue. The first was a belief that the most effective way to tackle a serious problem is to go to its roots—and the roots of *Humanae Vitae* are, or claim to be, primarily theological. The second thought was a comforting one: whenever the Roman Catholic Church has passed judgment upon scientific matters, it has almost invariably managed to be wrong. Thus, I could feel confident that my own batting average could hardly be much worse.

Just how firm a theological basis does the Church's opposition to birth control have? An incredibly weak one. The first really powerful Papal decree indicating disapproval comes not from the time of Christ, but from Pope Sixtus V on 29 October 1588. Here, the using or giving of contraceptives was equated literally with murder and was punishable as such.[5] Sixtus V Bull *(Effraenatum)* proved more embarrassing than successful, and was quietly laid to rest a few months after its author by his successor, Gregory XIV. The sort of reasoning behind it, however, did not die. It was to appear again in the mid-19th century under St. Pius IX (the same who proclaimed as dogma the Immaculate Conception of Mary and Papal infallibility). But it was not until 1930 that Rome really resurrected Sixtus V, with the issuance of Pius XI's *Casti connubii,* a masterful distillation of past doctrinal statements. St. Augustine's famous passage on the "cruel lust" of couples avoiding procreation is cited, as is the Thomistic view of the nature of coitus. But probably the tone and intent of *Casti connubii* are best conveyed by its statement that " . . . those who do such a thing (i.e., practice

contraception) are masked with a grave and total flaw" (yes, "flaw"!).

There were, however, still some grounds for hope. Even in 1930, many of the clergy were openly critical of *Casti connubii* and the French, in particular, tried to prevent it. Thus, prior to *Humanae Vitae,* the Church had really been inching its way back out on a limb on this matter for only about 35 years. Pope Paul could have easily enabled the Church to retreat rather gracefully, as well as perform a tremendous service to humanity. Indeed, as soon as Paul began to examine the birth control issue, the Patriarch of Antioch said to his Cardinal colleagues, "I beg of you, my brothers; let us avoid a new Galileo case: one is enough for the Church." But Pope Paul elected to ignore the lessons of history.

If contraception is really such a serious sin for Christians, one would have expected Christ to have devoted at least a little attention to it. He did not; nor did the apostles. In truth, as one Roman Catholic priest put it concerning *Humanae Vitae,* "Since there is no scripture and no history, there can be no theological ground either."

Early birth control bans gave as scriptural justification an obscure passage in the Old Testament book of Genesis, Chapter 38. Here is related the "Sin of Onan." In the story, Onan is ordered by his father to have sexual intercourse with his brother's widow. Onan does so but, not wishing to have his own sperm follow that of his brother, withdraws before having an orgasm and, as the Bible puts it, "spills his seed upon the ground." God then "slew" him.[6]

I invite any reader to read the story of Onan for himself. According to the Church, the incident showed that God disliked birth control. But this is a classic case of out-of-context interpretation. Once one reads the *entire* story of Onan, not just the part cited by the Church, it becomes perfectly evident that Onan was slain for his refusal to meet his responsibility to his brother and the clan, rather than for the means he used in not doing so. Even the Church now seems to realize it was a mistake to use Onan in support of

---

[4]Archbishop Davis, undoubtedly chastened by thoughts of drastically reduced collections in the plate, later denied statements issued from the Chancery to this effect.

[5]Sixtus V seems to have had an obsession to continue a pet project of Pope Paul V to stamp out prostitution in Rome, and actually had a woman who had procured for her daughter executed.

[6]"Slewing" people seemed to be almost an obsession with the God of the Old Testament, often on rather vaguely worded charges. Indeed, we read that Onan's brother was struck down merely for "displeasing" God. The American Civil Liberties Union would have been driven absolutely wild.

antibirth control activity, and it is perhaps a credit to Pope Paul that *Humanae Vitae* wisely omits any reference to it.

In terms of being consistent, the Church lost much of the strength of its argument against birth control when it allowed rhythm as a means of limiting family size. This meant the Church had changed its tune—it was no longer implying that for man to limit his numbers was necessarily wrong, but only the use of "unnatural" means of doing so was a "grave sin." Indeed, *Humanae Vitae* is quite explicit on this point. But what *are* these "unnatural" means? Even the Church admits that in some cases it does not know. There are certain means, such as the use of diaphragms, condoms, intrauterine devices, etc., that the Church says are definitely "unnatural." But even the pill is banned as "unnatural," which implies that the Church knows more about the precise biochemical means by which the pill works to effect birth control than do the scientists who developed it.

Thus, to date, the only method of birth control now considered as "natural" is rhythm. Ironically, the Roman Catholic physician John Rock, who had written a definitive paper on rhythm years before, recently expressed regrets that he had done so and clearly labeled rhythm as unnatural! Biologically speaking, it certainly is. The only thing that separates man sexually from the vast majority of lower animals is that he does not have certain periods of nonmating. In other words, man has no breeding schedule. Rhythm puts man right back onto a breeding schedule. Rome gets around this difficulty by suggesting that periods of abstinence be looked upon as personal sacrifices to the glory of God. But this merely reflects the scarcely hidden opinions of sex as dirty and immoral held by St. Paul and St. Augustine. ("Better to marry than to burn," is the way St. Paul is quoted.) Even as late as March 1954, Pius XII was stating in his encyclical, *Sacra Virginitae*, that marriage was not as high a state of life as holy virginity! Until very recently, obsession with the "evils" of sex permeate Catholic theology—indeed, Pope Paul IV insisted that for his coronation, loincloths be put upon Michelangelo's cherubs on the ceiling of the Sistine Chapel. It is not until 1874 that one finds a Roman Catholic theologian making any connection between sexual intercourse and love, and it

is only since the reign of Pope John XXIII (1958-63) that this anti-Augustinian, anti-Thomist heresy has crept in any significant way into the Church's viewpoint on these matters. Thus, while it is difficult to prove, one gets the impression that Rome has long considered sex as a necessary evil in order to have children, and that "if the chance of the procreation of life no longer remains open," then the act of sexual intercourse may be simply done because it's fun . . . and that's a "no no." And so the attacks of the Church against birth control have paralleled in intensity the rate at which birth control practices have become available to mankind.

The Catholic Scientist

Where does all of this leave the Roman Catholic scientist? In my opinion—and events since the encyclical has come out tend to support it—the Catholic scientist has three choices.

The first is to simply ignore both the Pope and the problem. This is no more nor less than many educated Roman Catholic laymen are doing, and many of them frankly admit it. But the person who *privately* feels the birth control encyclical is wrong, yet refuses to speak out against it, is adopting an unchristian form of behavior, for it is an intrinsically selfish one. The Catholic scientist who ignores the encyclical (which according to the encyclical is the same as disobeying it) may himself be intellectually free to do so. But he is guilty of turning his back on the vast majority of his fellow Catholics who have been deprived of a good education and who live out their lives in an environment which is both physically and intellectually a replica of the 13th century. To such persons, fears of the "fires of Hell" are both real and frightening.

As Bernard Hollowood put it in *Punch* (14 August 1968):

> Unfortunately, those who will suffer most from this philosophical nonsense will be the poor and underprivileged, those who lack the strength of mind and body to resist religious enslavement. Many of them will obey out of fear and ignorance, and as they do so they will bring increasing hardship upon themselves, increasing misery, and hopelessness. Religion is a terrible and terrifying force when it can be so abused.

The second type of Roman Catholic scientist is the one who goes right down

the line with the Church and publicly says so. While I do not myself see how any scientist can square what is now known with what is written in *Humanae Vitae*, I can say that I admire this sort of Roman Catholic scientist a great deal more than one who simply ignores the encyclical. At least the former has the courage of his convictions and speaks out for them.

The third kind of Roman Catholic scientist is the one our protest petition was written to support. The following words of a Roman Catholic biologist perhaps best describes this type of person.

> My first duty as a Catholic is to do what I believe is morally correct. There is no doubt in my mind that the position of the Church with respect to birth control is morally wrong. The price of doctrinaire insistence on unworkable methods of birth control is high. It contributes to misery and starvation for millions and perhaps the end of civilization as we know it. As a scientist I know that Catholic doctrine in this area is without biological foundation. It is therefore my duty, both to myself and to my Church, not just to ignore this doctrine, but to do everything within my power to change it. After all, without drastic world-wide measures for population control in the near future, there will be no Church anyway. If the Church, or, for that matter, any organized religion is to survive, it must become much more humanitarian in focus. If it does, the theology will take care of itself.

As if to echo these words, and in reference to *Humanae Vitae*, another scientist writes:

> Whilst respecting individual beliefs, the world can no longer afford to tolerate such undemocratic, authoritarian pronouncements which claim universal obedience. The great hope, as has been aptly shown in the past few weeks, is that people—Roman Catholics and others—are beginning to see the Roman Catholic Church for what it is—an institution concerned primarily with the maintenance of its own authority in a world it does not comprehend, and where the need to preserve the dogma of bygone centuries has priority over a concern for man.

What Can Be Done

It is too late, of course, to prevent *Humanae Vitae*. But it is not too late to prevent at least some of the tragedy and misery which will result from it.

In matters such as foreign policy, arms control, etc., the voice of the scientific academic community has had considerable effect. The same voice can be used to good effect in this matter also. Recently, three Roman Catholic biologists, one a priest, sent a copy of the scientists' protest statement to the 150 U.S. Roman Catholic bishops and stated in their accompanying letter their own conviction that "no leader, religious or otherwise, who speaks irresponsibly, can be allowed to go unchallenged." Twenty members of the Catholic University of Washington, D.C., signed a protest statement against the encyclical as soon as it was issued. The University is currently considering whether or not to take disciplinary action; if it does so, surely some sort of censure should be attempted by the academic community, both Catholic and non-Catholic. Indeed, it is the former who should be the most concerned, because any action of a punitive nature taken against faculty members acting out of intellectual and moral conviction would make the Catholic University's claim to academic respect a laughable one and, indeed, would be a serious blow to the intellectual respectability which some Catholic universities have only recently attained. In any community pretending to be an academic one, the channels of debate must be kept open on both sides of the question; if this is done, *Humanae Vitae* will collapse on its own merits (or lack of them).

There is a strong liberalizing force now at work in the Roman Catholic Church, a force attempting to make the Church adjust to the 20th century. While the problem is an internal one, more the concern of Catholics than non-Catholics, incidents such as *Humanae Vitae*, the dictatorial methods of Washington, D.C.'s Cardinal O'Boyle in suspending those priests who

protested it (methods recently supported by Pope Paul VI in a letter to O'Boyle), and other such transgressions on the rights of free men certainly offer focal points at which the non-Catholic academic community could and should lend its support.

Meetings of the American Roman Catholic bishops are usually followed by statements such as "American Roman Catholics believe . . . ," "American Roman Catholics will not support . . . ," etc. But the situation has obviously changed for the better; on birth control and other issues, Roman Catholics are now thinking for themselves. The medieval dogmatism which characterized the Church in the past is slowly dying out; ironically, *Humanae Vitae* seems to be hastening its demise. Just this year, the Dutch Roman Catholic clergy stated that "love is the only absolute and eternal law."

Humanae Vitae is not based upon love; as were statements made in the past by the Church, it is based upon biological ignorance. It thus is a perversion of the very religion it claims to represent. As is stated in the last sentence of the scientists' protest statement, "The fact that this incredible document was put forth in the name of a religious figure whose teachings embodied the highest respect for the value of human dignity and life should make the situation even more repugnant to mankind."

References

Pope Paul VI. *Humanae Vitae,* dated July 25, 1968, released to press July 29, 1968.

Fremantle, Ann (ed.). 1963. *The Papal Encyclicals in their Historical Context.* Mentor-Omega Books, New York & Toronto. This book extends only to the "Pacem in Terris" of Pope John XXIII, and thus does not contain *Humanae Vitae.* Mrs. Fremantle is a Roman Catholic and the book carries the

"Nihil Obstat" of John A. Goodwine, J. C. D., Censor Librorum, and the "Imprimatur" of the late Francis Cardinal Spellman, Archbishop of New York. A full reading of encyclicals is absolutely essential before one can begin to understand the sort of reasoning behind them. As the book's title suggests, the point is made that in order to be fully appreciated, the Papal encyclicals must be read in the context of the period in which they were written. This is certainly correct, but when one realizes that both *Humanae Vitae* and Pius X's encyclical, *Lamentable Sane* (which "condemns the errors of the Modernists"), were both written in the 20th century, one's "appreciation" is apt to be of another sort. On 31 May 1954, incidentally, Pope Pius XII canonized Pius X a saint, a happening that would appear to make the future bright for Paul VI.

Getlein, Frank. 1964. *The Trouble with Catholics.* Helicon Publishers of Baltimore, Maryland & Dublin, Ireland. This book is written by a Roman Catholic layman in a delightfully humorous tone. Mr. Getlein retains his faith in the Roman Catholic Church's ability to get over what he calls "its love affair with the 13th century." (This book was written before *Humanae Vitae.*)

Ehrlich, Paul R. 1968. *The Population Bomb,* Ballantine Books, New York. This book has received wide circulation, due primarily to the interest shown in it by many natural history societies, conservation groups and ecological societies. Professor Ehrlich has been a leading figure in putting in layman terms the danger of the current population growth rate.

Genesis, Chapter 38. Related in this chapter is the "Sin of Onan," which the Roman Catholic Church once used to justify scripturally its opposition to birth control.

Noonan, John T., Jr. 1965. *Contraception.* Mentor-Omega Books, New York & Toronto. A well-researched book, the author traces the history of the Church's oppositon to contraception from its origins in gnosticism, stoicism, and paganism to its modern day status in the Church.

Hardin, G. 1968. Remarkable reversal of time at 41.52 N. 12.37 E. *New Sci.,* September 5, 1968. A delightful tongue-in-cheek article by biologist Garrett Hardin of the University of California, Santa Barbara, in which the author sees *Humanae Vitae* as a case of time reversal leading to scientific predictability.

Optimum World Population

H. R. Hulett

Optimum population is hard to define. However, if the ability to provide current living standards in the United States is used as the criterion, the optimum world population at present is of the order of one billion people, compared to the actual population of about 3 billion 600 million. (BioScience 20, no. 3, p. 160-161)

No hunter of the age of fable
Had need to buckle in his belt
More game than he was ever able
To take ran wild upon the veldt.
Each night with roast he stocked his table
Then procreated on the pelt,
And that is how, of course, there came
At last to be more men than game.

A. D. Hope, *Texas Quarterly, Summer 1962*

The population explosion is now widely recognized as a worldwide problem. Many have attempted to calculate the ultimate supportable population of the world, with resulting numbers ranging from a few to many times the current population of about 3.5 billion (Schmidt, 1965). There is no reason to believe that such a population is optimum, unless it is assumed that it is innately desirable to have as many people as possible. On the other hand, there are many reasons why such a population would not be optimum—reasons concerned with such aspects of the quality of life as pollution, loss of open space and wildlife, overcrowding, and lowered individual allotments of food and other raw materials. It is probably impossible to come to any quantitative conclusions as to the most desirable value for any of these parameters. However, the average U.S. citizen would certainly assume that the amount and variety of food and other raw materials available to him are not greater than optimum. The ratio of current world pro-

The author is in the department of genetics, Stanford University School of Medicine, Stanford, Calif. 94305.

duction of these materials to current average American consumption then can be used as a rough indication of the upper limit of optimum world population at present production rates. This optimum population can increase no more rapidly than the production of these essential raw materials can increase.

Food

Food is probably the most useful indicator of supportable population. Even at current levels, which over most of the world entail much lower quantity and quality than American diets, there is not enough food in many areas to provide an adequate diet for the present population (F.A.O., 1968). The picture is much darker when the American diet is used as a reference standard. We each purchased about 3200 kcal/day in 1966, probably corresponding to about 2600 kcal/day consumed (USDA, 1968). Of this 3200 kcal/day about one-third came from meat, milk, eggs, and other animal products, with the remainder, about 2100 kcal/day or 7.5×10^5 kcal/yr, directly from plants. The animal products required 750×10^9 feed units (corn equivalent pounds) or about 6.3×10^6 kcal/person/yr, so total requirement was slightly over 7×10^6 kcal/person/yr—about six times what it would have been on a strictly vegetarian diet.

The increased primary calorie requirements because of use of animal products are not strictly comparable to calories available from cropland, since much of the land used by animals for grazing is

not suitable for cropland, and its produce would be wasted if it were not grazed. Some 1 billion acres are used for grazing in the United States, but its caloric yield is only equivalent to about 200 million cropland acres (Landsberg et al., 1963). There is an additional 16 million cropland acres equivalent from grazing on previously harvested fields, but about 66 million acres of cropland are included in the grazed area, giving a caloric output equivalent to that from about 150 million cropland acres from grazing areas not suitable to crops. There are a total of 465 million acres presently suitable for crops. Thus the increased yield from grazing is about one-third.

There is more grazing and cropland in the United States relative to total area than in most countries, but the ratio of the two is not far from average (Schmidt, 1965). However, let us assume optimistically that caloric output throughout the world from grazing land is equal to that from present cropland. The production of plant crops in the world is about 1.2×10^6 kcal/person yr or about 4.2×10^{15} kcal/yr (Schmidt, 1965). If this is doubled to include grazing by domestic animals, the total production would be less than 10^{16} kcal/yr, enough to provide for only about 1.2 billion people at American food standards. Other methods of calculation, based on present protein consumption in various areas, together with the efficiency of conversion of plant food by individual animal species, gives very similar results. These figures show the impossibility of lifting the rest of the world to our dietary standards without a several fold increase in world food production or a massive reduction in population.

In addition to food from the land, man utilizes some of the food in the ocean. However, the amount is relatively small—less than 1% of the total food calories and less than 4% of the total protein in the global diet (Schmidt, 1965). It may be possible to increase the harvest from the oceans in the future, but at present it has only a minimal effect on available food.

Other Renewable Resources

The other major renewable resources are lumber and other forest products such as paper. Here again the picture is dim. On a world basis, forest reserves are probably shrinking. Total worldwide wood production in 1965 was 2.0×10^9 m^3. Of this about 0.33×10^9 m^3 were used in the United States (USDA, 1968; UN Statistical Yearbook, 1969). If the present cut could be maintained, it would supply a world population of a little over one billion people at the U.S. level of consumption. The energy content in the wood used, estimated at 0.65 g/cm^3 of carbohydrate equivalent is about 4×10^6 cal/yr for each U.S. inhabitant, a large fraction of that utilized for food. If the energy in the wasted roots, branches, and leaves is included, the total is undoubtedly more than that used for food.

Of course the basic limitation on renewable resources is the photosynthetic process. Man tries to convert solar energy into various plant and animal products. Unfortunately, he is not yet able to attain high efficiency in the conversion. When irrigation water "makes the desert bloom," or when large-scale fertilizer applications remove natural limitations on plant food, man increases photosynthetic production. However, in many cases where agricultural crops are substituted for natural ecosystems, total photosynthesis is decreased because man keeps certain plants out of available ecological niches where they would utilize sunlight which is otherwise wasted. In addition, we take land out of production for cities and highways, vast areas of the earth have been made deserts by man's activities, and environmental pollution has drastically reduced plant growth in some areas. On balance, photosynthesis has been reduced by man.

Recent estimates of net photosynthetic production on land include about 10^{10} tons of carbon fixed/year (Lieth, 1963), 2.25×10^{10} tons (Wassick, 1968), and 2.2 to 3.2×10^{10} tons (Vallentyne, 1966). These figures correspond to between 2.5 and 10×10^{10} tons of dry plant material as carbohydrate. With a caloric value for such material of about 4 kcal/g, this is a total conversion of about 1 to 4×10^{17} kcal of solar energy into available plant energy. If all 3.5 billion inhabitants of the world utilized this energy for food and forest products at the same rate as U.S. citizens, from 10 to 40% of all material photosynthesized on land would be used for humans. When it is realized that most of the solar energy goes into roots, stalks, leaves, and other materials which are currently unusable by man, it is obvious that either the efficiency of photosynthesis will have to be greatly increased or some other energy source will have to be developed if the growing world population is to adopt U.S. patterns of using renewable resources.

Nonrenewable Resources

The picture is even bleaker in terms of present production and use of many nonrenewable resources (UN Statistical Yearbook, 1969). World production of energy in 1967 was equivalent to about 5.8 billion tons of coal, that of the United States was equivalent to almost 2 billion tons. Thus, fewer than 600 million people could have used energy at the rate we did. In theory, coal, oil, and gas can be considered renewable resources since they are derived ultimately from photosynthesis. If all the material currently photosynthesized on land were burned, it would provide energy at the U.S. rates of consumption for about one to four billion people (and, of course, there would be nothing left for food). Steel consumption of the world in 1967 was 443 million tons, in the United States, about 128 million. About 700 million could have used steel at this rate. Fertilizer use in the world was 44 million tons, in the United States, about 10 million. About 900 million people could have used fertilizer at our rate. Aluminum production was 7.5 million tons, U.S. production, almost 3 million. Thus, only 500 million people could have used aluminum at the rate we did. Practically all other mineral resources show similar ratios. The world's present industrial complex is sufficient to provide fewer than a billion people with the U.S. standard of affluence. Production of all these substances can be increased, but the increases will be slow because of the heavy capital investment required. In addition, of course, the increased production is accompanied by more rapid depletion of mineral reserves, and in many cases, by increased environmental pollution, certainly not a component of optimum conditions.

In all the areas treated, it appears that of the order of a billion people is the maximum population supportable by the present agricultural and industrial system (and the present work force) of the world at U.S. levels of affluence.

It would obviously be very difficult to produce food and raw materials at the present rate with the smaller work force consistent with a world population of about a billion people; therefore, this number is, if anything, too large to be self-supporting at U.S. affluence levels. As our technology, knowledge, and industrial and agricultural systems expand so can the optimum population, although it might be more desirable either to channel the increased production into an increased standard of living or to reduce the depletion rate of our nonrenewable resources rather than simply to produce more bodies. The differences between one billion people and the present world population is an indication of the magnitude of the problem caused by the population explosion.

References

F.A.O.: Third World Food Survey, Freedom from Hunger Campaign, Basic Study #1, 1963; *Mon. Bull. Agr. Econ. Statist.*, **17**: 1 (#5), 1968.

Landsberg, H. H., L. L. Fischman, and I. L. Fisher. 1963. *Resources in America's Future.* The Johns Hopkins Press, Baltimore, Md.

Leith, H. 1963. The role of vegetation in the carbon dioxide content of the atmosphere, *J. Geophys. Res.*, **68**: 3887-3898. (1.5×10^{10} tons C exchanged, with 30% lost on short time basis through respiration and direct exchange.)

Schmidt, W. R. 1965. The planetary food potential, *Ann. N.Y. Acad. Sci.*, **118**: 647-718.

United Nations Statistical Yearbook 1968. Statistical Office of the U.N., Department of Social & Economic Affairs, New York, 1969.

U.S. Dept. of Agriculture. 1968. *Agricultural Statistics.* Govt. Printing Office, Washington, D.C.

Vallentyne, J. R. 1966. New primary production and photosynthetic efficiency in the biosphere, p. 309. In: *Primary Productivity in Aquatic Environment*, C. R. Goldman (ed.), University of California Press.

Wassink, E. C. 1968. Light energy conversion in photosynthesis and growth of plants, p. 53-66. In: *Functioning of Terrestrial Ecosystems at the Primary Production Level*, F. E. Eckhardt (ed.), UNESCO.

Plants, People, and Politics

Arthur W. Galston

Many pressing social problems require the attention of botanists. These include the world's burgeoning population and our diminishing ability to feed it, the progressive degradation of man's natural environment, and the dilemma posed by our increasing dependence on chemical pesticides. The massive use of herbicidal chemicals in the Vietnam war has been largely ignored by botanists, but needs discussion in connection with proposals to ratify the Geneva Gas Protocol. (BioScience 20, no. 7, p. 405-410)

To anyone teaching at a university or college in the United States or anywhere in the western world, one of the key words of everyday conversation has come to be *relevance*. Students are questioning as never before the relevance of their studies to the real world outside the academy. While many of them recognize that important improvements in man's estate have stemmed from undirected, ivory-tower type pure research, they are also aware that many professors deliberately turn their backs on pressing social problems for which their expertise would be useful. They criticize modern academics as inheritors of a tradition which glorifies the impractical, demeans the applied, and excuses almost any kind of intellectual effort on the grounds that it may one day become important. Witnessing the huge gap between our advanced science technology and our imperfect social order, our students find it difficult to understand why we, who possess the knowledge that might contribute toward the solution of these pressing social problems, fail to volunteer our services. They wonder what it is that we find so all-encompassing in our laboratories that keeps us from the problems which are close at hand and which cry urgently for solution. In their inability to understand our apparent in-

difference, their voices grow more strident, their actions more violent. Their attitudes toward science change: science no longer promises the better life, but rather a harsher, depersonalized over-technologized existence, devoid of higher social values. They turn away from science, to other vocations.

Should we be concerned by a generation "turned off" by science? Are we not forging ahead technically, educationally, and scientifically as rapidly as we can afford to? Is our society not, in fact, the most prosperous in the history of man? Must we in any way respond to the cries of those who are disaffected with the present order? I suggest that to ignore the requests for dialogue from a large, or even a small, group of our student colleagues in educational adventure, is not only impolite, possibly arrogant, but also dangerous. For when discontent is not channeled into proper constructive pathways, violence and destruction frequently occur. So, I think we must delegate some of our best talent to grapple with the problems of society for which our expertise is relevant, and we must all be prepared to maintain long and searching dialogues with those who seek to change our institutions through democratic means. We must engage in a meaningful dialogue not only with this new generation of students but also with the society which supports our work. We must face our responsibilities, not only as the elders and teachers of students but also as citizens of our communities, of our country, and of the world.

What can one say to students who urge their professors to leave the quiet and solace of the research laboratory for the hurly-burly world of pressing practical problems and the debilitation which flows from confrontation and argumentation in the area of politics? In the first place, it must be clear that not all of us can easily shift from one role to the other, and so not all of us should be expected to. This, of course, may be construed by our critics as a convenient cloak behind which all of us can hide. But I would hope that in the large community of world botanists, sufficient practitioners of the various aspects of their science will step forward to assume socially responsible roles as to gain social acceptability for the entire field. Our critics must be made to understand that it is extremely important that we not leave our laboratories for the political and social battlefield. It has been said that a society that cares only about the present has no future. Some of those who remain in the laboratory conducting their apparently aimless researches, unrelated to the solution of any social problems, may, as we well know, be the most practical of all men. We need only recall the importance of Charles Darwin's researches on phototropism in the discovery of plant hormones and thus, indirectly, of herbicides. Had Darwin been in the employ of a chemical company that put him on the job of developing a new herbicide, he might never have come up with anything new at all. In the same way, B. O. Dodge, and later G. W. Beadle and E. L. Tatum, investigating the life cycle and inheritance

The author is a member of the department of biology, Yale University, New Haven, Conn.

This paper was the address of the retiring president of the Botanical Society of America, delivered at the International Botanical Congress, Seattle, Washington, 27 August 1969. It is scheduled for publication in the March 1970 newsletter of the Society, *Plant Science Bulletin*.

in the apparently useless red bread mold *Neurospora,* have probably contributed more to our knowledge of genetics, with its great potential for improving the lot of mankind, than platoons of some animal and plant breeders dedicated to the solution of practical problems. So, I think the first thing we need to tell our young friends who are challenging us to climb down out of the ivory tower into the cobblestone strewn streets is, "Fine, we will send you a delegation. But some will have to stay up here to keep the store running."

If we are going to send a delegation, clearly some criteria are required for the establishment of proper credentials for our representatives. In setting up these credentials, I think we shall discover paradoxically that we will want to call on the older, rather than the younger, members of the profession, and thus perhaps those who feel least sensitively attuned to the demands of the young proponents of change. Clearly, if our representatives are to retain their credentials with the scientific community, and be able to influence the outside world as well, they must have demonstrated competence in their field for some extended period. Since ventures into the sociopolitical arena are somewhat distracting from scientific work, it is to be expected that such men would be, in a sense, diminishing their scientific productivity. Since, also, they will be venturing into areas in which opinions are frequently not decisive, and where opinions may impinge on political prejudices, it might be well for them to enjoy the security which academic tenure affords. All this says that our representatives should probably be mature, respected, scientifically productive, and stably placed members of our profession.

What are some of the major and pressing problems for which the skills of the botanist are relevant tools? Certainly, if the botanist can make any one special claim, it is that he understands the plant. Since "all flesh is as grass," it is at once clear that the ability of this earth to sustain human life stands in direct relation to grow sufficient plants, especially food crops, to satisfy the requirements of man. Heretofore, this has not been much of a worldwide problem. While it is true that in the preagricultural era man's ability to increase his numbers was probably limited by his food supply, ever since the industrial revolution food has not been limiting to man's increase in numbers, at least not on a world scale.

Man is now reproducing at an absolutely catastrophic rate. There are now about three and a half billion humans on earth, increasing at about 1.8% per annum, with a doubling time of about 38 years. This means that by the year 2000 there will be almost 7 billion of us on this planet, and by that time we will probably be doubling our numbers every generation. How long can this go on? Guesses have been made and can continue to be made. There are, of course, some ridiculous outer limits. If we go on at this rate for about another 3000 years, then there will be about 10^{23} people on earth. Since this approximates Avogadro's number, we might say that at that time the earth will have become one molar with respect to people. If we allow 100 lb./person in such a crowded world, then the total weight of mankind on earth would exceed 10^{25} pounds, or just about the weight of the earth. At this point, all of the lithosphere, hydrosphere, and atmosphere would have been converted into one representative of the biosphere, and the earth would have become a true monoculture!

What are the real limits to the human population on earth? Let us note first that with our present population of 3.5 billion people, and with technology intruding into agriculture in most parts of the world, we are still chronically short of food, even if one assumes adequate means of distribution from areas of surplus to areas of hunger. Even if we were able to double total world food production, our progress would be annulled in 38 years in the next round of world population doubling. Let us remember that doubling agricultural productivity is no easy task. It takes not only the work of the plant breeder to produce new high-yielding genotypes, the plant pathologist to help us ward off diseases and predators, the agronomist to help us plan productivity rationally, the physiologist to develop new growth regulatory compounds and regimes, and the agricultural engineer to devise the apparatus required for rationalized production, but it requires the raw materials as well. Plants cannot grow without such elemental requirements as nitrogen, phosphate, and potassium, and as we go to more and more submarginal lands for a greater productivity, successively higher and higher quantities of these materials are required. But, as we do that, we must also remember that we have by now exhausted the highest grades and easily available supplies of such materials as phosphate rocks. It now becomes necessary to go to second- and third-rate sources which require more and more energy and technology before they are fit for agricultural use. Thus, while I think it is realistic for us to say that we can certainly do much to improve overall productivity on the earth's surface, there are limits to what we can perform, limits imposed by the earth's resources. We foresee in the not too distant future, certainly within another century, the moment of truth after which our efforts will perhaps be to no further avail. Any rational program for linking food supply to expanding population must necessarily deal with problems of population regulation as well.

As botanists, we can claim no special competence in human population dynamics, but because we can say authoritative things about the earth's capacity to produce foodstuffs to support mankind, what we say about population also has some relevance. I think we need to say clearly and in unmistakable terms that the earth's capacity to support mankind is not unlimited, that it is up to man to decide what kind of world he wants and then to so regulate the number of individuals permitted to come into that world that the kind of society which is considered most desirable can be brought about through the best workings of man's mind and hands. Our failure to take such a step will not prevent a decision from being made, but rather than being made rationally it will be imposed by the four horsemen of the apocalypse: hunger, disease, starvation, and possibly war.

It is alleged by some prognosticators that because it is so much less efficient to produce animal foods such as beefsteak and eggs than plant foods, it may be necessary for us in the crowded world of the future to be largely vegetarian. This is a prospect which few of us can face with equanimity, and I would like to ask us to consider whether there may not be other alternatives. For example, large acreages are now devoted to crops which are either not necessary, not beneficial to mankind, or easily supplantable by substitutes. One such crop is tobacco, whose high cash value causes it to be grown over many thousands of valuable acres in our own country as well as other parts of the world. Let us leave aside for a moment the question of the harmful effects of tobacco on health, which by now have been firmly established. Can we in all good conscience, in a crowded world hungering for more food, permit the use of many acres of potential food crop land for the production of a crop which yields absolutely no food value? In the years ahead, we may need to make a decision on such questions. Botanists might therefore be well advised to consider possible substitute crops for the areas which might be displaced from tobacco production, either because of its menace to public health or because it has become a luxury which man feels he cannot afford. Other crops with marginal food value for man, such as celery and lettuce, might have to go. Also rubber and fiber-producing plants may become marginal as synthetic substitutes become cheaper and better.

Not only must botanists be aware of the inefficient allocation of land for the production of the greatest quantity of food for the greatest number of hungry people but they must also sense and be prepared to correct our inadequate planning for catastrophes which could strike us in the future. Histories of agriculture tell us that modern Western man has failed to introduce a single important new food crop (Carrier, 1923). Almost all of our staple cereals, vegetables, fiber plants, spices, and beverage plants are heritages from the native peoples whose lands were conquered by the invading Westerners. It is true that in the hands of modern Western man, the rather primitively cultivated, poorly yielding original genotypes have been much improved into the highly efficient photosynthetic machines of the present day. Yet, we must all be aware of the fact that our dependence on restricted genotypes of the major food plants of the world could contribute to a catastrophe of astounding proportions. What, for example, if a new pathogen should arise for our highest producing strains of corn, or rice, or wheat? Would we have the resources to dip into new genotypes for the production of reasonably high-yielding strains resistant to the new predator? In a world sensibly geared to meet the needs of people everywhere, much more extensive international genotype banks of the world's most important crops should be maintained and fostered for diversity and hardiness to all known pathogens.

Some such efforts are now conducted in various parts of the world by separate national, state, and local governments as well as by universities, research institutes, and private breeders. I believe that some organization such as the International Union of Biological Sciences should take official cognizance of this problem, and that an international body of scholars should plan and maintain such an ongoing effort.

Another area of public responsibility to which the botanist, among others, owes some responsibility, is, of course, the preservation of the environment in which we all live. Of the immediate necessity for purifying the air we breathe and the water we drink, I will say little, since this topic has been well popularized in recent years and is beginning to receive official governmental attention. I would suggest, however, that we might lend ourselves to a revolutionary rededication to the ideal of a healthy, clean, and beautiful environment in many small ways that do not require national campaigns for implementation. The concept of the world outside one's house and automobile as a huge garbage pail available for deposition of all of one's waste must be altered. It is estimated that each day, each American produces 5 pounds of garbage, a total for the United States alone of one billion pounds per day. To preserve the spaceship Earth as a fit environment for life, we must become dedicated to orderly and complete disposal of these wastes, and to recycle many of them, through new technology, back into production.

One particularly insidious aspect of pollution of the environment is that which flows from man's desire to rationalize agricultural productivity by the use of ever-increasing quantities of chemicals which are dumped, sprayed, or dusted onto land and plants. We have become so dependent upon such chemicals for our continued high level of agricultural productivity that to advocate a return to the hoe or tractor as the sole means of controlling weeds and other pests would be folly. But we should be aware that just as chlorinated hydrocarbons like DDT, dieldrin, and aldrin are now regarded as public menaces because of their persistence in the biosphere and their potential poisoning of various kinds of creatures, so may some of our present highly regarded herbicides and plant growth

regulators come to seem less desirable. Research in this important area must continue. New products must be constantly developed, and they must be adequately tested as to agricultural effectiveness, ready biodegradability, lack of ecological side effects, low persistence in harvested foods, and nontoxicity of the quantities which do persist. Our current herbicidal chemicals may be likened to rather crude buckshot blasts; what we need are more precise weapons with a much more restricted range of damage.

One example of a highly successful, fairly specific, nontoxic, and easily biodegradable herbicide is, of course, 2, 4-D (2, 4-dichlorophenoxyacetic acid). Under normal conditions of agriculture and under proper formulation, this herbicide may be applied at appropriate dose rates to achieve desired broad-spectrum selective herbicidal action. So far as we can now tell, this can be done without harmful side effects; the applied herbicide is completely degraded and largely converted, in fact, into microbial bodies, so that soil fertility is not disturbed.

Some of the other more recently introduced herbicides, while they have impressive toxicities and even desirable specificities under proper formulation, do not give one the same feeling of comfort concerning their lack of undesirable perpetuated effects. In fact, some of them may be potential herbicidal analogs of DDT. I suspect that one such compound is 4-amino, 3, 5, 6 trichloropicolinic acid, also referred to as picloram or Tordon. While this material certainly has impressive credentials as a herbicide, and can even be used to denude an area of conifers which are insensitive to the halogenated phenoxyacetic acids, its persistence in soils is so great as to constitute a source of worry. Under optimal conditions in some soils, 20% to 50% of applied Tordon disappeared after 467 days (Youngson et al., 1967). However, on other soils, poor in inorganic matter, low in moisture and aeration, only 3.3% of the applied material disappeared in a similar period. Repeated application of such a material to productive crop lands could lead to the buildup of a dangerous titer of herbicidally active material, which could diminish growth in desirable as well as weedy plants. In view of the fact that no microorganisms are now known which can degrade Tordon as a sole carbon source, and in view of the fact that between 10,000 and 100,000 parts of exogenous carbon are required to oxidize one part of Tordon (Tschirley, 1969), it would appear important that the further introduction of this herbicide into agriculture be delayed until the problem of its persistence in soils can be further clarified. Similarly, atrazine, which has performed so well as a selective herbicide in corn fields, is currently causing some worry, since it appears to have produced a diminution of yield in soybeans rotated onto the same soil in subsequent years.

Under certain circumstances, even 2, 4-D can become a menace. It has been reported that applications of 2,4-D can cause such a massive increase in the nitrate content of pasture plants as to sicken animals eating these plants (Stabler and Whitehead, 1950). The toxicity presumably has to do with the fact that nitrate is reduced to nitrite in the tissue of the animal, and it is the latter compound which causes the symptoms of malaise. The safe use of 2,4-D also depends on proper environmental conditions surrounding its application. For example, if much of the applied material is carried off into streams which find their way into quiet lakes, then 2,4-D may persist in the cool, relatively anaerobic environment of the bottom muds where the aerobic bacteria that degrade it cannot prosper. Whether such an accumulation could cause eventual alteration of the algal components of the lake is unknown. We do know that 2,4-D can affect the vigor of *Daphnia* and other lake animals which serve as food for fish (Crosby and Tucker, 1966). It is difficult to avoid the conclusion that no herbicide is without its dangers to the ecology, and must be used under carefully regulated conditions.

Some currently used pesticides are fabricated around heavy metals, such as lead and mercury, or around elements such as arsenic, which although relatively benign in one valence state (+5) may become very toxic if reduced (+3 valence state). The important difference between such pesticides and the completely organic ones is that there is no way to achieve complete detoxification after application. The metal remains, no matter to what form it is converted after metabolism by plant, soil, or animal. Once deposited in the biosphere, it may persist for longer than we would like to admit. We should note, in this connection, the growing concern in public health circles over the rising quantities of lead and mercury in the environment surrounding man.

What I propose to discuss in closing involves a somewhat more difficult problem. It is the deliberate application of botanical knowledge for destructive, rather than constructive, ends; for the production of barren areas, devoid of vegetation, rather than rich, green rolling fields; for the destruction of food crops, rather than their enhanced growth; for the desecration of a natural environment, rather than its preservation. This misapplication of botany for destructive ends is a relatively new phenomenon. Not so long ago, to be a botanist was to be assured of being included in the ranks of those whose works could only benefit mankind. The botanist worked for the discovery of new plant resources useful to man. He selected the most desirable varieties of such materials and by careful breeding brought them into commercial production. He studied their growth, rationalized their agriculture, devised useful chemicals to control their growth and to ward off predators. All these activities could only improve man's estate. With knowledge, however, comes power, and with power comes the ability to control events in destructive as well as constructive ways. Society must continually be on its guard against the misapplication of science. For our normal peace-time activities, we have many safeguards built into the legal structure to protect us against the wrongdoer. In war, when there is a breakdown in the fabric of law, harmful practices which have been banned may suddenly emerge to be used against the enemy as a potent weapon of war. It is unfortunate, I believe, that herbicides which have done so much to improve man's productivity have recently been used in a massive way to create ecological havoc.

In the years since 1962, we have dumped more than 100 million pounds of herbicides into Vietnam to defoliate the jungles; to prevent ambush along roads, trails, waterways; to prevent infiltration by the Vietcong and their allies; and to deprive outlying communities of the food which they derive from cultivated rice patches. The chemicals used in this operation have been largely herbicides which are in use all over the Western world in peacetime agriculture. These include 2,4-D and its relative, 2,4,5-T, picloram, about which we have spoken earlier, and the arsenical cacodylic acid, which has been used exclusively to kill rice, elephant grass, and other materials largely insensitive to the halogenated phenoxyacetic acids. The use of these materials has conferred upon the United States forces certain military advantages. The removal of dense cover from around encampments and along roads and rivers has certainly spared American lives. As such, it must be adjudged a successful military weapon. Yet some aspects of our use of herbicidal chemicals as instruments of war in Vietnam have been unwise, and could react in the future to the disadvantage of the United States.

Many militarily useful weapons are not employed in warfare either because of the sense of abhorrence that their use produces or because of fear that retaliation in kind might do the initial user more harm than good. Thus, for example, we have not used even small tactical nuclear weapons in Vietnam because of the suspicion that the introduction of this new quantum jump in destructiveness would bring us that much closer to a possible confrontation with other nuclear powers, such as the Soviet Union. Like nuclear weapons, chemical and biological weapons have seen scattered use in warfare. Biological weapons are said to have been used by Lord Jeffrey Amherst who, in the French and Indian wars, distributed among the Indians blankets which had been previously used for smallpox patients (Dept. of Army, 1964). The resulting smallpox epidemic is said to have been severe and of military advantage to the British. But that was more than 200 years ago, and there are happily no authenticated reports of the use of biological weapons since them. Chemical weapons have seen greater use. In World War I, chlorine, phosgene, and mustard gas took more than a hundred thousand lives and maimed many others. In the Yemen, poison gas was apparently used by the Egyptians on behalf of their allies, the Yemeni Republicans, against the Yemeni Royalists as recently as 1963 (Salvia, 1967). In Vietnam, in addition to the chemical warfare against plants, we have used more than 14 million pounds of so-called riot control gases, especially CS (ortho chlorobenzalmalononitrile) against personnel (Congr. Record, 1969). The

Geneva Protocol of 1925, which was drafted by the United States, signed by the United States, but never ratified by the U.S. Senate, prohibits the use in warfare "of asphyxiating, poisonous or other gases, and all analogous liquids, materials or devices." While we never became party to the Geneva Protocol of 1925, President Roosevelt, in a statement dated 12 June 1943, stated categorically that "We shall under no circumstances resort to the use of such weapons unless they are first used by our enemies." On 5 December 1966, the General Assembly of the United Nations adopted a resolution calling for strict observance by all states of the principles and objectives of the Protocol signed in Geneva in 1925. While resolutions of the General Assembly are normally not binding as such on member states, they do provide clear evidence of the state of the law. This UN resolution was passed unanimously, with only three abstentions, from Cuba, France, and Gabon. Thus, the United Nations resolution of 1966, to which we are a party, declares that the Geneva Protocol today constitutes a general international law, and is no longer a mere contract for the actual parties to it. It extends both to chemical and bacteriological warfare. The question then arises whether, in the eyes of the world, the United States, by its use of chemical weapons in Vietnam, has contravened these limitations. Our United Nations Ambassador Nabrit specifically stated his views to the contrary as follows (1969):

> The Geneva Protocol of 1925 prohibits the use in war of asphyxiating and poisonous gas and other similar gases and liquids with equally deadly effects. It was framed to meet the horrors of poison-gas warfare in the First World War and was intended to reduce suffering by prohibiting the use of poisonous gases such as mustard gas and phosgene. It does not apply to all gases. It would be unreasonable to contend that any rule of international law prohibits the use in combat against an enemy, for humanitarian purposes, of agents that Governments around the world commonly use to control riots by their own people. Similarly, the protocol does not apply to herbicides, which involve the same chemicals and have the same effects as those used domestically in the United States, and the Soviet Union and many other countries to control weeds and other unwanted vegetation.

Professor Ian Brownlie of Wadham College, Oxford University, states (Brownlie, 1969) "Practices which must result in depriving peasant communities permanently of their food resources constitute a crime against humanity, and if persisted in, when large scale distress is manifest, would amount to genocide. Large-scale destruction of the fertility of the countryside is an operation which is probably more strikingly indiscriminate as between combatants and noncombatants than any technique other than resort to nuclear weapons. . . . Large scale crop destruction must fall foul of these rules, especially when it is carried out from the air."

The U.S. Field manual (USFM 27.10.-1949, paragraph 24, and 1956, paragraphs 40 and 41) is very precise on this point. It states that destruction of food crops and food supplies is prohibited unless it can be shown that these are for the use of enemy combatant personnel. The United States has said repeatedly that intended victims of its food destruction campaign are male, combatant personnel in isolation from the community, and that civilians are warned in advance, and told where to go. According to Donald Hornig, President Johnson's Science Advisor, the real purpose of the anticrop program was directed at moving the population out of the NLF-controlled areas into those controlled by the Saigon regime. If this is true, and it appears to be borne out by a survey of defoliated areas, it puts quite a different perspective on the entire operation. Crop destruction has been most marked not in the sparsely occupied areas where the effect would be largely confined to the NFL guerrillas but in the densely populated fertile Mekong delta, the rice bowl of Southeast Asia (see Brownlie, 1969).

What, in fact, are the ecological consequences of the widespread massive application of herbicides? With respect to Vietnam, it should be noticed that in 1968 approximately a million and a half acres of forested land and a quarter of a million acres of crop land were sprayed with an average of about 3 gal/acre (or ca 27 lb./acre) of chemical. This means that almost 50 million pounds of assorted herbicides were dumped on the countryside in that one year. Most of this was in the form of the phenoxyacetic acids; some was in the form of picloram; some, probably about three-quarters of a million pounds, in the form of cacodylic acid.

It is frequently alleged that a single spray with a defoliating chemical, such as 2,4-D or 2,4,5-T, produces no permanent damage to a forested area. This, it seems to me, is a pious hope in view of the paucity of hard data available; recent observations on mangrove associations indicate extensive kill after one spray (Tschirley, 1969; Brownlie, 1969). Certainly no experiments have been done previously in Vietnam with its particular collection of plants, soil, and climate, and often-cited studies done in the Philippines and in Puerto Rico are relevant but not exactly transferable (USDA, 1968). Defoliation, at the very least, promotes the growth of understory vegetation such as bamboo, which may then gain a competitive advantage. It may also temporarily deprive soil microflora of photosynthate, which comes to it in the form of organic matter excreted through the roots. This deficient microbial action may not be serious but if extended by repeated defoliation operations may lead to significant loss of productivity and may also result in soil erosion. Permanent denudation of an area by repeated spraying can, of course, lead to more serious consequences, such as the complete transformation of the forest to a bamboo thicket, and possible laterization of lateritic soils. It is estimated in a UNESCO report that more than half of the soils of Vietnam are laterizable (Maignien, 1966). Although it is widely supposed that 2,4-D and 2,4,5-T are nontoxic[1] they may be washed into the anaerobic rice paddy bottoms and may there do harm to vegetation, crustaceans, and possibly fish which are raised as a by-product.

With regard to cacodylic acid, whose lethal dose in mice is one gram per kilogram of weight, it can only be said that transformation of this material to the more toxic methylarsonic acid, or to some trivalent form of arsenic, is not excluded in the cycle of nature, and the indiscriminate dumping of large quantities of this material over the Vietnamese countryside is in no way to be considered a beneficial exercise. When one adds to this the dan-

---

[1] Both compounds, but especially 2,4,5-T, are now suspected of being teratogenic in mice and rats (Report of the Secretary's Commission on Pesticides and their Relationship to Environmental Health, Parts I and II, U.S. DHEW, 1969, Chap. 8). The toxicity may possibly be due to an impurity of the dioxin type (FDA fact sheet on 2,4,5-T, 1970). The entire situation is well reviewed in "Chemical-Biological Warfare: U.S. Policies and International Effects" - Hearings before the Subcommittee on National Security Policy and Scientific Developments of the Committee on Foreign Affairs, House of Representatives, November-December 1969.

gers of the opening of the Pandora's box of CBW, and the possible indiscriminate damage done to children, pregnant and lactating women, and the aged and the infirm of the civilian population by our food deprivation program, then I think the picture is one with which most Americans will not feel particularly happy.

All American citizens, and scientists and botanists in particular, need to concern themselves with a practice that, in the eyes of some, is outside accepted international law. One constructive move, at the present time, would be to aid and support a House Joint Resolution No. 691, proposed by Representatives Edward Koch and Richard D. McCarthy of New York State, which calls for the setting up of an International Commission for investigation of the ecological damage caused by the widespread use of herbicides in Vietnam. The same two Congressmen (House Joint Resolution 457) are also proposing that we ratify the Geneva Protocol of 1925. Even at this late date, such a move would be in the public interest, and in the waning days of the Vietnam war, might actually spur our disengagement from that area and promote other arms control measures which we are currently negotiating with the Russians.

In closing, let me make the following suggestions. I believe in the collective wisdom of the people of a democracy to decide important matters concerning their own fate. The American public has been deprived, by the Department of Defense, of information concerning our CBW operations in Vietnam. Only muckraking and reportorial snooping activities have caused them to come to light recently. We should demand that the books on CBW be opened as completely as is consonant with the national security. We should learn where the annual CBW allocation of one-third of a billion dollars goes. We should learn how, out of this figure, $71 million in herbicidal chemicals were used. We should have clear statements on the responsibility for the death of the thousands of sheep in Dugway, the stockpiling of nerve gases overseas, and the disposition of overaged chemical munitions. We should have clear discussions of the desirability of the continued production of nerve gases, botulinus toxin, and other CBW weapons.

President Nixon has moved encouragingly in the last months by announcing a high-level review of all CBW operations (Semple, 1969). The United Nations has recently released a report pointing out the need for a ban on all such weapons (NYT, 1969), and Great Britain has recommended a total ban on the manufacture and use of biological weapons (*New Haven Register*, 1969). A Senate committee has recently seen fit to delete from the budget all funds for offensive CBW weapons (Finney, 1969). The move to ratify the Geneva Protocol is being pushed in some administration quarters. I believe that we botanists, as citizens of our country, and citizens of the world, must get ourselves involved with these important questions. Discussion of these matters at annual meetings, at business meetings, and at International Conventions is entirely essential as a prelude to individual action. To do less is to fail in our responsibility as socially concerned scientists and citizens.

References

Brownlie, I. 1969. Legal Aspects. In: *CBW,* Steven Rose (ed.), Beacon Press, Boston, Mass.

Carrier, L. 1923. *The Beginnings of Agriculture in America.* McGraw-Hill Book Co., New York.

Chemical and Biological Weapons: Some possible approaches for lessening the threat and danger. Prepared for the Special Subcommittee on the National Science Foundation of the Committee on Labor and Public Welfare of the U.S. Senate, May 1969.

Congressional Record, H4775, 12 June 1969.

Crosby, D. G., and K. R. Tucker. 1966. Toxicity of aquatic herbicides to *Daphnia magna. Science,* **154:** 289-290.

Department of the Army. 1964. *Military Biology and Biological Agents.* Technical Manual No. 3-216, March.

Finney, John W. Pentagon denied funds to develop gas-germ agents. *New York Times,* 4 July 1969.

Maignien, R. 1966. *Review of Research on Laterites.* UNESCO Natural Resources Research IV.

New Haven Register, 10 July 1969.

New York Times, 3 July 1969.

Pfeiffer, E. W., and G. H. Orians. 1969. Mission to Vietnam. *Sci. Res. Part I,* 9 June 1969, p. 22-30; *Part 2,* 23 June 1969, p. 26-30.

Salvia, J. 1967. Gas in Yemen. *Sci. Citizen,* **9** (7): 149-152.

Semple, Robert B. Nixon orders study of policy on germs and gas in warfare. *New York Times,* 18 June 1969.

Stabler, L. M., and E. I. Whitehead. 1950. The effect of 2,4-D on potassium nitrate levels in leaves of sugar beets. *Science,* **112:** 749-751. (*See also* Berg & McElroy. 1963. *Can. J. Agr. Sci.,* **33:** 354. Freiberg Clark. 1952. *Bot. Gaz.,* **113:** 322. Frank & Grisby. 1957. *Weeds,* **5:** 206-217.)

Tschirley, F. H. 1969. Defoliation in Vietnam. *Science,* **163:** 779-786.

U.S. Dept. of Agriculture. 1968. Response of tropical and subtropical woody plants to chemical treatments. Research Report CR-13-67.

Youngson, C. R. et al. 1967. Factors influencing the decomposition of Tordon herbicide in soils. In: *Down to Earth* (published by the Dow Chemical Co.) **23** (2): 3-11.

Federal Action for Population Policy—
What More Can We Do Now?

Robert W. Lamson

The Federal Government commands many resources to do more now through research and planning and operational programs to implement the goal of zero population growth which Dr. Lee DuBridge, the President's Science Advisor, has given top priority. Failure to use these resources promptly and effectively increases the likelihood that we will limit our population through some combination of manipulation, repression, war, famine, and disease, instead of through voluntary limitation. (BioScience 20, no. 15, p. 854-857)

A critical problem and a question confront us. The United States and World Population will not increase forever. There are limits. How will they be imposed?

We have roughly three options.[1]

1) *Physical limits—war, famine, and disease:* to approach more closely the physical capacity of the earth, and thereby, to bring into play the traditional agents—war, famine, and disease—which have helped to limit growth of populations in the past.

2) *Repression:* to risk, by delaying action now, the use later of more manipulative and repressive social and political techniques, which some individuals now advocate and governments may come to

The author is a Staff Associate in the Office of Planning and Policy Studies, National Science Foundation, Washington, D.C. 20550.

This article represents only the views of the author and not those of the National Science Foundation.

[1]Provision of means to limit births and family size include abortion, sterilization, pills, chemicals, various types of contraceptives, rhythm, abstinence, and delayed marriage.

Methods for motivating people to limit family size include clinics, information, and propaganda, removal of incentives for having additional children beyond a given number through the tax and social security system, raising the legal age for marriage, provision of careers for women which will serve as viable alternative means to the self-fulfillment now attained through having and raising children.

Manipulative and repressive techniques include putting contraceptive chemicals in food and water supplies; greatly increasing the legal age for marriage and government licensing of the right to bear children with harsh penalties for violation; compulsory sterilization, abortion, and contraceptive inoculation or immunization against fertility via implantation of fertility-reducing drugs and chemicals; and infanticide.

For a Malthusian anti-utopia, see Anthony Burgess. 1962. *The Wanting Seed.* W. W. Norton & Company, Inc., New York.

use, in order to avoid the "traditional" physical limiting agents.

3) *Voluntary limitation:* to control our size and growth, voluntarily, by increasing human awareness and individual decision to regulate family and population size. This option is based on widespread provision of the means to limit births as well as on democratic creation of policies to influence the intent of individuals to use these means.

Current concern over the environment has led to increased discussion of the need to control population size, primarily via the third option.

Consider for example, the following statements which reflect the concern of the Executive Branch as well as the Congress of the United States:

Dr. Roger Egeberg, Assistant Secretary for Health and Scientific Affairs, the Department of Health, Education and Welfare: "What does freedom of choice in family planning imply in the present state of our society? It implies enormous population growth for the simple reason that the typical American family, if it can, will elect to have three children, not two. . . . I think we are going to have to work for a change in national mores, a change based on the public acceptance of the demographic facts of life. I think we are going to have to help the people of this country understand that their vital interest and that of their children demands that we control the growth of population."

Secretary Robert H. Finch, Department of Health, Education and Welfare,

when asked at a meeting in Washington, D.C., what young people can do to protect the environment, replied: "I'd begin by saying, have only two children."

The House Committee on Government Operations: "We fully agree that one of the most serious challenges in the last third of this century will be the growth of population and that our response to that challenge will be determined by what we do today."

The House Republican Task Force on Earth Resources and Population: "The overriding concern of the Task Force is for realization that the time for action is now and that the need is urgent."

Dr. Lee DuBridge, Science Advisor to the President: "Do we need more people on the earth?" We all know the answer to that is 'no.' Do we have to have more people? Also 'no.' . . .

"Our spaceship called the Earth is reaching its capacity. Can we not invent a way to reduce our population growth rate to zero? Of ensuring that there be no more births than deaths?

"That is the first great challenge of our time. And we are the first generation to come face to face with this challenge and recognize it. Will we do something about it? Every human institution, school, university, church, family, government—and international agencies, such as UNESCO—should set this as its prime task."

If the nation and the U.S. government are serious about the importance of the population problem and about zero popu-

74

lation growth, which the President's Science Advisor stated as a desirable goal for national policy, then we must ask ourselves several questions, and begin to implement the answers.

What can we do now, with existing resources, to carry out this goal through voluntary limitation.

In the future, what measures can we take for which we will need additional funds, personnel, equipment, facilities, authority, and new organizational arrangements?

The federal government can, immediately, with existing authority and resources, take many actions in the areas of research, planning, and operations to cope with our critical domestic population problem—the additional 100 million projected for the year 2000, if current trends continue.

Research

On 1 July 1969, an interagency Ad Hoc Group on Population Research made a report, "The Federal Program in Population Research," to the Federal Council for Science and Technology.

The Group recommended that the government create an interagency Standing Committee on Population Research to review and evaluate federal population research activities; to advise on gaps, priorities, and uses, as well as appropriate ways to support and administer research; to review efforts to collect, store, and disseminate information; to review federal mechanisms to identify research underway and further research needed in the future; and to identify organizations involved in research.

The federal government, particularly the new Commission on Population Growth and the American Future, now has an opportunity to help implement these actions. In addition, much research remains to be done.

Population Growth Rates and National Goals: For example, we need to analyze the effects of alternate trends in population growth and distribution on the success and cost of federal programs as well as on the capacity of the United States to protect and enhance its values and to meet its goals.

There are many goals and programs affected by population growth as well as agencies which should, therefore, have an interest in this research. Too large a pop-

ulation and too rapid growth make it more difficult for us to achieve these goals. Consider the various agencies with responsibilities for meeting the need to:

—protect and enhance the environment, and meet increasing demands for resources and services (Departments of Agriculture; Health, Education and Welfare; Housing and Urban Development; Transportation; and Interior; Smithsonian Institution; Water Resources Council; National Water Commission; Corps of Engineers)

—provide energy (Atomic Energy Commission; Federal Power Commission; Department of the Interior)

—supply housing and other urban functions (Department of Housing and Urban Development)

—provide transportation (Department of Transportation)

—solve manpower and unemployment problems (Department of Labor)

—solve problems of trade, industrial production, economic growth, location of population and industry, and examine and cope with the effects of population stability on the economy (Council of Economic Advisors; Departments of Commerce and Labor)

—provide for education, health, and welfare services (Department of Health, Education and Welfare)

These agencies could introduce their analysis of the impact of population trends into their Annual Reports, public information materials, and reports on proposed legislation.

Environment and Population Policies: Based on its survey of ongoing population research supported by federal agencies as of 30 April 1969, the Ad Hoc Group on Population Research found that, of a total of some $55 million spent for population research, about $20,000 or 0.04% of it concerned the environment, and about $153,000 or 0.3% concerned population policy and its implementation.

Even allowing for some error in reporting, there does seem to be a need for more research emphasis in such areas as the implementation of alternate population growth rates and policies for the achievement of environmental quality values, goals, and programs. In this regard, population study centers could be encouraged to examine the environmental policy aspects of population growth and distribution; and, environment and

resource study centers could be encouraged to analyze the relation between population trends and environmental problems. Federal activities with an interest in such research include: the Council and Cabinet Committee on Environmental Quality; the Departments of Interior; Agriculture; Commerce; and Health, Education and Welfare; The Atomic Energy Commission; and The Federal Power Commission.

Incentives: In addition to creating, through biomedical research, more efficient means to limit births, we also need more analysis of incentives to use these means and to limit family size. The physical and social environment can be designed to restructure incentives for having children, for example, through housing and community arrangements, and by creating alternate careers for women which provide opportunities, in addition to having and raising children, through which women can find personal self-fulfillment. The Council on Urban Affairs; the Departments of Housing and Urban Development; Labor; and Health, Education and Welfare, all have interests and responsibilities in this area. In addition, the tax and social security system as well as federal and state laws can accelerate or retard population growth and influence population distribution. There are opportunities here for the Departments of Justice; Commerce; Health, Education and Welfare; Treasury; and Internal Revenue Service; and the Council on Environmental Quality.

Zero Population Growth: Finally, we need more research on the problem of stabilizing U.S. (and world) population at various levels—less than its present size, or double its present size, or greater by a factor of 2.5, 3, or 4. The critical research questions are: What are the requirements for, and effects of, achieving a stable population, at what level, at what rate, and when—in 40, 60, 76, 100, or 200 years?

Planning and Operations

We can take, immediately, many practical steps to plan and implement policies for zero population growth, and to translate the results of research into action. Consider the following opportunities.

Planning: In our plans to support science, we can aim directly at developing the manpower, institutions, and medical and social technology necessary to

Framework for Analyzing Federal Actions for Population Policy—
to Influence Capacity and Intent to Limit Births

Research[a]	Planning	Operations	Goals	Options
Reproductive Biology	Plan to control population growth as well as to meet the needs (for resources and services) generated by population growth	Public Information	Zero Population Growth via	Voluntary Limitation
Fertility Regulation Techniques and Materials		Annual Reports		
Description of Population Size, Distribution, Characteristics and Trends		Reports on Legislation		Manipulation and Repression
Determinants of Population Size, Distribution, Characteristics and Trends	Contingency planning for a range of Alternative Demographic Futures	Family Planning Programs - Clinics		War, Famine and Disease
		Programs with States and Cities		
Consequences of Population Size, Distribution, Characteristics and Trends	Use of Planning, Programming and Budgeting System	Possible Futures; Use of Tax and Social Security		
Research on Operational Aspects of Population Problems		Careers for Women		
Programs to Support Institutions Which Perform Research on Population		Urban Design		

[a]This list of research categories is taken from the report by the Ad Hoc Group on Population Research.

achieve zero population growth. The Office of Science and Technology, the Department of Health, Education and Welfare, and the National Science Foundation have important responsibilities and opportunities in this area.

We can include considerations of population growth, distribution and control in planning, programming, and budgeting studies conducted throughout the government. The Bureau of the Budget can make sure that all agencies plan for a range of alternative demographic futures, based on alternate patterns of population growth, distribution, and use of technology. For example, federal water resource planning should consider a range of contingencies based on the difference between high and low population projections for the nation as a whole as well as for specific river basins.

River Basin Commissions, Regional Commissions and States, in addition to attempting to meet demands for resources, could be encouraged to look at a range of population projections, and to consider the problem of limiting demands for resources by influencing population growth and distribution within a particular river basin or region. In addition to the Bureau of the Budget, agencies in a

position to encourage this activity include the Departments of Interior, Agriculture, and Commerce; the Corps of Engineers; Water Resources Council; and National Water Commission.

In commenting on proposed legislation, especially proposals which attempt to meet the demand for some resource or service, agencies of the Executive Branch can discuss the relation of the proposal to population growth, what difference it would make for the success of the legislation if the high or low population projection came true, and the limits to the proposal's ability to meet the demands which population growth creates. The Bureau of the Budget, in coordinating comments on legislation, has an opportunity to encourage agencies to include such considerations in their reports.

Public Information and Education: This activity is important in influencing people's intent to limit births. To some degree, public information can substitute for positive and negative incentives.

As we have seen, most agencies have interests and programs which are affected by population growth. They could, therefore, adapt their public information programs to convey to the public the interaction between: (1) alternate popu-

lation growth rates; (2) family size; and (3) the ability of the agency to continue to solve the problems which it is chartered to solve. Federal agencies can do much more to develop public awareness of the population problem through conferences and seminars, and by developing needed public information and media materials, T.V. programs, speechs, charts, graphs, posters, pamphlets, movies, and policy exhibits.

For example, the National Aeronautics and Space Administration, with the Departments of Interior; Health, Education and Welfare; and Agriculture could develop a series of posters on the theme "Spaceship Earth," the need to take proper care of it, and the relation of this theme to population growth, environmental quality, and average family size. The Department of Health, Education, and Welfare could develop teaching aids for use in acquainting students at various grade levels with the demographic facts of life, how to prevent conception, and what needs to be done to preserve and extend the quality of the environment.

The Post Office Department could (1) create a series of stamps concerning the relation between population growth, family planning, family size, and problems of resources, the environment, and society—air, water, and land pollution, transportation, food, housing, medical and welfare services, and education; (2) provide free distribution of information and publicity via pamphlets and posters; and (3) increase the opportunity for employment of housewives.

The Government Printing Office and the Department of Health, Education, and Welfare could create and maintain a special list of available government publications, charts, exhibits, posters, stamps, films, etc., on population and family planning.

All federal agencies could include in their Annual Reports information on the relation between trends in population growth and distribution, and the success or failure of their mission.

Federal agencies such as the Department of Health, Education, and Welfare and Office of Economic Opportunity which have family planning programs could, in addition to enabling families to control births, also attempt to influence their intent to do so, for example, through information concerning the relation between family size, population growth, and other social problems.

Finally, most federal agencies have programs with regions, states, and cities and could encourage them to consider alternatives for population growth and distribution in their planning, programs, and public information.

Conclusion

As this article demonstrates, the government currently commands many resources to do more *now,* through research, planning, and operational programs, to implement Dr. DuBridge's priority, no-growth goal for U.S. population.

However, we urgently need the wisdom, will, and decisions to put these many existing capacities to work—to increase quickly public discussion of the population problem and of the goals and means to cope with it, and to expand, among policy makers and the public, the awareness, concern, and understanding which, are necessary for effective action.

What do we do now, with the resources at hand, and with the time we have left, will help to determine how, at some future date, we will achieve the inevitable limits to the world and U.S. population growth.

Our lack of foresight and prompt action increases the likelihood that we will limit our population through some combination of manipulation, repression, war, famine, and disease. Thus, we will fail to protect and promote our values of economic well-being, environmental quality, democratic government, and individual freedom.

Bibliography

Ad Hoc Group on Population Research, "The Federal Program in Population Research, a Report to the Federal Council for Science and Technology," Office of Science and Technology, Executive Office of the President, 1 July 1969. See also Center for Population Research, National Institute of Child Health and Human Development, "Population Research: Scope of the Field and Programs of the Center for Population Research at the National Institute of Child Health and Human Development," April 1970.

Committee on Government Operations, U.S. House of Representatives. Report No. 91-738 to accompany H.R. 15165, To Establish a Commission on Population Growth and the American Future, 91st Congress, 1st Session, 1969, p. 3.

DuBridge, L. A. 1969. Speech before the 13th National Conference of the U.S. National Commission for UNESCO, San Francisco, California, 23 November 1969.

Egeberg, R. O. 1969. Speech, "Population Growth—The Challenge," Before the Annual Meeting of Planned Parenthood—World Population, Inc., New York, 30 October 1969.

Finch, R. Quoted in *U.S. News and World Report,* 2 March 1970, Vol. LXVIII, No. 9, p. 36.

Task Force on Earth Resources and Population, Republican Research Committee, U.S. House of Representatives. "Federal Government Family Planning Programs—Domestic and International," 22 December 1969, reprinted in the Congressional Record, 29 December 1969, 91st Congress, 1st session, 1969. p. E11018.

How Green is the Green Revolution?

William C. Paddock

Warnings were issued about 3 years ago of impending famine in the under-developed countries of Asia, Africa, and Latin America. None occurred, however, because of increased agricultural output termed "The Green Revolution," brought about by the introduction and rapidly spreading use of the so-called miracle grains—rice and wheat. In addition, unexpectedly favorable weather conditions improved yield per acre and increased use of fertilizer and irrigation also assisted greatly. However, despite these obvious gains, we cannot afford to become overly optimistic about man's ability to continue to feed himself adequately at the rate of population growth today. (BioScience 20, no. 16, p. 897-902)

Three years ago, any agricultural specialist worth his salt was warning of impending famine in the underdeveloped nations of Asia, Africa, and Latin America. The less developed world, it was said, was losing the capacity to feed itself. Disaster lay as close as the year 1975.[1]

Today the warnings are of a wholly different sort. The world has an overabundance of grain. Wheat stocks have reached the level of 60 million tons. If anything, the danger immediately ahead would seem to be oversupply and glut.

In three short years, a startling turn-around has apparently taken place in the agricultural output of several parts of the developing world. The Philippines report achieving self-sufficiency in rice for the first time in history this year. Malaysia and South Vietnam are predicting the same for 1971 and Indonesia for 1973. Pakistan says it will shortly be self-sufficient in all cereals, and India expressed a similar hope. Optimism, clearly, rides tall in the saddle this year.

The increases are laid to a "Green Revolution" which is based on the introduction and the rapidly spreading use of so-called "miracle grains" in the rice paddies and wheat stands of South Asia. These are new, high-yielding varieties of wheat researched in Mexico by the Rocke-

feller Foundation and rice developed at the International Rice Research Institute in the Philippines, co-sponsored by the Rockefeller and Ford Foundations.

Among many agriculturalists, there is euphoria about man's potential for feeding himself for years and even centuries ahead of a kind that has not been seen since the introduction of the potato into Ireland. Reams of prose are being written and conferences held on the potential of the new seeds. The general theme is that now, at last, the chance exists to eradicate hunger from our planet.

At the risk of offending some good friends who are writing so hopefully, I say . . . no. The revolution is green only because it is being viewed through green-colored glasses. (Remember the Emerald City in the Wizard of Oz? It could be seen only when you put on a pair of green glasses.) Take off the glasses, and the revolution proves to be an illusion—but devastating in the damage it can do to mankind's tardy efforts to limit the world's horrendous population growth. For optimism about man's ability to feed himself as today's rate of population growth continues is precisely what we do not need and cannot afford in the race with the population bomb.

The Green Revolution, in short, could do us all in—if it worked. The cruel joke is that it does not work.

To many, the Green Revolution is a turning point in man's long war against the biological limitations of the earth. On examination, however, "skirmish" seems

a more accurate description. Because, win or lose this round, the final outcome of the war will not be altered.

Here is the "official" U.S. AID story of the Agricultural Revolution in South Asia:

> What has happened in less than three years is revealed in a few statistics . . . overall food production has risen 14 percent in the period 1967-69. And, in South Asia alone—the crucial countries of India and Pakistan—the increase has been 27 percent. AID worked with foundations, universities and others in developing new farming methods, including the most efficient use of "miracle" wheat and rice seeds that have brought about the Green Revolution. (Tollefson, 1970)

The statement is misleading for it places all the emphasis on new technology. Consider the following items.

Weather

1965 and 1966 were poor weather years for the farmer of South Asia, and the succeeding years have been good. A drought followed by rain will cause a spurt in production with or without new technology! In the last 3 years, India, for instance, has increased her production of barley, chickpeas, tea, jute, cotton, and tobacco by 20 to 30% and did so with no new high-yielding varieties.

Throughout Asia, agricultural yields on virtually all crops are up. Thus, rubber production in West Malaysia was 12% higher last year than the year before. Pakistan's peanut crop is double that of

Adapted from address given at the symposium, "Man: His Environment, His Future," at North Carolina State University at Raleigh, 25 February 1970.

[1]The writer (a Washington, D.C.-based consultant in tropical agricultural development) speaks with experience. His book *Famine—1975!* was published 3 years ago.

4 years earlier. Even Red China, which has only recently been reported to have the new high-yielding grains, has been able to perform agriculturally as well as India and the rest of Asia. This has been possible although fertilizer shipments to China have been interrupted (because of the closed Suez Canal and the civil disturbances of the Cultural Revolution).

Far and away the most important factor for increased production is the improvement in weather. But weather seldom gets the credit it deserves. When crops are *poor,* governments blame it on the weather. When crops are *good,* governments take the credit for the foresight and wisdom of providing fertilizer and loans to the farmer and for the clairvoyance of having conducted the research needed to develop improved crop varieties.

Thus, AID, when asking Congress for this year's money, said, "India's current successes in agriculture are largely due to a reappraisal of its agricultural strategy . . . with the help of the United States, the World Bank and other interested agencies and countries, India developed a new strategy which placed top priority on investment in agriculture. . . ."[2]

High-Yielding Varieties

Since the early 1950s, most of the developing world has been increasing its total agricultural production and yields per acre. This has been possible through greater use of fertilizer and irrigation, improved varieties, and the opening up of new agricultural land. The concern of most who study the problem is whether or not this increase can continue to keep pace with the growth in population.

Thus, India from 1951 to 1961 was able to increase agricultural production by 46%. This was done partially with new technology but primarily by putting new land into production. As new land became scarce, the increase tapered off. To simply maintain current per capita consumption levels, India must now increase cereal production by three million tons each year (Shertz, 1970). If the Green Revolution is to be a reality, production must now grow faster than it has in the past. Bernard Nossiter, whose book on

India will be published this fall, has looked at India's grain production figures from 1965 to 1970 and says that the increase "is something less than 2.5 percent. In other words, the 'revolution' has not yet increased food supply at the same rate as the growth in population" (Nossiter, 1970).

This does not mean that the new high-yielding wheats in India and Pakistan have not increased production spectacularly. Where irrigated and fertilized, crops have flourished. The same has been true in southeast Asia with rice. But while there is a promise of other crops on which to base a Green Revolution, to date there are only the two: wheat and rice.

The development of the new wheat and rice varieties having high fertilizer response without lodging resulted from imaginative research justifiably meriting recognition. However, the press agent's "miracle" and "wonder" appellation given these cereals distorted out of proportion their impact on the world.

In India, where one-third of Asia's population lives, *only* the new wheats have made an impact. This is unfortunate since in India wheat is a far less important crop than is rice (the production of which is three times that of wheat). Actually, according to a recent study by economic forecaster Louis Bean, the trend in increased rice yields which began in the early 1960s as a result of new technology has leveled off and stagnated at the 1964-65 level. Thus, the "miracle" rice has produced no miracle in India or in East Pakistan, the traditional rice-growing area of that country, although it has done extremely well in West Pakistan, an area not normally recognized as a major rice producer.

In discussing the new rice varieties for India, a recent U.S. Department of Agriculture report ended by saying: "For the immediate future, modest increases in yield from local (i.e., *not* the "miracle" rice) varieties through improved fertilizer use offer the most promise" (Haviland, 1969).

Bean calls it the "Brown and Green Revolution" to underscore its sporadic influence. In India, for instance, a third of the wheat land has been affected, but only 3% of the rice production has been touched, with the rest of the crops escaping its influence.

Irrigation

Irrigation is the life blood of the new cereals. For those who are accustomed to seeing wheat grown only in the United States, where no wheat is irrigated, this point needs to be underscored. Virtually all the new wheats in Mexico, India, Pakistan, and Turkey—the areas where they have made an impact—are grown under artificial irrigation. They are grown, then, on the very best land in the nation, the most expensive land, the land which receives the largest capital investment, and the land with the best farmers. In the United States, we consider wheat too low in value to put on irrigated land.

The new rice varieties also require carefully controlled irrigation. In the Philippines, where the new rice is grown under irrigation, harvests are reported as two to three times that of the traditional local varieties. However, on nonirrigated land, the new varieties do no better than the standard ones.

This is important to understand. Ford Foundation's Lowell S. Hardin says that if one looks at a map "the land where this new technology, this Green Revolution, applies is a postage stamp on the face of the earth" (Hardin, 1969). The major reason is that, unfortunately, there is very little irrigated land in this world. To expand the current Green Revolution, therefore, will require expanding the amount of irrigated land, an extremely expensive operation. Even with capital, the potential land for irrigation is limited by its location, slope, and availability of water.

The hungry nations have been and are hungry because they have a poor piece of real estate. The soils are too dry, too wet, too rocky, too thin, or too mountainous to fulfill adequately the agricultural needs of the country. A Green Revolution may minimize these disadvantages, but it can never do away with them.

Subsidies

Green Revolution advocates ignore the cost at which wheat and rice production has been achieved in some countries. To understand the role of subsidies, the Department of Agriculture's Director of Economics Don Paarlberg says:

> This is the inescapable fact that a price artificially held above the competitive level will stimulate production, retard consumption and create a surplus. This

---

[2]Agency for International Development Congressional Presentation, p. H-3, 29 May 1969.

will be true even if the commodity was originally in deficit supply. Thus a surplus is the result of deliberate intervention in the market. It is the product of human institutions, not simply a consequence of rapid, technological advance. It may or may not be accompanied by a scientific revolution. We could create a surplus of diamonds or uranium or of avocadoes or rutabagas simply by setting the price above where the market would have it and foregoing cost production control. A surplus is not so much a result of technology as it is a result of intervention in the market.[3]

The much-heralded Philippine rice self-sufficiency is a classic example of how Paarlberg's statement applies to the developing world. In 1966, the Philippine Rice and Corn Administration initiated a self-sufficiency program. Within a year, it increased the price support paid for rice by 50%. The support price of corn was also raised but to a lesser degree than rice. Rice production went up. Corn became cheaper to eat than rice, thus more people ate corn—result: a "surplus" of rice in the Philippines. With much fanfare, it was publicized that the Philippines were now able to export rice. Yet this was done at a *loss* because the world market price for rice was less than the government paid the Philippine farmer. In the words of James Keefer of the U.S. Department of Agriculture, the Philippines have "administered self-sufficiency" because they have artificially defined the level of consumption in the country. The nation's people could consume more rice, but the people cannot buy more at the price at which the government pays for it.

While many of the Green Revolution countries not only subsidize in part the price of fertilizer, pesticides, and irrigation water, *all* subsidize the production of the new cereals. Thus, Mexico supports her wheat at $1.99 a bushel or 33% above the world's market price for quality grain; Turkey, at 63%; India and Pakistan, at 100%. But since the quality of the grain from the new miracle cereals is low and they are sold at a discount, the subsidies are, in real terms, significantly higher. Currently, there is fear of a glut in world cereal markets, but the fear "is

largely attributable to expansion of production in the developed world" (Shertz, 1970) rather than to any Green Revolution in the hungry nations. The current glut is related to the support policies which all grain-producing nations follow (wheat supports range from $1.40 a bushel in the United States to $4.29 a bushel in Switzerland), policies which are often used as justification for similar subsidies in Asia, Africa, and Latin America. It should be obvious, however, that what a developed nation may do with ease an undeveloped nation might find nearly impossible to do.

The United States will subsidize her farmers with a sum approaching $4 billion this year, but this is in a nation where agriculture generates only 3% of the gross national product. India's agriculture accounts for 49% of her GNP; Pakistan's, for 47%; and the Philippines', for 33%. In these countries, there are not enough other sources of income to generate for long the money needed to subsidize the large agriculture segment of the economy.

It was interesting that the *very* day the House Foreign Affairs Subcommittee was holding its recent symposium on the Green Revolution and repeatedly pointing out to all the attendees the self-sufficiency achieved in rice production by the Philippines, the Philippine Government asked the United States for an advance of $100 million on its 1970 payments (due it for our use of military bases) in order to "stave off the emergency" arising from threatened bankruptcy.

Unfortunately, most of the developing world totters on the brink of bankruptcy with little hope of improving its situation. Within the next few years, the debt service of countries such as Indonesia, India, and Pakistan will equal nearly 50% of their export earnings.

Yet, the new varieties require irrigation water, fertilizer, and additional labor. All are expensive. For the farmer, this means financial risks. For him, risk is justified because of the support price. But, take that crutch away and fewer would take the risk.

With these high support prices, one of two things becomes obvious. Either the farmers are getting rich on the government subsidies or else the new technology

is much more costly to use. There are reports of land prices skyrocketing in the area of the Green Revolution, of incipient social revolution with formerly absent landlords returning to farm their land and evicting their tenants. All of this may be true, but to what extent?

My guess is that the best farmers on the best land are profiting substantially from the Green Revolution. But the report that "hundreds of millions of rural people" (Borlaug et al., 1969) are benefiting is open to question.

In 1969, during the wheat harvest, this writer visited Sonora, Mexico, to see the experiment station where the new wheats were developed.

While there, a delegation of wheat farmers from this area left for Mexico City to ask the government to raise still higher their wheat subsidy. This may have been simply a ploy to keep pressure on the government and prevent it from lowering the subsidy. Yet the U.S. Department of Agriculture's Vernon Harness has studied the incomes of these farmers and concluded that the "man with average yields is not making much of a profit." In Sonora, the average wheat farmer made $12.00 an acre while in adjacent Sinaloa, he *lost* $12.00 (Harness, 1969).

The U.S. Department of Agriculture's Dana Dalrymple cites two surveys of farmers in the Philippines who decided to stop growing improved rice varieties. Over 50% gave as their reason the "low price or added expenses" while another 10 to 15% said the new rice involved too much additional labor. He also cites a Burmese village which reduced its acreage because of the poor consumer demand for the miracle rice on both the free and black markets. The Burmese wanted to raise the rice if the government would buy the production but not otherwise. Dalrymple says, "It has been widely assumed that the increased returns from growing the new variety have exceeded the cost. Incomes have probably generally been increased in the short run. Yet there is little solid evidence on this point" (Dalrymple, 1969).

The Green Revolution and the 1970s

In his book, *Seeds of Change*, Lester Brown has projected a highly hopeful

[3]Don Paarlberg, Address before the 12th Annual Meeting of the Agricultural Research Institute, National Academy of Sciences, Washington, D.C., 18 October 1963.

agricultural future because of the Green Revolution. He reflects the opinions of many who feel that "thanks to the breakthrough in the cereal production, the problems of the seventies will be much more political and less technological than were those of the sixties. Their solutions lie more in the hands of politicians, less in the hands of scientists and farmers" (Brown, 1970).

Such a view would be correct if the new varieties were as good as the press often suggests. But to overcome the biological limitations imposed by the land on agricultural production will require greater technological breakthroughs in the 1970s than anything we have ever seen. "What we have accomplished so far in the Green Revolution is the easiest part," says Will Meyers, Vice-President of the Rockefeller Foundation (Horne, 1969).

The new wheat varieties are essentially a transfer of temperate zone technology to temperate zone areas in Mexico, India, Pakistan, and Turkey. Tropical rice has so far had only limited success. Corn is going to be a more difficult crop with which to work because of its inability to be moved from latitude to latitude.

The "wonder" wheats and "miracle" rice varieties have been quickly accepted in Asia partly because governments encouraged their acceptance. Farmers who grew them were the ones who found loans for fertilizer and pesticides available to them. Governments were encouraged to do this partially out of fright stemming from the crop failures of 1965 and 1966 and partially from the pressure and salesmanship of foreign scientists and aid givers. Already many fear the consequences of this action.

The U.N.'s Food and Agriculture Organization recently held a round-table discussion on the "genetic dangers in the Green Revolution" and concluded that progress in one direction "represents a calamitous loss in the other." Plant breeders unanimously agree that it is dangerous to produce over large areas varieties with similar disease-resistant characteristics. By eliminating the great number of genetically different types of wheat and rice and replacing them with substantially the same variety, there is a loss of variability from which to select resistance to new and still unknown diseases. Speaking of this, Dr. Jack R. Har-

lan, professor of Plant Genetics at the University of Illinois, says, "The food supply for the human race is seriously threatened by any loss of variability" (Anonymous, 1969).

The danger of a disastrous attack by either insect or disease is greatly enhanced when a region is planted to genetically similar varieties. The consequences of this are surely to be seen in the 1970s.

"All across southern Asia (not just India) there has been a rush toward one dominant family of wheats prized for its yielding ability. . . . All of this wheat carries the same kind of rust resistance, which means that if a new race of rust to which it would be especially susceptible were suddenly to appear, much of the wheat crop of that whole vast stretch of the world could be devastated almost overnight."[4]

This is not theory without precedent. In 1946, 30 million acres of U.S. land were planted to a new group of oats (two-thirds of the oat crop), all having what was called "Victoria type" resistance to rust. Within 2 years, these oats had virtually disappeared from the country's oat fields. The reason was the emergence of a new disease which had been unknown only 4 years earlier.

In 1950, there was probably no single phase of the plant sciences more highly developed than that related to the control of a disease on wheat known as "stem rust." A strain of that rust (called 15B) had been known and watched in the United States for 10 years. Nevertheless, 15B was able to build up to epidemic levels and, in 1953 and 1954, cause the almost total destruction of our durum-wheat crop. If this were to happen in India today, the results would be disastrous.

Yet a country like India is particularly vulnerable. She has too few technicians to keep track of what is going on in her wheat and rice fields as well as too few scientists to develop new disease-resistant varieties and have them ready when needed. Furthermore, her seed industry cannot quickly multiply a new variety and get it into the hands of the farmer if a crisis arises.

The recent epiphytotics of the developed world involved highly selected crop

[4]Streeter, Carroll P. 1969. A partnership to improve food production in India, A report from the Rockefeller Foundation.

varieties derived from a narrow genetic base. The hungry world has had a degree of protection against this because of the multiplicity of types found within its unselected crops. However, the sudden introduction and widespread use of the new Mexican wheats and Philippine rice into South Asia shows how quickly this can change.

If the 1970s is to see an agricultural revolution, another problem must be solved: the efficient use of fertilizer and water. Fertilizer is expensive; most countries lack the natural resources to produce it. What the subsidies now do is make it economically possible for the farmer to use the high-cost fertilizer and water required by the new cereals.

Where the Green Revolution is said to exist, it would die tomorrow without any one of its three legs: subsidies, irrigation, and fertilizer. The economies of the developing world make all three legs fragile supports.

Finally, for the Green Revolution to produce a revolution in this coming decade, some way must be found to bring it to the tropics where a majority of the free world's hungry live. Little technological progress has been made with the basic food crops of the tropics, and virtually no aspect of the Green Revolution has reached Africa south of the Sahara or Latin America south of Mexico.

The Danger in the Green Revolution Optimism

Many believe that the Green Revolution has bought time to solve the world's population problem.

To me this hope is premature at best and disastrous at worst.

The potential of the current Green Revolution is too limited to expect it to provide anywhere near adequate time in which to find a solution to the population problem. Bert Tollefson, Assistant Administrator of the Agency for International Development, recently told a campus group that "AID hopes to see a breakthrough similar to the Green Revolution in individual country efforts to control population growth" (Tollefson, 1970). Like a litany, our AID officials tell of Taiwan, Hong Kong, Singapore, and South Korea lowering their birth rate without adding that even these prize examples will double, on the average, their population size within 27 years—one year longer than the rest of the developing world!

The 1969 study of India's population by Emerson Foote puts the hungry world's population growth in true perspective. When India began her population control program 17 years ago, her population was growing at the rate of 6 million a year; today, it grows at an annual rate of 15 million. If things continue this way, Foote says, the population of India would be one billion in 2000. He continues: "Long before the one billion figure would be reached, the break point would occur . . . it is entirely possible that in India and in other parts of the world for the next three years, five years or even a bit longer, the 'Green Revolution' will increase food production faster than population grows. But if this is the case, it will be a very temporary and misleading solace—only postponing the day of reckoning. . . . (The) growth will be slowed either by rational means or by indescribable catastrophe" (Foote, 1969).

Premature hope stemming from the Green Revolution contains two dangers. They are (1) the governments of the hungry nations will once again turn their thoughts away from the No. 1 problem of solving the agricultural and rural problems of their countries and resume their emphasis on pacifying the cities and worshipping the idol of industrialization; (2) of greater danger, however, is the likelihood of lessening concern over the exploding world population.

In 1968, at the Second International Conference on the War on Hunger, the Philippine "success" with the Green Revolution (although it was yet to be called the Green Revolution) was a major topic. In fact, the Philippine Undersecretary for Agriculture, Dr. Dioscoro Lopez Umali, came to Washington and brought with him a Philippine farmer who had markedly increased his production through the use of the new "miracle" rice. Before a distinguished audience, Umali translated the farmer's story as he spoke. The farmer had 10 children and said that because of the new high-yielding variety, he and his neighbors would now have enough food for all, and all could enjoy seeing their women in the condition in which they were most beautiful—pregnant. This sudden switch from concern about food short-

ages to praise for pregnancy was a frightening specter to some of the audience. The Philippino farmer cannot be criticized for waxing poetic over the beauties of his pregnant wife. But some felt that the Undersecretary for Agriculture, with a Cornell University Ph.D., might have suggested the danger such beauties held for his country. The Philippines, which among the world's 15 largest nations has the fastest population growth rate, will double the number of her citizens in 20 years.

Some time earlier, the Rockefeller Foundation's Norman Borlaug, while discussing the impact of the high-yielding varieties said, "It seems likely that through a combination of improvements in conventional and non-conventional food production methods, man can feed the world's mushrooming human population for the next 100-200 years" (Borlaug, 1965). More recently, however, he shortened the time to "two or three decades" (Borlaug et al., 1969).

Green Revolution Not Enough

Virtually all authorities accept the fact that if the developing world is to be fed, the purchasing power of its people must be raised. Yield per acre is only part of the equation. *Cost* of production is of equal importance. Even with its highly efficient agricultural productivity, the United States has 5 million citizens who are malnourished because they cannot afford to buy the food they need.

Jean Mayer, President Nixon's Advisor on Food and Nutrition, says that it would take $3.5 billion more than is now being spent to solve the U.S. hunger problem. Much more than just food for the hungry is involved in Dr. Mayer's $3.5 billion figure because food cannot be separated from other problems of poverty. Nevertheless, if such a figure is accurate, think what the cost will be to solve the food needs of the developing world.

In 1967, the President's Science Advisory Committee's report on the "World Food Problem" said that it is meaningless to consider a nation's demand for, and supply of, foodstuffs independently from overall economic growth. That report put a price tag for achieving the goal at approximately $12 billion more a year in external investment than was then going

into the hungry nations.

The report of the Commission on International Development to the World Bank (commonly known as the Pearson Report) stated in September, 1969 (when the Green Revolution was already a household phrase among development people) that in order to achieve the goals to which the Commission had addressed itself, foreign assistance must be increased by $10 billion annually during the next 7 years.

The FAO's enormous new Indicative World Plan, which was 6 years in the making and was presented to the Second World Food Conference at The Hague in June, "indicates" what the hungry nations must do. By 1985, the plan says, food demand in developing countries will be nearly two and a half times the level of 1962 (two-thirds of the extra demand will be a consequence of population growth). The FAO plan to meet this food requirement calls for an expenditure of $112 billion ($37 billion alone is required for expanding irrigation!). In the understatement of the decade, the plan says that the need for foreign aid will continue and "is likely to increase."

So, taking your pick among the authorities, you still need from $7 to $12 billion more a year for the developing world to feed its expanding population. Because that part of the world can barely handle its current $3 billion annual debt servicing charges, this extra demand placed on the area's agriculture must come from the developed nations. But such aid to the developing countries is now at a low ebb with no upswing in sight. Without outside financing, the Green Revolution will never get out from behind the barricades.

The conclusion is clear: Current optimism that the world food problem is being solved is premature.

Production Versus Reproduction

Whether the Green Revolution is a fact or a myth, the consequences of an agricultural breakthrough without an accompanying breakthrough in population control are ominous.

To feed today's world population requires the use of agricultural chemicals, the pollutants of which will have a deleterious effect on our children and on their children. But we have seen nothing yet!

By 1985, the demand for food in the hungry world will more than double. If the hungry world is to then feed itself, it must increase its use of fertilizers by 100% and pesticides by 600% (President's Science Advisory Committee 1967). Such an increase in the use of chemicals to feed the projected populations could wreck our environment.

Man has, through the use of his land, turned far more into desert than he has reclaimed through irrigation. Lord Richie Calder says that in the Indus Valley in West Pakistan the population grows at the rate of 10 more mouths to be fed every 5 minutes. In that same 5 minutes in that same place, an acre of land is being lost through water-logging and salinity.

Paul Ehrlich says, "Those clowns who are talking of feeding a big population in the year 2000 from make-believe 'green revolutions' . . . should learn some elementary biology, meteorology, agricultural economics and anthropology."

Today's accelerating rate of population growth is due primarily to the consequences of modern medicine which has lowered the world's death rate without an accompanying lowering of the birth rate.

Rereading the 1936 best seller, *An American Doctor's Odyssey,* is today a disturbing experience. The author, Victor Heiser, tells of activities when he headed the Asian section of the Rockefeller Foundation's International Health Division. In a chapter entitled, "Dividends from Philanthropy" he tells not only of the successful attack on hookworm and other diseases but of the "great progress" achieved by 1934 in upgrading the "backward public health situation of 1914 for which I rejoice to feel the Foundation is largely responsible (this progress) fairly staggers the imagination."

In retrospect, the highly motivated, well-intentioned staff of the Rockefeller Foundation and other similar good Samaritans might well have been advised to slow down the dissemination of modern medicine until Asia's resources could be developed, until educational facilities and agricultural technology could be expanded, *and* some way found to motivate man to limit his population. Herman Kahn, reflecting on the good and bad effects of prematurely bringing modern medicine to a nation says, perhaps only half facetiously, the United States was

fortunate to develop her resources before the Rockefeller Foundation began its good works.

Agriculturalists (and this writer is one) too glibly damn modern medicine while striving to do exactly the same thing through improved agricultural technology. More food will certainly mean that more people will live. This will accelerate the population explosion still more. Obviously, without effective population control, an agricultural breakthrough resulting in increased yields might be as detrimental to some countries as was the use of DDT on the malaria-bearing anopheles mosquito.

Perhaps no one, with a clear conscience, can deny a hungry nation the technology for an agricultural revolution. Even if he wanted to, he could not. Today's transistor radio and the jet provide the means for the knowledge and the theft of the new seeds.

However, simultaneously with the release of improved food crop varieties to a hungry nation, an effort must be made to limit that nation's population growth. Not to do so is to ignore history, and he who ignores history, the axiom says, is condemned to relive it. In this case, to relive history is to endure still another spurt in population growth.

Should we then be disappointed that the Green Revolution is neither very green nor very revolutionary? Indeed, is the world ready for a Green Revolution?

Malthus' dismal theorem said, essentially, that if the only check on the growth of population is starvation and misery, then no matter how favorable the environment or how advanced the technology, the population will grow until it is miserable and starves. Kenneth Boulding has, however, what he calls the "Utterly Dismal Theorem." This is the proposition "that if the only check on growth of population is starvation and misery, then any technological improvement will have the ultimate effect of increasing the sum of human misery as it permits a larger proportion to live in precisely the same state of misery and starvation as before the change" (Boulding, 1956).

Boulding uses Ireland as an example of this "Utterly Dismal Theorem." In the 17th century, the population of Ireland had come into balance with the carrying capacity of her land. Two million Irish lived there destitute.

Then came the 18th Century truly Green Revolution. The Irish potato was introduced to the Emerald Isle from the Western Hemisphere. Agricultural production shot up. The carrying capacity of the land increased. The Irish multiplied accordingly. By 1835, eight million Irish lived where only two million had lived in the previous century.

Then arrived a totally new plant disease caused by the previously unknown fungus *Phytophthora infestans* and the potato crop was destroyed. In the resulting Irish famines of the 1840s, two million Irish starved to death, two million Irish emigrated, and four million Irish were left on the land in abject poverty.

When there is such a thing as a Green Revolution, its name will be disaster if it arrives ahead of a Population Control Revolution.

References

Anonymous. 1969. Genetic dangers in the green revolution. *Ceres,* Sept.-Oct., 1969: 35-37.

Borlaug, Norman. 1965. Wheat, rust and people. *Phytopathology,* 55: 1088-1097.

Borlaug, Norman, Ignacio Narvaez, Oddvar Aresvick, and R. Glenn Anderson. 1969. A green revolution yields a golden harvest. *Colombia J. World Bus.,* 4: 1019.

Boulding, Kenneth. 1956. *The Image.* University of Michigan Press, Ann Arbor.

Brown, Lester R. 1970. *Seeds of Change.* Published for the Overseas Development Council by Praeger Publishers.

Dalrymple, Dana. 1969. *Technological Change in Agriculture, Effects and Implications for the Developing Nations.* Foreign Agriculture Service, U.S. Dept. of Agriculture, p. 41.

Foote, Emerson. 1969. *Observations and Recommendations on Mass Communications in Family Planning.* Foreword by S. Chandrasekhar, Minister of State for Health and Family Planning, and Works, Housing and Urban Development. New Delhi, India.

Hardin, Lowell S. 1969. Symposium, Subcommittee on National Security Policy and Scientific Developments, House Committee on Foreign Affairs, 5 Dec. 1969.

Harness, Vernon L. 1969. Mexican cotton production—a 1969 closeup. *For. Agr.,* 28 July.

Haviland, Guy L. 1969. Rice in India, promising new varieties still face problems. *For. Agr.,* 22 Dec., p. 20-21.

Horne, A. D. 1969. *Washington Post,* 6 Dec.

Nossiter, Bernard D. 1970. *Washington Post,* 17 February.

President's Science Advisory Committee. 1967. *The World Food Problem,* Vol. 1, p. 22.

Schertz, Lyle P. 1970. The Green Revolution: production and world trade. *Colombia J. World Bus.,* 5: 9-19.

Tollefson, Bert. 1970. Agency for International Development press release 24 Feb.